Decoding the TOEFL® iBT

Advanced

LISTENING

INTRODUCTION

For many learners of English, the TOEFL® iBT will be the most important standardized test they ever take. Unfortunately for a large number of these individuals, the material covered on the TOEFL® iBT remains a mystery to them, so they are unable to do well on the test. We hope that by using the *Decoding the TOEFL® iBT* series, individuals who take the TOEFL® iBT will be able to excel on the test and, in the process of using the book, may unravel the mysteries of the test and therefore make the material covered on the TOEFL® iBT more familiar to themselves.

The TOEFL® iBT covers the four main skills that a person must learn when studying any foreign language: reading, listening, speaking, and writing. The *Decoding the TOEFL® iBT* series contains books that cover all four of these skills. The *Decoding the TOEFL® iBT* series contains books with three separate levels for all four of the topics, and it also contains *Decoding the TOEFL® iBT Actual Test* books. These books contain several actual tests that learners can utilize to help them become better prepared to take the TOEFL® iBT. This book, *Decoding the TOEFL® iBT Listening Advanced*, covers the listening aspect of the test. Finally, the TOEFL® iBT underwent a number of changes in August 2019. This book—and the others in the series—takes those changes into account and incorporates them in the texts and questions, so readers of this second edition can be assured that they have up-to-date knowledge of the test.

Decoding the TOEFL® iBT Listening Advanced can be used by learners who are taking classes and also by individuals who are studying by themselves. It contains eight chapters, each of which focuses on a different listening question, and one actual test at the end of the book. Each chapter contains explanations of the questions and how to answer them correctly. It also contains passages of varying lengths, and it focuses on asking the types of questions that are covered in the chapter. The passages and question types in *Decoding the TOEFL® iBT Listening Advanced* are the same difficulty levels as those found on the TOEFL® iBT. Individuals who use *Decoding the TOEFL® iBT Listening Advanced* will therefore be able to prepare themselves not only to take the TOEFL® iBT but also to perform well on the test.

We hope that everyone who uses *Decoding the TOEFL® iBT Listening Advanced* will be able to become more familiar with the TOEFL® iBT and will additionally improve his or her score on the test. As the title of the book implies, we hope that learners can use it to crack the code on the TOEFL® iBT, to make the test itself less mysterious and confusing, and to get the highest score possible. Finally, we hope that both learners and instructors can use this book to its full potential. We wish all of you the best of luck as you study English and prepare for the TOEFL® iBT, and we hope that *Decoding the TOEFL® iBT Listening Advanced* can provide you with assistance during the course of your studies.

Michael A. Putlack
Stephen Poirier
Maximilian Tolochko

TABLE
OF
CONTENTS

ABOUT THE TOEFL® iBT LISTENING SECTION

Changes in the Listening Section

TOEFL® underwent many changes in August of 2019. The following is an explanation of some of the changes that have been made to the Listening section.

Format

The Listening section contains either two or three parts. Before August 2019, each part had one conversation and two lectures. However, since the changes in August 2019, each part can have either one conversation and one lecture or one conversation and two lectures. In total, two conversations and three lectures (in two parts) or three conversations and four lectures (in three parts) can appear. The possible formats of the Listening section include the following:

Number of Parts	First Part	Second Part	Third Part
2	1 Conversation + 1 Lecture	1 Conversation + 2 Lectures	
	1 Conversation + 2 Lectures	1 Conversation + 1 Lecture	
3	1 Conversation + 1 Lecture	1 Conversation + 1 Lecture	1 Conversation + 2 Lectures
	1 Conversation + 1 Lecture	1 Conversation + 2 Lectures	1 Conversation + 1 Lecture
	1 Conversation + 2 Lectures	1 Conversation + 1 Lecture	1 Conversation + 1 Lecture

The time given for the Listening section has been reduced from 60-90 minutes to 41-57 minutes.

Passages and Questions

The lengths of the conversations and the lectures remain the same as before. The length of each conversation and lecture is 3 to 6 minutes.

It has been reported that some conversations have academic discussions that are of high difficulty levels, making them almost similar to lectures. For example, some questions might ask about academic information discussed between a student and a professor in the conversation. In addition, questions for both the conversations and the lectures tend to ask for more detailed information than before.

The numbers of questions remain the same. The test taker is given five questions after each conversation and six questions after each lecture. The time given for answering each set of questions is either 6.5 or 10 minutes.

Each conversation or lecture is heard only once. The test taker can take notes while listening to the passage and refer to them when answering the questions.

Question Types

TYPE 1 Gist-Content Questions

Gist-Content questions cover the test taker's basic comprehension of the listening passage. While they are typically asked after lectures, they are sometimes asked after conversations as well. These questions check to see if the test taker has understood the gist of the passage. They focus on the passage as a whole, so it is important to recognize what the main point of the lecture is or why the two people in the conversation are having a particular discussion. The test taker should therefore be able to recognize the theme of the lecture or conversation in order to answer this question correctly.

TYPE 2 Gist-Purpose Questions

Gist-Purpose questions cover the underlying theme of the passage. While they are typically asked after conversations, they are sometimes asked after lectures as well. Because these questions focus on the purpose or theme of the conversation or lecture, they begin with the word "why." They focus on the conversation or lecture as a whole, but they are not concerned with details; instead, they are concerned with why the student is speaking with the professor or employee or why the professor is covering a specific topic.

TYPE 3 Detail Questions

Detail questions cover the test taker's ability to understand facts and data that are mentioned in the listening passage. These questions appear after both conversations and lectures. Detail questions require the test taker to listen for and remember details from the passage. The majority of these questions concern major details that are related to the main topic of the lecture or conversation rather than minor ones. However, in some cases where there is a long digression that is not clearly related to the main idea, there may be a question about the details of the digression.

TYPE 4 Making Inferences Questions

Making Inferences questions cover the test taker's ability to understand implications made in the passage and to come to a conclusion about what these implications mean. These questions appear after both conversations and lectures. These questions require the test taker to hear the information being presented and then to make conclusions about what the information means or what is going to happen as a result of that information.

TYPE 5 Understanding Function Questions

Understanding Function questions cover the test taker's ability to determine the underlying meaning of what has been said in the passage. This question type often involves replaying a portion of the listening passage. There are two types of these questions. Some ask the test taker to infer the meaning of a phrase or a sentence. Thus the test taker needs to determine the implication—not the literal meaning— of the sentence. Other questions ask the test taker to infer the purpose of a statement made by one of the speakers. These questions specifically ask about the intended effect of a particular statement on the listener.

TYPE 6 Understanding Attitude Questions

Understanding Attitude questions cover the speaker's attitude or opinion toward something. These questions may appear after both lectures and conversations. This question type often involves replaying a portion of the listening passage. There are two types of these questions. Some ask about one of the speakers' feelings concerning something. These questions may check to see whether the test taker understands how a speaker feels about a particular topic, if a speaker likes or dislikes something, or why a speaker might feel anxiety or amusement. The other category asks about one of the speaker's opinions. These questions may inquire about a speaker's degree of certainty. Others may ask what a speaker thinks or implies about a topic, person, thing, or idea.

TYPE 7 Understanding Organization Questions

Understanding Organization questions cover the test taker's ability to determine the overall organization of the passage. These questions almost always appear after lectures. They rarely appear after conversations. These questions require the test taker to pay attention to two factors. The first is the way that the professor has organized the lecture and how he or she presents the information to the class. The second is how individual information given in the lecture relates to the lecture as a whole. To answer these questions correctly, test takers should focus more on the presentation and the professor's purpose in mentioning the facts rather than the facts themselves.

TYPE 8 Connecting Content Questions

Connecting Content questions almost exclusively appear after lectures, not after conversations. These questions measure the test taker's ability to understand how the ideas in the lecture relate to one another. These relationships may be explicitly stated, or you may have to infer them from the words you hear. The majority of these questions concern major relationships in the passage. These questions also commonly appear in passages where a number of different themes, ideas, objects, or individuals are being discussed.

HOW TO USE THIS BOOK

Decoding the TOEFL® iBT Listening Advanced is designed to be used either as a textbook in a classroom environment or as a study guide for individual learners. There are 8 chapters in this book. Each chapter provides comprehensive information about one type of listening question. There are 5 sections in each chapter, which enable you to build up your skills on a particular listening question. At the end of the book, there is one actual test of the Listening section of the TOEFL® iBT.

▌ Question Type

This section provides a short explanation of the question type. It contains examples of typical questions so that you can identify them more easily and hints on how to answer the questions. There is also a short listening passage with one sample question and explanation.

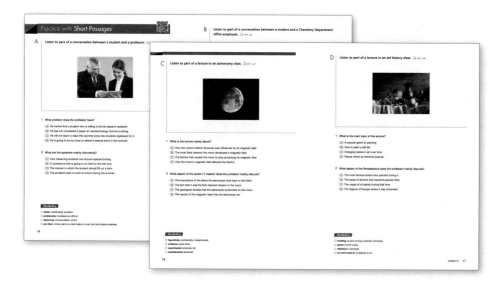

▌ Practice with Short Passages

This section contains 4 passages. There are usually 2 conversations between 300 and 350 words long and 2 lectures between 500 and 600 words long. However, depending on the question type, there may be more conversations and fewer lectures or more lectures and fewer conversations. Each passage contains 2 questions of the type covered in the chapter and has a short vocabulary section.

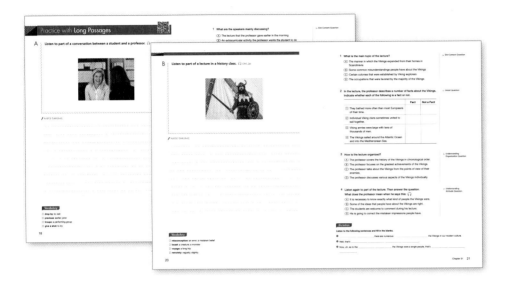

Practice with Long Passages

This section contains 2 passages. There are normally 1 conversation between 400 and 500 words long and 1 lecture between 600 and 700 words long. However, depending on the question type, there may be either 2 conversations or 2 lectures. There is at least 1 question about the type of question covered in the chapter. The other questions are of various types. There are also a short vocabulary section and a dictation section to practice your listening skills.

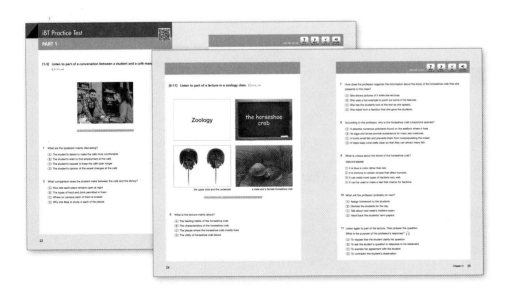

iBT Practice Test

This section has 2 full-length conversations with 5 questions and 3 full-length lectures with 6 questions each.

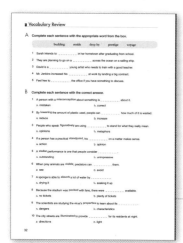

▨ Vocabulary Review

··

This section has two vocabulary exercises using words that appear in the passages in the chapter.

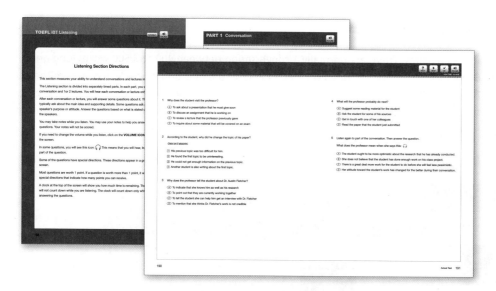

▨ Actual Test (at the end of the book)

··

This section has 1 Listening test, which contains 3 full-length conversations with 5 questions and 4 full-length lectures with 6 questions.

Chapter 01

Gist-Content

Question Type | **Gist-Content**

◢ About the Question

Gist-Content questions focus on how well you comprehend the talk as a whole. You are asked to understand the gist of the talk, so you have to recognize the main point of the lecture or the reason that the people are having a conversation. The information asked about in these questions is always about the theme of the lecture or conversation. These questions appear after both lectures and conversations.

Recognizing Gist-Content questions:

- What problem does the man have?
- What are the speakers mainly discussing?
- What is the main topic of the lecture?
- What is the lecture mainly about?
- What aspect of X does the professor mainly discuss?

Helpful hints for answering the questions correctly:

- Think about the main idea of the talk and ignore any minor points that are mentioned.
- For lectures, focus on what the professor is mostly talking about. For conversations, determine what problem or issue the speakers are discussing.
- The main idea of either a lecture or conversation is usually stated at the beginning of the talk. Listen closely to this part to find the correct answer.

◢ Sample Question

What is the main topic of the lecture?

- (A) The manner in which pearls are created
- (B) The different types of pearls
- (C) The shellfish capable of making pearls
- (D) The amount of time it takes to make a pearl

| Script | Listen to part of a lecture in a marine biology class.

M Professor: We normally think of the sea as a place that provides riches in the guise of fish, lobster, shrimp, crab, and other marine creatures rather than a region that produces other things of value such as, uh, gold and silver. Nevertheless, there are still some treasures to be gleaned from the sea, the best known of which is this one that I'm holding in my hand. Can anyone tell me what it is . . . ? Yes, you by the window with your hand up . . .

W Student: It's a pearl, sir.

M: Indeed it is. Right now, I'd like to speak with you about how oysters make pearls. Oh, uh, and just so you know, it is possible for clams and mussels, both of which are shellfish similar to the oyster, to produce pearls, but it's quite rare, so I'm going to ignore them for the purpose of this lecture.

So what allows oysters to produce pearls? Well, you should know that oysters have two shells, each of which has a layer called the mantle. The mantle is responsible for protecting the oyster's internal organs. Sometimes, an irritant, uh, something like a grain of sand, for instance, may go into the oyster and get between its shell and mantle. At that point, the oyster starts producing a substance called nacre, which is otherwise known as mother-of-pearl. Basically, it's calcium carbonate crystals. Anyway, the oyster covers the irritant in layers upon layers of nacre, which eventually results in the creation of a pearl.

Of course, what I just said makes it seem as though this process happens relatively quickly, but don't be mistaken. While pearls may take only half a year to develop at times, they require a few years to develop in some oysters. Let me show you a video now that will let you see how a pearl develops in an oyster over a period of time. I think you'll find it rather enlightening.

| Answer Explanation |

Choice (A) is the correct answer. The professor spends most of his time explaining to the students how pearls are created by oysters.

A | Listen to part of a conversation between a student and a professor. 🎧 CH1_2A

1 What problem does the professor have?

    (A) He cannot find a student who is willing to be his research assistant.

    (B) He has not completed a paper on nanotechnology that he is writing.

    (C) He will not teach a class this summer since few students registered for it.

    (D) He is going to be too busy to attend a special event in the summer.

2 What are the speakers mainly discussing?

    (A) How deserving students can acquire special funding

    (B) A conference that is going to be held for the first time

    (C) The manner in which the student should fill out a form

    (D) The student's plan to work at school during the summer

---

Vocabulary

☐ **stellar:** outstanding; excellent

☐ **problematic:** troublesome; difficult

☐ **deserving:** commendable; worthy

☐ **per diem:** money paid on a daily basis to cover food and lodging expenses

Listen to part of a conversation between a student and a Chemistry Department office employee. 🎧 CH1_2B

1 What problem does the student have?

- Ⓐ He is not being allowed to take a lab he registered for.
- Ⓑ He has to take a class at a time inconvenient for him.
- Ⓒ He is not permitted to enroll in a class until next year.
- Ⓓ He forgot to sign up for a class that he wants to take.

2 What are the speakers mainly discussing?

- Ⓐ The materials that the student needs for one of his classes
- Ⓑ Some problems regarding a class in the Chemistry Department
- Ⓒ The necessity of the student to take one of his core courses
- Ⓓ Some ways the student can convince the professor to let him take a class

Vocabulary

☐ **slot:** a spot; a position

☐ **packed:** full

☐ **core course:** a class that is important to a major

☐ **regret:** to feel bad about something, especially an action done in the past

C | Listen to part of a lecture in an astronomy class. 🎧 CH1_2C

1 What is the lecture mainly about?

   Ⓐ How the moon's interior structure was influenced by its magnetic field

   Ⓑ The most likely reasons the moon developed a magnetic field

   Ⓒ The factors that caused the moon to stop producing its magnetic field

   Ⓓ How the moon's magnetic field affected the Earth's

2 What aspect of the *Apollo 11* mission does the professor mainly discuss?

   Ⓐ The importance of the items the astronauts took back to the Earth

   Ⓑ The fact that it was the first manned mission to the moon

   Ⓒ The geological studies that the astronauts conducted on the moon

   Ⓓ The results of the magnetic tests that the astronauts ran

---

Vocabulary

☐ **figuratively:** symbolically; metaphorically

☐ **evidence:** proof; facts

☐ **superheated:** extremely hot

☐ **sophisticated:** advanced

D | **Listen to part of a lecture in an art history class.** CH1_2D

1 What is the main topic of the lecture?

Ⓐ A popular genre of painting

Ⓑ How to paint a still life

Ⓒ Changing tastes in art over time

Ⓓ Places where art became popular

2 What aspect of the Renaissance does the professor mainly discuss?

Ⓐ The most famous artists who painted during it

Ⓑ The types of artwork that became popular then

Ⓒ The usage of oil paints during that time

Ⓓ The regions of Europe where it was influential

Vocabulary

☐ **budding:** up and coming; potential; promising

☐ **genre:** a kind; a type

☐ **depiction:** a portrayal

☐ **try one's hand at:** to attempt to do

A Listen to part of a conversation between a student and a professor. 🎧 CH1_3A

✏ NOTE-TAKING

Vocabulary

☐ **drop by:** to visit

☐ **previous:** earlier; prior

☐ **troupe:** a performing group

☐ **give a shot:** to try

1 What are the speakers mainly discussing?

← Gist-Content Question

   Ⓐ The lecture that the professor gave earlier in the morning

   Ⓑ An extracurricular activity the professor wants the student to do

   Ⓒ The differences between modern and classical dancing

   Ⓓ A performance that was given by some students on the weekend

2 According to the professor, what recently happened to the dance troupe?

← Detail Question

   Ⓐ It received additional funding from the school.

   Ⓑ Its members began learning some new steps.

   Ⓒ The group sold all of the tickets for a performance.

   Ⓓ Two of its members had to stop participating.

3 What is the student's attitude toward the professor's suggestion?

← Understanding Attitude Question

   Ⓐ She is eager to become a part of the group.

   Ⓑ She is afraid she will not know anyone else.

   Ⓒ She is unwilling to give up her free time.

   Ⓓ She is nervous about performing in front of others.

4 Listen again to part of the conversation. Then answer the question.
What does the student imply when she says this: 🎧

← Understanding Function Question

   Ⓐ She got low grades in the previous semester, so she quit her part-time job.

   Ⓑ She is hoping to find some part-time employment before the semester ends.

   Ⓒ She received a scholarship so no longer needs to work part time.

   Ⓓ She has worked part time at school during previous semesters.

Dictation

Listen to the following sentences and fill in the blanks.

❶ There's something I'd like to _____ _____ _____ _____ .

❷ _____ _____ _____ _____ in participating in an extracurricular activity?

❸ We need a couple of _____ dancers, _____ _____ we won't be able to put on the performance.

B Listen to part of a lecture in a history class. 🎧 CH1_3B

🖊 NOTE-TAKING

Vocabulary

☐ **misconception:** an error; a mistaken belief

☐ **beast:** a creature; a monster

☐ **voyage:** a long trip

☐ **remotely:** vaguely; slightly

1 What is the main topic of the lecture?

← Gist-Content Question

    Ⓐ The manner in which the Vikings expanded from their homes in Scandinavia

    Ⓑ Some common misunderstandings people have about the Vikings

    Ⓒ Certain colonies that were established by Viking explorers

    Ⓓ The occupations that were favored by the majority of the Vikings

2 In the lecture, the professor describes a number of facts about the Vikings. Indicate whether each of the following is a fact or not.

← Detail Question

	Fact	Not a Fact
① They bathed more often than most Europeans of their time.		
② Individual Viking clans sometimes united to sail together.		
③ Viking armies were large with tens of thousands of men.		
④ The Vikings sailed around the Atlantic Ocean and into the Mediterranean Sea.		

3 How is the lecture organized?

← Understanding Organization Question

    Ⓐ The professor covers the history of the Vikings in chronological order.

    Ⓑ The professor focuses on the greatest achievements of the Vikings.

    Ⓒ The professor talks about the Vikings from the points of view of their enemies.

    Ⓓ The professor discusses various aspects of the Vikings individually.

4 Listen again to part of the lecture. Then answer the question.
What does the professor mean when he says this: 🎧

← Understanding Attitude Question

    Ⓐ It is necessary to know exactly what kind of people the Vikings were.

    Ⓑ Some of the ideas that people have about the Vikings are right.

    Ⓒ The students are welcome to comment during his lecture.

    Ⓓ He is going to correct the mistaken impressions people have.

Dictation

Listen to the following sentences and fill in the blanks.

❶ _____ _____ , there are numerous _____ _____ the Vikings in our modern culture.

❷ Well, that's _____ _____ _____ _____ .

❸ Now, uh, as to the _____ _____ the Vikings were a single people, that's _____ _____ _____ .

iBT Practice Test

PART 1

[1-5] **Listen to part of a conversation between a student and a café manager.**

🎧 CH1_4A

---

1   What are the speakers mainly discussing?

    Ⓐ The student's desire to make the café more comfortable

    Ⓑ The student's wish to find employment at the café

    Ⓒ The student's request to keep the café open longer

    Ⓓ The student's opinion of the recent changes at the café

2   What comparison does the student make between the café and the library?

    Ⓐ How late each place remains open at night

    Ⓑ The types of food and drink permitted in them

    Ⓒ Where on campus each of them is located

    Ⓓ Why she likes to study in each of the places

3 In the conversation, the student describes a number of facts about the café. Indicate whether each of the following is a fact or not.

Click in the correct box for each statement.

	Fact	Not a Fact
1 It remains open until midnight every night of the week.		
2 It has chairs that are more comfortable than the ones at the library.		
3 The café is located in the university's student center.		
4 The food that is sold in the café is nutritious.		

4 Why does the man tell the student about the wages that the employees receive?

Ⓐ To discourage her from applying for a job at the café

Ⓑ To explain why he has to reject the request she made

Ⓒ To claim that they make more than most other students do

Ⓓ To mention why the café is currently losing money

5 What does the man imply about the café?

Ⓐ The changes made to it have attracted many more students.

Ⓑ It is likely going to close at the end of the semester.

Ⓒ The owner is considering changing the café's business model.

Ⓓ It could extend its business hours if more customers visited it.

[6-11] **Listen to part of a lecture in a zoology class.** 🎧 CH1_4B

Zoology

the upper side and the underside

a male and a female horseshoe crab

6   What is the lecture mainly about?

    Ⓐ The feeding habits of the horseshoe crab

    Ⓑ The characteristics of the horseshoe crab

    Ⓒ The places where the horseshoe crab mostly lives

    Ⓓ The utility of horseshoe crab blood

7   How does the professor organize the information about the body of the horseshoe crab that she presents to the class?

   Ⓐ She shows pictures of it while she lectures.
   Ⓑ She uses a live example to point out some of its features.
   Ⓒ She has the students look at the text as she speaks.
   Ⓓ She reads from a handout that she gave the students.

8   According to the professor, why is the horseshoe crab a keystone species?

   Ⓐ It absorbs numerous pollutants found on the seafloor where it lives.
   Ⓑ Its eggs and larvae provide sustenance for many sea creatures.
   Ⓒ It hunts small fish and prevents them from overpopulating the ocean.
   Ⓓ It helps keep coral reefs clean so that they can attract many fish.

9   What is unique about the blood of the horseshoe crab?

   Click on 2 answers.

   ☐1 It is blue in color rather than red.
   ☐2 It is immune to certain viruses that affect humans.
   ☐3 It can resist most types of bacteria very well.
   ☐4 It can be used to make a test that checks for bacteria.

10 What will the professor probably do next?

   Ⓐ Assign homework to the students
   Ⓑ Dismiss the students for the day
   Ⓒ Talk about next week's midterm exam
   Ⓓ Hand back the students' term papers

11 Listen again to part of the lecture. Then answer the question.

   What is the purpose of the professor's response?

   Ⓐ To request that the student clarify his question
   Ⓑ To ask the student a question in response to his statement
   Ⓒ To express her agreement with the student
   Ⓓ To contradict the student's observation

Listen to part of a lecture in an anthropology class. 🎧 CH1_4C

12 What aspect of the potlatch does the professor mainly discuss?

- Ⓐ The reasons it was held
- Ⓑ The role of gifts in it
- Ⓒ The actions of tribe members at it
- Ⓓ The foods served during it

13 In the lecture, the professor describes a number of facts about the potlatch. Indicate whether each of the following is a fact or not.

Click in the correct box for each statement.

	Fact	Not a Fact
1 It was held to celebrate various occasions.		
2 It always lasted more than one day.		
3 It could be used to solve problems between various tribes.		
4 All the members of the tribe gave gifts to one another during the ceremony.		

14 What comparison does the professor make between potlatches held in pre-Columbian times and after the arrival of Europeans in North America?

   Ⓐ The way that the natives regarded their own ceremonies

   Ⓑ The importance of slaves during the ceremonies

   Ⓒ The length of time that the ceremonies usually lasted

   Ⓓ The types of presents that were given away during them

15 According to the professor, why do some anthropologists believe Native American tribes fought so many wars against one another?

   Ⓐ To acquire slaves to use in potlatches

   Ⓑ To obtain better hunting grounds

   Ⓒ To get more wealth from opposing tribes

   Ⓓ To avenge insults made at potlatches

16 What is the professor's opinion of the potlatch?

   Ⓐ It is extremely primitive.

   Ⓑ It is a beautiful ceremony.

   Ⓒ It represents outdated thinking.

   Ⓓ It is a cause of jealousy.

17 Listen again to part of the lecture. Then answer the question.

What does the professor imply when he says this:

   Ⓐ The potlatch has influenced some modern-day gift-giving events.

   Ⓑ Many tribal chiefs stepped down as leaders after holding a potlatch.

   Ⓒ The chief of a tribe expected to die soon after a potlatch ended.

   Ⓓ It is uncommon for modern-day people to destroy their belongings.

[1-5] **Listen to part of a conversation between a student and a professor.** 🎧 CH1_4D

1 What are the speakers mainly discussing?

    Ⓐ Some questions on a lecture that the student has

    Ⓑ The quality of the student's term paper on mosses

    Ⓒ A presentation that the student must give in class

    Ⓓ The student's recent performance on an exam

2 Why does the student apologize to the professor?

    Ⓐ He forgot to submit his term paper on time.

    Ⓑ He did not give her a note that she requires.

    Ⓒ He was unable to attend a recent class.

    Ⓓ He has been late for class several times.

3 Why does the student ask the professor about the height of mosses?

    Ⓐ He believes that his friend's notes are inaccurate.

    Ⓑ He wants to confirm that mosses with roots can grow high.

    Ⓒ He is curious about how height affects the growth rate of mosses.

    Ⓓ He thinks that most mosses are several centimeters high.

4 According to the professor, where can mosses grow?

Click on 2 answers.

    ☐1 In areas that are very foggy

    ☐2 On the northern sides of trees

    ☐3 In places with bodies of water

    ☐4 In regions that are dark and damp

5 What is the professor's attitude toward the student?

    Ⓐ She is unhappy about his frequent absences from class.

    Ⓑ She is impatient with him because she has a meeting soon.

    Ⓒ She is pleased with his overall performance in class.

    Ⓓ She is willing to answer all of the inquiries he makes.

Architecture

6   What is the main topic of the lecture?

Ⓐ Discoveries that allowed artificial light to displace natural light

Ⓑ Different types of light that are used to illuminate buildings

Ⓒ The ways that indoor lighting has improved people's lives

Ⓓ The main advantages that artificial light has over natural light

7   According to the professor, what is a disadvantage of a building having many glass windows?

Ⓐ Electricity bills increase during the summer and winter months.

Ⓑ The structure may be weaker than buildings without windows.

Ⓒ The natural light might be too bright on some sunny days.

Ⓓ Only the northern side of the building will get enough natural light.

8   What can be inferred about sources of artificial light in the past before electricity?

    Ⓐ They were able to illuminate some buildings completely.

    Ⓑ They allowed people to preserve local natural resources.

    Ⓒ They resulted in buildings being cool during the summer months.

    Ⓓ They occasionally caused some buildings to burn down.

9   What comparison does the professor make between incandescent light bulbs and fluorescent light bulbs?

    Ⓐ The toxic substances used in both of them

    Ⓑ The amount of electricity they each use

    Ⓒ The ways they can both affect people's health

    Ⓓ The people who invented each of them

10 Based on the information in the lecture, indicate which type of lighting the statements refer to.

Click in the correct box for each statement.

	Natural Lighting	Artificial Lighting
① May have an effect on people's circadian rhythms		
② Cannot be used to entirely light up a building		
③ Can be used effectively as directional lighting		
④ Lets people get more sleep and feel better		

11 How is the lecture organized?

    Ⓐ The professor explains why most people prefer natural light to artificial light.

    Ⓑ The professor focuses primarily on artificial light and then covers natural light.

    Ⓒ The professor compares and contrasts the advantages of natural and artificial light.

    Ⓓ The professor discusses natural light first and then focuses on artificial light.

■ Vocabulary Review

A Complete each sentence with the appropriate word from the box.

budding	reside	drop by	prestige	voyage

1 Sarah intends to _____ in her hometown after graduating from school.

2 They are planning to go on a _____ across the ocean on a sailing ship.

3 David is a _____ young artist who needs to train with a good teacher.

4 Mr. Jenkins increased his _____ at work by landing a big contract.

5 Feel free to _____ the office if you have something to discuss.

B Complete each sentence with the correct answer.

1 A person with a **misconception** about something is _____ about it.

   a. mistaken   b. correct

2 By **lowering** the amount of plastic used, people can _____ how much of it is wasted.

   a. reduce   b. increase

3 People who speak **figuratively** are using _____ to stand for what they really mean.

   a. opinions   b. metaphors

4 If a person has a practical **standpoint**, his _____ on a matter makes sense.

   a. action   b. opinion

5 A **stellar** performance is one that people consider _____.

   a. outstanding   b. unimpressive

6 When prey animals are **visible**, predators can _____ them.

   a. see   b. avoid

7 A sponge is able to **absorb** a lot of water by _____.

   a. drying it   b. soaking it up

8 Because the stadium was **packed** with fans, there were _____ available.

   a. no tickets   b. plenty of tickets

9 The scientists are studying the virus's **properties** to learn about its _____.

   a. dangers   b. characteristics

10 The city streets are **illuminated** to provide _____ for its residents at night.

   a. directions   b. light

Chapter **02**

Gist-Purpose

Question Type | Gist-Purpose

◢ About the Question

Gist-Purpose questions focus on the theme of the talk. You are asked to determine why the conversation is taking place or why the professor is lecturing about a specific topic. These questions begin with "why." They do not ask about the details of the talk. Instead, they ask about why it is happening. These questions sometimes follow lectures but are more common after conversations.

Recognizing Gist-Purpose questions:

- Why does the student visit the professor?

- Why does the student visit the Registrar's office?

- Why did the professor ask to see the student?

- Why does the professor explain X?

Helpful hints for answering the questions correctly:

- Think about why the lecture or conversation is taking place.

- For conversations, listen closely to the description of the problem that the student has as well as the solution. Knowing both of these can help you determine why the student is speaking with the professor or visiting a certain office.

- In many instances, the student explains the reason he or she is visiting the professor or office at the beginning of the conversation. Always listen carefully to this part.

- In other instances, the student sums up the conversation at the end and therefore provides the answer to the question.

Why did the professor ask to see the student?

(A) To give him a new writing assignment

(B) To show him how he needs to correct his homework

(C) To tell him one of his papers will be published

(D) To ask him to subscribe to an economics journal

| Script | Listen to part of a conversation between a student and a professor.

W Professor: Hi, Leo. Thanks for coming by so quickly after you got my message.

M Student: Good afternoon, Professor Edgerton. Uh, what's going on? The email you sent me only read that I ought to get to your office as soon as possible but didn't provide any details.

W: Ah, well, I wanted this to be a big surprise for you.

M: A surprise? Um, so . . . what is it?

W: Do you remember the article you gave me to submit to the economics journal a couple of months ago back in February?

M: Oh, yeah. Sure. What about it?

W: Well, this morning, I received an email from the journal, and they mentioned that they've decided to print the article in an upcoming edition. Congratulations, Leo. You're going to be a published writer soon.

M: Wow, that's amazing news. I, uh, I can't believe they chose to print my article. So, uh, what do I have to do to get it published?

W: They provided a list of changes and improvements you need to make to the paper. I looked at them, and it shouldn't take too much time to do everything. Do you happen to have time to go over them now?

M: Sure, I can do that.

W: Okay, then let me show you the letter. We can look at their comments together.

M: Sounds good.

| Answer Explanation |

Choice Ⓒ is the correct answer. The professor tells the student, "Well, this morning, I received an email from the journal, and they mentioned that they've decided to print the article in an upcoming edition." So she wanted to see him to give him that news.

A Listen to part of a conversation between a student and a student center employee.

🎧 CH2_2A

1 Why does the student visit the student center?

Ⓐ To ask why he was not allowed into the library

Ⓑ To get directions to a campus orientation session

Ⓒ To find out where to get a student ID card made

Ⓓ To learn the locations of some buildings on campus

2 Why does the student center employee explain what happened during the spring semester?

Ⓐ To complain about the actions taken by the dean of students

Ⓑ To point out that the problems from then are still going on

Ⓒ To tell the student why he needs to carry his student ID card

Ⓓ To instruct the student that he should be careful while on campus

Vocabulary

☐ **solely:** only; exclusively

☐ **alumni:** graduates of a school

☐ **obligatory:** required; mandatory

☐ **institute:** to start something new

Listen to part of a conversation between a student and a professor. 🎧 CH2_2B

1 Why does the student visit the professor?

   Ⓐ To talk about some work he did in her class

   Ⓑ To ask her for some guidance in a course he is taking

   Ⓒ To discuss doing some research as a senior

   Ⓓ To declare his intention to attend graduate school

2 Why does the student explain his options for the future?

   Ⓐ To emphasize his desire to become a TA or RA

   Ⓑ To claim that he would prefer to get a job upon graduating

   Ⓒ To explain why he thinks graduate school will be too hard

   Ⓓ To point out that he is unsure which of them to choose

Vocabulary

☐ **option:** a choice

☐ **precisely:** exactly

☐ **focus:** an emphasis; attention

☐ **strike:** to occur to

C Listen to part of a conversation between a student and a dining services employee.

🎧 CH2_2C

1 Why does the student visit the dining services employee?

Ⓐ To complain about the quality of food in the dining halls

Ⓑ To request a change in her student meal plan

Ⓒ To purchase a meal plan for the coming semester

Ⓓ To ask about the food used in the dining halls

2 Why does the student explain her eating habits?

Ⓐ To give the reason that she dislikes most of the food in the dining halls

Ⓑ To say why she does not visit the dining halls very often

Ⓒ To point out that she is a very picky eater

Ⓓ To state why the food served in the dining halls should be changed

Vocabulary

☐ **reduce:** to lower

☐ **waste:** to spend or use something in an inefficient manner

☐ **simply:** merely

☐ **definitely:** clearly

D   Listen to part of a conversation between a student and a professor. 🎧 CH2_2D

1 Why did the professor ask to see the student?

(A) To inquire about her activities during the break

(B) To discuss a book that he recently wrote and published

(C) To learn why she is not studying with him this semester

(D) To find out how her research on mercantilism is going

2 Why does the student explain what happened at the Registrar's office?

(A) To say that she was not allowed to register for his class

(B) To mention that a form she needs was not there

(C) To complain about the way that she was treated there

(D) To state that she failed to turn in some forms there on time

Vocabulary

☐ **mercantilism:** an economic system based upon trade

☐ **inform:** to tell someone about something

☐ **drop:** to quit; to stop taking a class

☐ **enroll:** to register for a class

A   **Listen to part of a conversation between a student and a professor.** 🎧 CH2_3A

✏ NOTE-TAKING

Vocabulary

☐ **have a word with:** to speak to; to chat with

☐ **embarrassed:** ashamed

☐ **go downhill:** to decline in quality

☐ **conducive:** beneficial; helpful

1   Why does the student visit the professor? ← Gist-Purpose Question

    (A) To find out why he did not receive his exam in class

    (B) To ask the professor a question about the day's lecture

    (C) To request some assistance due to his poor grade

    (D) To talk about his study habits with the professor

2   What does the professor imply about the student? ← Making Inferences Question

    (A) The student should consider changing his major.

    (B) The student ought to drop the professor's class and retake it later.

    (C) The student will probably do poorly on the final exam.

    (D) The student should quit skipping so many classes.

3   What does the professor suggest that the student do to improve his grade? (Choose 2 answers.) ← Detail Question

    (A) Take better notes in class

    (B) Do his studying in the library

    (C) Hire a graduate student as a private tutor

    (D) Become a member of a study group

4   Listen again to part of the conversation. Then answer the question. Why does the professor say this: 🎧 ← Understanding Function Question

    (A) To encourage the student to work harder in class

    (B) To point out that the student's study habits are sufficient

    (C) To express his disagreement with the student

    (D) To criticize the student for failing to study at all

Dictation

Listen to the following sentences and fill in the blanks.

❶ I didn't want _____ _____ _____ _____ in front of your friends.

❷ I _____ _____ _____ _____ tell me about your study habits.

❸ I _____ _____ _____ _____ one of the following.

Listen to part of a conversation between a student and a study abroad office employee. 🎧 CH2_3B

✎ NOTE-TAKING

Vocabulary

☐ **ruins:** the remains of buildings, especially old ones

☐ **sidetracked:** diverted; unfocused

☐ **be affiliated with:** to have an official connection with

☐ **corresponding:** equivalent

1 Why does the student visit the study abroad office?   ← Gist-Purpose Question

    Ⓐ To get some information about studying in another country

    Ⓑ To talk about the experience she had while she was in Greece

    Ⓒ To learn how to get credit for some courses that she took

    Ⓓ To find out which Greek schools are affiliated with the university

2 Why does the student tell the study abroad office employee about her friend?   ← Understanding Function Question

    Ⓐ To mention that her friend had a problem similar to hers

    Ⓑ To say that her friend had a negative experience while abroad

    Ⓒ To note that her friend encouraged her to study in Greece

    Ⓓ To claim that her friend told her she could get a form in the office

3 What does the study abroad office employee tell the student to do? (Choose 2 answers.)   ← Detail Question

    Ⓐ Contact the university in Greece that she studied at

    Ⓑ Have some professors at the university sign a form

    Ⓒ Visit the Registrar's office to pick up some papers

    Ⓓ Come back later so that the student can speak to her boss

4 Listen again to part of the conversation. Then answer the question. What does the student mean when she says this: 🎧   ← Understanding Attitude Question

    Ⓐ She is ashamed of how some students acted while abroad.

    Ⓑ There are not enough students lucky enough to study abroad.

    Ⓒ It is unfortunate that some students had bad times abroad.

    Ⓓ Some students should try harder when they are in other countries.

Dictation

Listen to the following sentences and fill in the blanks.

❶ I _____ _____ _____ to waste my time in Greece like that.

❷ I'm _____ _____ _____ _____ my grades from my school in Greece transferred here, and

  I'm _____ _____ _____ _____ _____ .

❸ That's true, but _____ _____ _____ _____ .

[1-5] **Listen to part of a conversation between a student and a professor.** CH2_4A

1 Why does the student visit the professor?

    Ⓐ To speak about her upcoming class

    Ⓑ To ask him for some letters of recommendation

    Ⓒ To find out if he thinks she should attend graduate school

    Ⓓ To discuss her volunteer work with him

2 What is the student's opinion of the volunteer work she is doing?

    Ⓐ She believes it is a waste of her time.

    Ⓑ She is upset she is not getting paid for it.

    Ⓒ She thinks it is beneficial to her.

    Ⓓ She finds it more useful than her classes.

3   What does the professor imply about the head of the Sociology Department?

  Ⓐ He is still just a junior member of the faculty at the university.

  Ⓑ He is the person that the student should speak to about graduate school.

  Ⓒ He is close friends with Dr. Richards at the healthcare center.

  Ⓓ His thoughts on the requirement for volunteering are wrong.

4   What will the student probably do next?

  Ⓐ Go to the healthcare center

  Ⓑ Make a call to Dr. Richards

  Ⓒ Attend her next class

  Ⓓ Visit the head of the Sociology Department

5   Listen again to part of the conversation. Then answer the question.

  What does the professor imply when he says this:

  Ⓐ He has a great deal of respect for Dr. Richards.

  Ⓑ Dr. Richards helped his career in the past.

  Ⓒ He knows Dr. Richards better than most people.

  Ⓓ There are many articles about Dr. Richards on the Internet.

[6-11] Listen to part of a lecture in a sociology class. 🎧 CH2_4B

Sociology

6 What aspect of motion pictures does the professor mainly discuss?

- Ⓐ The technology that was used to make them so entertaining
- Ⓑ The actors and actresses who performed in them
- Ⓒ The manner in which they affected the American people
- Ⓓ The genres of motion pictures that were the most popular

7 Why does the professor explain how people entertained themselves in the late 1800s?

- Ⓐ To help the students understand how motion pictures influenced society
- Ⓑ To stress how many free-time activities were done by families together
- Ⓒ To argue that many Americans had little time to entertain themselves then
- Ⓓ To point out that most people either read or did other activities at their homes

8   What was a nickelodeon?

    Ⓐ A theater in which vaudeville performances were held

    Ⓑ A place where people could view short film strips

    Ⓒ An eating establishment that featured live entertainment

    Ⓓ An area in which actors put on live dramatic performances

9   Based on the information in the lecture, indicate whether the statements refer to causes or effects of the rise of motion pictures.

Click in the correct box for each statement.

	Cause	Effect
① Watching a movie was inexpensive for most people.		
② Fewer people attended theatrical performances.		
③ Some social barriers between people in different classes were dismantled.		
④ Vaudeville performers started to act in motion pictures.		

10   Why does the professor mention Charlie Chaplin?

    Ⓐ To say that he was a vaudeville performer who started acting in movies

    Ⓑ To name him as one of the first movie idols in the motion picture industry

    Ⓒ To claim he helped Hollywood become the center of the American movie industry

    Ⓓ To explain why Americans were so fascinated by his personal life

11   What will the professor probably do next?

    Ⓐ Start lecturing on the automobile

    Ⓑ Answer one of the student's questions

    Ⓒ Show the students something on the screen

    Ⓓ Give the students a homework assignment

Listen to part of a lecture in an environmental science class. 🎧 CH2_4C

Environmental Science

ice ages

12 What is the lecture mainly about?

Ⓐ How ice ages change the appearance of the Earth

Ⓑ What causes ice ages to occur at certain times

Ⓒ Which parts of the Earth ice ages mostly affect

Ⓓ When ice ages have happened and how long they lasted

13 What is the professor's attitude toward the student?

    Ⓐ He is interested in the theories that she mentions.

    Ⓑ He is complimentary of the knowledge she exhibits.

    Ⓒ He is pleased that she completed her assignment on time.

    Ⓓ He is bothered by some of the questions she asks.

14 What is a result of the albedo effect?

Click on 2 answers.

    ☐1 Solar radiation is deflected back into space.

    ☐2 Less heat is absorbed by the Earth's surface.

    ☐3 There is an increase in the amount of snow that falls.

    ☐4 Fewer parts of the Earth's oceans freeze.

15 Why does the professor explain the reasons that people believe ice ages happened in the past?

    Ⓐ To note that he thinks the Earth is currently in the middle of an ongoing ice age

    Ⓑ To argue against most of the theories that have been proposed regarding the matter

    Ⓒ To examine the evidence that exists for several ice ages to have happened in the past

    Ⓓ To state why he believes there will be another ice age in a few thousand years

16 What can be inferred about the professor?

    Ⓐ He supports the notion that humans can affect global temperatures.

    Ⓑ He believes that volcanic eruptions caused past ice ages.

    Ⓒ He expects the next ice age to happen in a few decades.

    Ⓓ He is a supporter of the Milankovitch Cycle Theory.

17 Listen again to part of the lecture. Then answer the question.

What does the professor mean when he says this:

    Ⓐ Events in the present were used to make guesses about what happened in the past.

    Ⓑ The glaciers that exist in modern times are much smaller than those that once existed.

    Ⓒ Most of the ice ages that happened in the past lasted for thousands of years.

    Ⓓ By knowing about the past, scientists can predict what will happen in the future.

[1-5]   Listen to part of a conversation between a student and a job counselor.

🎧 CH2_4D

1   Why did the job counselor ask to see the student?

- Ⓐ To recommend that he major in History
- Ⓑ To offer him some part-time employment
- Ⓒ To discuss his job prospects in the future
- Ⓓ To encourage him to select different classes

2   According to the job counselor, what is an advantage of the student's choice of major?

Click on 2 answers.

- 1 The student will become a good public speaker.
- 2 The student will improve his writing skills.
- 3 The student will get hands-on experience in laboratories.
- 4 The student will learn how to think critically.

3   What is the student's opinion of being a middle school teacher?

    Ⓐ He has no interest in doing that.

    Ⓑ He has not given it much thought.

    Ⓒ He believes he would be a good teacher.

    Ⓓ He hopes to do that after he graduates.

4   What will the job counselor probably do next?

    Ⓐ Respond to the student's question

    Ⓑ Give the student a pamphlet

    Ⓒ Have the student sign a paper

    Ⓓ Ask the student to provide more information

5   Listen again to part of the conversation. Then answer the question.

Why does the student say this: 🎧

    Ⓐ To show his relief at having finally been offered a job

    Ⓑ To say that he is planning to change his major to Art History

    Ⓒ To indicate his lack of confidence in the major he chose

    Ⓓ To explain the reason why he wants to major in History

[6-11] **Listen to part of a lecture in a zoology class.** 🎧 CH2_4E

Zoology

grooming

6 What is the lecture mainly about?

- Ⓐ The benefits of grooming and how chimpanzees do it
- Ⓑ The chimpanzee hierarchy and how it influences grooming
- Ⓒ The grooming done by chimpanzees and other primates
- Ⓓ The activities chimpanzees prefer during periods of relaxation

7   What is a benefit of grooming for chimpanzees?

Click on 2 answers.

1 It teaches them how to interact with others.

2 It allows them to bond with their mothers.

3 It provides them with clean coats.

4 It lets them get small amounts of food.

8   What comparison does the professor make between human mothers and chimpanzee mothers?

Ⓐ How frequently they provide their babies with milk

Ⓑ How they wean their babies off mother's milk

Ⓒ How they act to calm down stressed babies

Ⓓ How they manage to get agitated babies to sleep

9   Why does the professor explain about the hierarchy in chimpanzee troops?

Ⓐ To discuss how well differently ranked chimpanzees groom one another

Ⓑ To mention that low-ranked chimpanzees rarely get groomed

Ⓒ To prove that only high-ranked chimpanzees benefit from grooming

Ⓓ To show how some chimpanzees use grooming to prevent violence

10 What is the professor's opinion of grooming by chimpanzees?

Ⓐ It has both benefits and drawbacks.

Ⓑ It is often abused by high-ranked chimpanzees.

Ⓒ It is generally advantageous for them.

Ⓓ It is necessary to maintain social order.

11 What will the professor probably do next?

Ⓐ Assign the students a group project to do

Ⓑ Show the students a short film on grooming

Ⓒ Discuss an exam the students will take soon

Ⓓ Answer a question that a student asked

▪ Vocabulary Review

A Complete each sentence with the appropriate word from the box.

apprehensive	obliged	lavish	ruins	strikes

1 Chris felt _____ to work overtime for his boss on the weekend.

2 Linda is feeling _____ about the results of her medical test.

3 There are _____ of old Roman buildings in places around Europe.

4 The company put on a _____ banquet for all of its employees.

5 When a thought _____ a person, she should write it down to avoid forgetting it.

B Complete each sentence with the correct answer.

1 **Hygienic** behavior is necessary to make sure that someone _____ .

   a. becomes stronger   b. stays clean

2 Please **inform** me of any problems by _____ me about them at once.

   a. telling   b. avoiding

3 _____ animals such as many dinosaurs were **gargantuan** in size.

   a. Very large   b. Very dangerous

4 The _____ quality of the company's products caused the firm to **go downhill** quickly.

   a. outstanding   b. poor

5 Mr. Maxwell will **institute** some new rules that will _____ next Monday.

   a. go into effect   b. be important

6 When the workers **dismantle** the building, they _____ .

   a. take it apart   b. renovate it

7 I got **sidetracked**, so my attention was _____ what I was supposed to be doing.

   a. only on   b. not focused on

8 We are **definitely** encountering bad weather as you can _____ see by looking at the sky.

   a. clearly   b. possibly

9 Something lasting for an **extended** period of time is useful _____ .

   a. for a short time   b. for a long time

10 The strongest animals **dominate** the others and _____ .

   a. hunt very well   b. rule over them

Chapter **03**

Detail

Question Type | Detail

■ About the Question

Detail questions focus on your ability to understand the facts that are mentioned in the talk. You need to listen closely to the details in the talk and remember them. These questions cover major details, not minor ones. However, if a speaker makes a long digression not related to the main topic, there may be a question about the details covered in it. These questions appear after both lectures and conversations.

Recognizing Detail questions:

1 Most Detail questions have four answer choices and one correct answer. These questions appear on the test like this:

- According to the professor, what is one way that X can affect Y?

- What are X?

- What resulted from the invention of the X?

- According to the professor, what is the main problem with the X theory?

2 Other detail questions have two or more correct answers though. These questions either require you to click on two answer choices or ask you to check if several statements are true or not. These questions appear on the test like this:

- According to the professor, what caused the Roman Empire to decline? [Click on 2 answers.]

- In the lecture, the professor describes a number of facts about polar bears. Indicate whether each of the following is a fact about polar bears. Click in the correct box for each sentence.

Helpful hints for answering the questions correctly:

- Be sure to recognize the main idea or topic of the talk. Then, focus on any facts that are mentioned which are related to it. If you are not sure about the correct answer, select the answer choice which is closest to the main idea or topic of the talk.

- Ignore facts about minor details in the talk.

- The correct answers to these questions are often paraphrased from the talk. Be careful of answer choices that use the exact words from the talk. These are sometimes intentionally misleading.

HELP　NEXT　OK　VOLUME

According to the professor, what influenced the work of George Inness?

Click on 2 answers.

1 Artists from Venice

2 The Renaissance

3 The Hudson River School

4 The Barbizon School

| Script |　Listen to part of a lecture in an art history class.

W Professor: Take a look at this picture . . . and this one . . . Both show the clear influence of the Hudson River School, which we discussed in our previous lecture. Here's a painting that's a bit different . . . and here's another one . . . You may be able to recognize the hand of the Barbizon School of France. Here's a picture of Venice . . . and this is a landscape . . . These paintings are all different from one another and show various influences, but they were painted by the same man. Can anyone tell me who it is?

M Student: I know. George Inness painted them.

W: Well, I'm impressed, David. In all the years I've been teaching, you're the only student who's guessed correctly. How did you know Inness painted them?

M: Oh, uh, one of the slides was *Autumn Oaks*, which is my favorite painting. I'm a big fan of Inness's work.

W: I am too. He happens to be one of my favorite painters. There's something, uh, spiritual about his paintings. But I'm getting ahead of myself, so let me go back to the beginning.

George Inness lived from 1825 to 1894 and was one of the most influential landscape artists in nineteenth-century America. Beginning his career, he was heavily influenced by the Hudson River School, particularly the artwork of Thomas Cole and Asher Durand. Here is one of Inness's early works . . . and here is another.

As a young man, Inness headed abroad and sailed across the Atlantic to Europe. That's where he came to be influenced by the Barbizon School, which I spoke about at the beginning of my lecture today. Notice how dark this picture . . . and this picture are . . . That's a direct influence of the Barbizon School. It also, I hope you remember, emphasized loose brushwork and stressed mood. But before he came under the influence of the Barbizon School, he went to Rome and Florence and saw many works by Renaissance masters.

| Answer Explanation |

Choices 3 and 4 are the correct answers. While showing some of Inness's paintings, the professor says, "Notice how both show the clear influence of the Hudson River School, which we discussed in our previous lecture." Then, she mentions, "That's where he came to be influenced by the Barbizon School," and, "That's a direct influence of the Barbizon School."

Practice with **Short Passages**

A | **Listen to part of a conversation between a student and a student housing office employee.** 🎧 CH3_2A

1 Why does the student want to check out of his dormitory room?

- Ⓐ He is going to graduate soon.
- Ⓑ The semester has just ended.
- Ⓒ He is going to live elsewhere.
- Ⓓ He cannot afford to pay for it.

2 What does the woman instruct the student to do?

- Ⓐ Return to the office to speak with another person
- Ⓑ Complete a form and turn in his dormitory room key
- Ⓒ Wait in the office until another individual returns
- Ⓓ Call the office as soon as lunch break is finished

Vocabulary

- ☐ **check out of:** to leave; to vacate
- ☐ **guess:** to suppose; to think
- ☐ **turn in:** to submit; to give something to someone
- ☐ **procedure:** a method; a way of doing something

B Listen to part of a conversation between a student and a professor. 🎧 CH3_2B

1 According to the student, why will he have trouble completing the assignment on time?

    Ⓐ He has been feeling ill lately so cannot work very much.

    Ⓑ An extracurricular activity will prevent him from doing the work.

    Ⓒ He has too many other class assignments to complete this week.

    Ⓓ The assignment is too difficult for him to complete everything.

2 In the conversation, the student and professor describe a number of facts about the assignment. Indicate whether each of the following is a fact or not.

	Fact	Not a Fact
1 The work must be completed by Friday.		
2 The assignment will count ten points on the student's grade.		
3 The student must write about some pages in the textbook.		
4 The professor will only accept assignments submitted by email.		

Vocabulary

☐ **misspeak:** to say something incorrectly or in error

☐ **unacceptable:** not allowed

☐ **analysis:** a study; an examination

☐ **suffice:** to be sufficient; to be enough

Listen to part of a lecture in a marine biology class. 🎧 CH3_2C

1   How is the giant squid like the kraken?

   Ⓐ They are both capable of sinking large ships.

   Ⓑ They can grab things with their tentacles.

   Ⓒ Their existence has been verified by experts.

   Ⓓ They may attack humans for no specific reason.

2   According to the professor, what could make sailors think the oarfish was a sea serpent?
    (Choose 2 answers.)

   Ⓐ It often swims close to the surface.

   Ⓑ It has a body that is shaped like a snake.

   Ⓒ It has long spines down its back.

   Ⓓ It has been known to attack small ships.

Vocabulary

☐ **superstitious:** having various beliefs not based upon reason or knowledge

☐ **fanciful:** imaginary; unbelievable

☐ **tentacle:** one of the long arms of an octopus, squid, or similar creature

☐ **specimen:** a sample

D Listen to part of a lecture in a chemistry class. 🎧 CH3_2D

1 According to the professor, what feature do all snowflakes have?

(A) They are combinations of both ice and water particles.

(B) They have arms that stick out from their various sides.

(C) They fall to the ground when they become a certain weight.

(D) They begin as simple structures that have six sides.

2 Why might one part of a snowflake be bigger than another part?

(A) The area in which the snowflake is in changes all of a sudden.

(B) The snowflake becomes too big and heavy, so a part of it breaks off.

(C) The temperature of the region the snowflake is in goes above freezing.

(D) The humidity in the area drops, so there is little moisture in the air.

Vocabulary

☐ **impurity:** something that contaminates another thing

☐ **lattice:** a structured arrangement in a regular pattern

☐ **humidity:** the amount of moisture in the air

☐ **symmetrical:** well-proportioned; regular in form

Practice with **Long Passages**

A Listen to part of a conversation between a student and a librarian. 🎧 CH3_3A

✏ NOTE-TAKING

☐ **input:** to enter data onto a computer

☐ **particular:** specific

☐ **consult:** to check

☐ **technician:** a machine specialist

1 What problem does the student have?

← Gist-Content Question

- Ⓐ The library does not have any of the books she needs.
- Ⓑ She cannot find anything by using the library's computer.
- Ⓒ One of the books that she wants has been checked out.
- Ⓓ Some reference books she needs are not on the shelves.

2 What does the man say about the author the student mentions?

← Detail Question

- Ⓐ The library recently acquired his most recently published work.
- Ⓑ He knows that the library has no books written by him.
- Ⓒ One of his books was checked out in the past month.
- Ⓓ There are two or more books authored by him in the library.

3 What will the man probably do next?

← Making Inferences Question

- Ⓐ Tell the person in charge about the problem
- Ⓑ Try to fix the computer system by himself
- Ⓒ Show the student where she can find some books
- Ⓓ Continue searching for books on the computer

4 Listen again to part of the conversation. Then answer the question. What is the purpose of the student's response? 🎧

← Understanding Function Question

- Ⓐ To state her agreement with the man's statement
- Ⓑ To confirm that the man will be able to assist her
- Ⓒ To express her surprise at the man's comment
- Ⓓ To inquire about the nature of the repairs that must be made

---

Dictation

Listen to the following sentences and fill in the blanks.

❶ I need some books, but I'm _____ _____ _____ _____ the computerized search system.

❷ I _____ _____ some different subjects, but _____ _____ _____ on the screen.

❸ I need to _____ _____ to let her know about this issue _____ _____ the technicians can get to work on fixing the system.

Listen to part of a lecture in an oceanology class. 🎧 CH3_3B

🖉 NOTE-TAKING

Vocabulary

☐ **enlightening:** educational; informative

☐ **collide:** to hit or run into something

☐ **water vapor:** water in its gaseous form

☐ **theoretical:** speculative; hypothetical

1 Why does the professor discuss the formation of the solar system?

← Understanding Organization Question

    Ⓐ To point out why the Earth is the only planet with oceans

    Ⓑ To explain how long it took for the layers of the Earth to be formed

    Ⓒ To focus on how it affected the creation of the Earth

    Ⓓ To argue that the Earth's oceans formed billions of years ago

2 According to the professor, where do people believe the water in the Earth's oceans came from? (Choose 2 answers.)

← Detail Question

    Ⓐ Heat from the sun caused great amounts of ice to melt on the Earth.

    Ⓑ Hydrogen and oxygen molecules combined to form water over millions of years.

    Ⓒ Asteroids and comets that contained water collided with the Earth.

    Ⓓ Outgassing from volcanic activity released water in its gaseous form.

3 In the lecture, the professor describes a number of facts about the Earth's oceans. Indicate whether each of the following is a fact or not.

← Detail Question

	Fact	Not a Fact
1 Around seventy percent of the water on the Earth is located in the oceans.		
2 The oceans formed billions of years ago right after the Earth was created.		
3 The Earth's oceans are larger than those that are on other planets and moons.		
4 Ultraviolet radiation burns off some of the water in the oceans.		

4 Listen again to part of the lecture. Then answer the question.

What can be inferred about the professor when he says this: 🎧

← Understanding Attitude Question

    Ⓐ He intends to give a detailed answer to the student's questions.

    Ⓑ The student needs to listen more carefully to what he is saying.

    Ⓒ He believes that there may be some truth to the student's theory.

    Ⓓ The argument that the student is making has been proved correct.

Dictation

Listen to the following sentences and fill in the blanks.

❶ Before we _____ _____ _____ _____ on the oceans today, I'd like to _____ _____ how they were initially formed with you.

❷ Firstly, you should be _____ that there are two major theories _____ the formation of the oceans.

❸ The second theory _____ _____ asteroids and large comets hit the Earth.

[1-5] Listen to part of a conversation between a student and a professor. 🎧 CH3_4A

1 Why does the student visit the professor?

Click on 2 answers.

- ☐1 To get the professor's opinion regarding some internships
- ☐2 To ask the professor for help applying for summer jobs
- ☐3 To inquire about some aspects of the final exam in her class
- ☐4 To discuss some of the theories of David Ricardo

2 What does the professor say the student needs to focus on?

- (A) Everything that the class has studied during the semester
- (B) The material that the class has not been tested on yet
- (C) The material that the class has learned in the past two weeks
- (D) The material that the class is going to learn starting next week

3   What can be inferred about the student's father?

    Ⓐ He has met the professor in person before.

    Ⓑ He is currently employed by Philips Consulting.

    Ⓒ He is encouraging the student to attend summer school.

    Ⓓ He has a job that is in the financial sector.

4   What is the professor's opinion of Wilson Financial?

    Ⓐ It is not run as well as it should be.

    Ⓑ It is a better company than Philips Consulting.

    Ⓒ It ought to be one of the world's most profitable companies.

    Ⓓ It is highly overrated by the majority of people.

5   Listen again to part of the conversation. Then answer the question.

    What does the student mean when she says this:

    Ⓐ She will pay closer attention during the next lecture.

    Ⓑ She intends to read some of the professor's articles on David Ricardo.

    Ⓒ She plans to discuss a possible future in economics with the professor.

    Ⓓ She will visit the professor to discuss some works after reading them.

6   What is the lecture mainly about?

(A) The relationship between the Bodele Depression and the Amazon Rainforest

(B) The weather that causes such intense dust storms in the Bodele Depression

(C) The reason that the land in the Amazon Rainforest has become so fertile

(D) The similarities that the Bodele Depression and the Amazon Rainforest have

7 What can be inferred about the Bodele Depression?

(A) Very little is known about it because it is so isolated.

(B) It is a dry land that gets a small amount of rainfall.

(C) It covers a majority of the land in the nation of Chad.

(D) There are few people and animals that live in it.

8 What is diatomite?

(A) A marine lifeform that resembles a type of alga

(B) A type of sedimentary rock formed from dead creatures

(C) A plant that lived when the Bodele Depression was covered by water

(D) A mineral commonly found in the Amazon Rainforest

9 Why does the professor tell the students about the wind?

(A) To state that it almost never stops blowing in the Bodele Depression

(B) To note that the Bodele Depression is one of the windiest places on the Earth

(C) To describe the speed it must blow at to lift dust into the atmosphere

(D) To explain how it is able to blow so much dust in Africa to Brazil

10 How is the Amazon Rainforest affected by dust?

(A) The dust increases the fertility of the soil.

(B) It causes some animals to have trouble breathing.

(C) The dust makes the water in the rivers there muddier.

(D) It helps plants create larger amounts of oxygen.

11 What is the likely outcome of the future disappearance of the mineral-rich soil in the Bodele Depression?

(A) The amount of oxygen and carbon dioxide in the atmosphere will increase.

(B) The Amazon Rainforest will begin to expand in size.

(C) Fewer plants will be capable of growing in the Amazon Rainforest.

(D) The amount of biomass in Africa will fluctuate over time.

[12-17] Listen to part of a lecture in an art history class. 🎧 CH3_4C

Art History

12 What aspect of Roman art does the professor mainly discuss?

Ⓐ The reason Roman sculptors preferred making portrait sculptures

Ⓑ The manner in which it was influenced by the Greeks

Ⓒ The different painting styles of the republic and empire eras

Ⓓ The various types of materials that Roman artists utilized

13 What comparison does the professor make between the Greeks and the Etruscans?

Ⓐ The types of art that they mostly created

Ⓑ The poses that their sculptors put their figures in

Ⓒ The ways that their artists depicted the human body

Ⓓ The materials that their artists preferred working with

14 Why does the professor mention the Arch of Constantine?

(A) To name the largest of all of the Roman statues

(B) To compare its appearance with that of Trajan's Column

(C) To show some slides of it to the students

(D) To describe the figures that are depicted on it

15 In the lecture, the professor describes a number of facts about Roman statues. Indicate whether each of the following is a fact or not.

Click in the correct box for each statement.

	Fact	Not a Fact
1 Large numbers of them were imitations of Greek statues.		
2 Miniature statues were popular with the Roman people.		
3 Statues of Roman gods were preferred to statues of men and animals.		
4 Roman sculptors attempted to make their statues highly realistic.		

16 According to the professor, how did Roman sculptors tend to depict Roman emperors?

Click on 2 answers.

1 By showing them leading armies of men

2 By portraying them riding on horses

3 By having them extending one of their arms

4 By making them wearing clothes worn by regular people

17 Listen again to part of the lecture. Then answer the question.

What does the professor imply when she says this:

(A) Many Roman statues made of metal were recycled by people in later times.

(B) Roman stone statues were very fragile so often broke when they were moved.

(C) Roman statues made of metal are more valuable than those made of stone today.

(D) Most Roman statues made of stone took longer to make than those made of metal.

[1-5] **Listen to part of a conversation between a student and an event organizer.**

🎧 CH3_4D

1 What are the speakers mainly discussing?

- (A) Preparations for a school event
- (B) The budget for an upcoming concert
- (C) The cancelation of the school's spring fling
- (D) Expected attendance at a school festival

2 What does the student imply about the Bogeys?

- (A) They perform at the school every year.
- (B) Some of their members currently attend the school.
- (C) She enjoys listening to the music they play.
- (D) They are a group that plays rock music.

3   What does the man ask the student to give him?

  (A) A list of student volunteers

  (B) Tickets for the concert

  (C) Some application forms

  (D) Copies of some flyers

4   Why does the man ask the student about the student activities office?

  (A) To determine how the negotiations with a band are proceeding

  (B) To find out if the student has gotten permission to post the flyers

  (C) To ask if Ms. Worthy is still the person who is running the office

  (D) To inquire as to when tickets for the event will be ready for sale

5   When does the man want to meet the student again?

  (A) At lunchtime

  (B) In the evening

  (C) The following day

  (D) On the weekend

Listen to part of a lecture in a child studies class. 🎧 CH3_4E

Child Studies

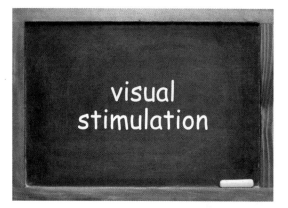

visual stimulation

6 What aspect of visual stimulation does the professor mainly discuss?

   Ⓐ The manner in which it might cause stress for some babies

   Ⓑ The primary disadvantages of visual stimulation for babies

   Ⓒ The ways that it can help stimulate brain growth in babies

   Ⓓ The effects on it on neurons growing in the brain

7 According to the professor, how do mobiles provide stimulation for babies?

Click on 2 answers.

☐1 Babies can understand that objects do not disappear if they cannot see them.

☐2 Babies can follow the colorful objects in them with their eyes.

☐3 Babies often attempt to grab the objects they are made of.

☐4 Babies can learn the words for the objects that are in the mobiles.

8 What is the professor's attitude toward taking babies outside in strollers?

(A) She believes it can be beneficial in certain situations.

(B) She considers it better than letting babies move around the house.

(C) She thinks parents should not do that until babies are older.

(D) She says that it might result in babies being overstimulated.

9 What is the likely outcome of a baby growing up in poverty during the child's first year of life?

(A) The child will have a very large amount of stress to deal with.

(B) The child will respond more negatively to some types of visual stimulation.

(C) The child will not be able to think as well as a baby living in better conditions.

(D) The child will see brain development twice as fast as in normal circumstances.

10 How can parents avoid causing too much stress for their babies?

(A) By exposing their babies to constant visual stimulation

(B) By planning surprises for their babies from time to time

(C) By letting their babies play with toys that some might consider scary

(D) By eliminating negative visual stimulation from their babies' lives

11 Why does the professor tell the students about the study done on tadpole brains?

(A) To prove that tadpole brains operate the same way as baby brains

(B) To show how exposure to light and darkness affected them

(C) To express her doubt about the validity of the results of the study

(D) To encourage the students to consider alternative methods of visual stimulation

◼ Vocabulary Review

A Complete each sentence with the appropriate word from the box.

superstitious	suffice	activates	negotiates	removal

1 A good businessperson always _____ to get a better deal.

2 The harvest this year should _____ for the entire winter and spring.

3 The medicine _____ cells in the body to fight the disease.

4 The _____ of pollution from the water is an important topic these days.

5 There are many _____ people who believe in things like good and bad luck.

B Complete each sentence with the correct answer.

1 Cindy **lacks** the time to finish the work, so she _____.

   a. should finish soon   b. cannot do it

2 If you know a good **procedure** to follow, then we can do the work _____.

   a. your way   b. at your pace

3 The **enlightening** speech was both _____ and entertaining.

   a. educational   b. humorous

4 The car nearly **collided** with ours, but the driver managed to keep it from _____.

   a. avoiding us   b. hitting us

5 The **replica** of the *Mona Lisa* was so good that nobody knew it _____.

   a. was a fake   b. was very old

6 The **impurities** in the chemicals _____ them, so the scientist threw everything away.

   a. combined with   b. contaminated

7 John's ideas were so **intriguing** that many people became _____.

   a. upset about them   b. interested in them

8 Fertilizer can **enrich** the soil by making it _____ to grow plants well.

   a. more capable   b. unable

9 If you are looking for a **particular** item, please be _____ when describing it.

   a. general   b. specific

10 There are a **multitude** of ways to do the experiment, so let's think of _____ of them.

   a. many   b. a couple

Chapter 04

Making Inferences

◢ About the Question

Making Inferences questions focus on your ability to understand the implications that are made in the talk. You are asked to determine the meanings of these implications. These are sometimes replay questions, or you may simply need to make a conclusion based on the information in a talk. These questions appear after both lectures and conversations.

Recognizing Making Inferences questions:

- What does the professor imply about X?

- What will the student probably do next?

- What can be inferred about X?

- What does the professor imply when he says this: (replay)

Helpful hints for answering the questions correctly:

- Learn how to read between the lines to understand what implications speakers are making. Don't focus on the literal meanings of some sentences.

- For replay questions, listen to all of the excerpted sentences since they often provide context clues and hints that can help you find the correct answer.

- Pay close attention to the end of a talk. That is when the student or professor often mentions what is going to happen next.

HELP **NEXT** **OK** **VOLUME**

What does the professor imply about the student?

Ⓐ She is going to do poorly on the upcoming final exam.

Ⓑ She did not do enough research on the paper that she wrote.

Ⓒ She needs to review her notes more in the future.

Ⓓ She normally does good work in the professor's classes.

| Script | Listen to part of a conversation between a student and a professor.

M Professor: Good afternoon, Janet. What brings you to my office today?

W Student: Hi, Professor Watkins. If you have a couple of minutes, um, I'd like to speak with you about the paper that you handed back to me in class today.

M: Sure, I can talk to you now. May I assume that you're disappointed with your grade?

W: Uh, yeah. How did you know?

M: Janet, you've taken three courses with me in the past two years, and that's by far the worst grade you've ever gotten on one of your assignments. Personally, I'm surprised it took you this long to make it to my office.

W: Yeah, I suppose you're right.

M: So . . . What happened?

W: That's a good question. I guess I must have misinterpreted the requirements for the paper.

M: That's what I thought since you wrote on a topic that was so much different than what everyone else in the class wrote about.

W: Do you think that I could, uh, you know . . . rewrite the paper and then submit it to you for you to grade again?

M: Normally, I don't do that sort of thing, but I think I'll make an exception in your case. However, I need to have that paper in my hands no later than forty-eight hours from now.

W: It's a deal. I'll do it. Thanks so much, Professor Watkins.

| Answer Explanation |

Choice Ⓓ is the correct answer. The professor comments, "Janet, you've taken three courses with me in the past two years, and that's by far the worst grade you've ever gotten on one of your assignments." In saying that, the professor implies that the student usually does good work in her classes and that only this assignment has been poor.

A

Listen to part of a conversation between a student and a student activities office employee. 🎧 CH4_2A

1 What can be inferred about the student?

Ⓐ She is a student in the Fine Arts Department.

Ⓑ She hopes to become a professional artist.

Ⓒ She is well acquainted with Mr. Martinson.

Ⓓ She is taking classes at the school part time.

2 What will the student probably do when the conversation ends?

Ⓐ Complete a form

Ⓑ Pay a registration fee

Ⓒ Show the man some samples

Ⓓ Visit her dormitory room

Vocabulary

☐ **handicraft:** a work of art made by hand

☐ **ambitious:** motivated; desiring to obtain success in the future

☐ **harsh:** severe

☐ **comply with:** to follow; to obey

Listen to part of a conversation between a student and a professor. 🎧 CH4_2B

1 What does the professor imply about foreign languages?

   Ⓐ They can be learned more easily at a young age.

   Ⓑ Not enough of them are taught at the university.

   Ⓒ People ought to study them with an instructor.

   Ⓓ European languages are easier to learn than Asian ones.

2 **Listen again to part of the conversation. Then answer the question.**

   What does the student imply when he says this: 🎧

   Ⓐ He got his lowest grades during his first year at school.

   Ⓑ He believes that the price of school is too high.

   Ⓒ He needs to think seriously about his future.

   Ⓓ He regrets not choosing a major during his freshman year.

Vocabulary

☐ **luncheon:** a formal lunch, often one that a meeting is held at

☐ **contemplate:** to consider; to think seriously about

☐ **concern:** something a person is interested in or cares about

☐ **make sense:** to be logical; to seem right

Listen to part of a lecture in an ecology class. 🎧 CH4_2C

1 What can be inferred about salmon?

  (A) There would be fewer trees in certain areas without them.

  (B) They are an endangered species in some parts of Canada.

  (C) Most of them are caught by bears before they can lay any eggs.

  (D) Some years, female salmon do not lay any eggs.

2 Listen again to part of the lecture. Then answer the question.

  What does the professor imply when he says this: 🎧

  (A) He is shocked by the comment that the student just made to him.

  (B) The student has an erroneous opinion about what they are discussing.

  (C) He has seen firsthand how many bears live in some parts of Canada.

  (D) The salmon that the bears eat provide a surprisingly high amount of nutrients.

Vocabulary

☐ **spawning ground:** a place where fish leave their eggs

☐ **gravel:** very small rocks

☐ **feces:** manure

☐ **estimate:** a guess

Listen to part of a lecture in a geology class. 🎧 CH4_2D

1   What does the professor imply about carbonado?

    Ⓐ Scientists believe that it may be found on other planets.

    Ⓑ It is much older than other types of diamonds found on the Earth.

    Ⓒ Its clarity makes it more valuable than regular diamonds.

    Ⓓ Some high-tech cutting machines are equipped with it.

2   What will the professor probably do next?

    Ⓐ Show the students some samples of carbonado

    Ⓑ Have the students look at some pictures in their books

    Ⓒ Begin speaking about another type of gemstone

    Ⓓ Answer some questions and then take a short break

Vocabulary

☐ **impurity:** dirtiness; a contamination

☐ **dense:** thick; solid

☐ **massive:** huge; enormous

☐ **dismiss:** to disqualify

A Listen to part of a conversation between a student and a housing office employee.

🎧 CH4_3A

✏️ NOTE-TAKING

1 What problem does the student have?

← Gist-Content Question

   (A) She argues with her roommate very often.

   (B) She tends to be late for her morning classes.

   (C) She dislikes the dormitory she is staying in.

   (D) She has not made any friends in Kenwood Hall.

2 In the conversation, the student describes a number of facts about Kenwood Hall. Indicate whether each of the following is a fact or not.

← Detail Question

	Fact	Not a Fact
1 The student chose to live in it this semester.		
2 It is located far away from the student's classes.		
3 The noise level in it causes the student problems when she studies.		
4 It has many students who are eager to study living in it.		

3 Why does the student tell the woman about her roommate?

← Understanding Function Question

   (A) To complain about the manner in which she acts

   (B) To emphasize that they argue almost every day

   (C) To point out that they get along well at times

   (D) To say that they are taking some of the same classes

4 What will the student probably do next?

← Making Inferences Question

   (A) File a complaint about the problems in Kenwood Hall

   (B) Check on the availability of some dormitory rooms

   (C) Call her roommate to arrange a counseling session

   (D) Turn in her key in order to check out of her room

Dictation

Listen to the following sentences and fill in the blanks.

❶ _____ _____ _____ I'd like to change dormitory rooms.

❷ I simply _____ _____ _____ _____ the current situation I'm in.

❸ Yeah, we've received _____ _____ _____ that dormitory from other students.

Listen to part of a lecture in an archaeology class. 🎧 CH4_3B

🖊 NOTE-TAKING

Vocabulary

☐ **herald:** to signal; to announce

☐ **elaborate:** ornate; intricate

☐ **denomination:** a specific value, such as for money

☐ **standard:** normal; usual

1 What is the lecture mainly about? ← Gist-Content Question

(A) The development of Roman coins

(B) The history of coins in the ancient world

(C) A comparison of Greek coins from different eras

(D) Minting techniques used in Greece and Rome

2 Based on the information in the lecture, indicate which period the statements refer to. ← Connecting Content Question

	Archaic Period	Classical Period	Hellenic Period
1 Was when silver and gold coins were first made			
2 Includes coins minted by the generals of Alexander the Great			
3 Saw the usage of the coins of Athens become widespread			
4 Lasted until the conquests of Alexander the Great			

3 According to the professor, what types of images did the Romans put on the first coins they made? (Choose 2 answers.) ← Detail Question

(A) Their gods

(B) Roman emperors

(C) Great achievements

(D) Animals

4 What will the professor probably do next? ← Making Inferences Question

(A) Continue lecturing about Roman coins

(B) Assign some homework to the students

(C) Show the students some ancient coins

(D) Answer any questions the students have

Dictation

Listen to the following sentences and fill in the blanks.

❶ Since Greece is the older of the two, _____ _____ _____ _____ its coinage first.

❷ _____ _____ _____ the Greek coins after Alexander died?

❸ _____ _____ the Romans . . . Roman coinage started around the fourth century B.C.

[1-5] **Listen to part of a conversation between a student and a professor.** 🎧 CH4_4A

1 What are the speakers mainly discussing?

- Ⓐ The research the student ought to do for a current course
- Ⓑ The preparations the student must do for an upcoming project
- Ⓒ The trip to Africa that the student and his parents went on
- Ⓓ The classes that the student should take during the summer

2 What does the professor imply about the student?

- Ⓐ His French language skills need to be improved.
- Ⓑ He should be more familiar with the school's faculty.
- Ⓒ He has to spend most of his free time in the library.
- Ⓓ His travels abroad should help him as a scholar.

3   What is the professor's opinion of the Paris Institute?

    Ⓐ It does not always hire the most qualified teachers.

    Ⓑ It is effective at teaching students written French.

    Ⓒ It provides good quality at reasonable prices.

    Ⓓ It is the best place in the city to study French.

4   Why does the professor tell the student about Professor Mankins?

    Ⓐ To suggest that Professor Mankins could assist the student with his thesis

    Ⓑ To recommend that the student ask Professor Mankins to be his advisor

    Ⓒ To state that Professor Mankins has done some excellent work on West Africa

    Ⓓ To mention some of the books Professor Mankins has written on African empires

5   What does the professor say that she is going to do for the student?

Click on 2 answers.

    1 Provide him with a list of books to read

    2 Speak with one of her colleagues about him

    3 Give him some of her research material

    4 Tutor him in the French language

[6-11] Listen to part of a lecture in an education class. 🎧 CH4_4B

Education

6 What is the main topic of the lecture?

- (A) How to teach all kinds of students
- (B) The various learning styles students have
- (C) How to get students interested in learning
- (D) The best way to teach groups of students

7 In the lecture, the professor describes a number of facts about visual learners. Indicate whether each of the following is a fact or not.

Click in the correct box for each statement.

	Fact	Not a Fact
1 They tend to be both talkative and social individuals.		
2 They are able to remember people's faces but not their names.		
3 They learn well by using flashcards and blocks.		
4 They like taking large amounts of notes in their classes.		

8   How do physical learners prefer to learn?

   Ⓐ By sitting still, reading, and writing

   Ⓑ By trying to figure out things by themselves

   Ⓒ By looking for patterns and making connections

   Ⓓ By reading detailed instructions first

9   Why does the professor tell the students what kind of learner she is?

   Ⓐ To stress that she is a social learner rather than a solitary one

   Ⓑ To respond to a student's question regarding that

   Ⓒ To enable the students to understand her preferences better

   Ⓓ To point out how people can learn in multiple ways

10 What can be inferred about the professor?

   Ⓐ She is teaching this class for the first time.

   Ⓑ She expects her students to become teachers in the future.

   Ⓒ She prefers to teach by using verbal learning methods.

   Ⓓ She dislikes when students interrupt her lecture with questions.

11 Listen again to part of the lecture. Then answer the question.

What can be inferred about the student when he says this:

   Ⓐ He is not sure which of the two terms is correct.

   Ⓑ He has never heard the term the professor uses before.

   Ⓒ He does not understand what the professor just said.

   Ⓓ He would like for the professor to repeat herself.

[12-17] **Listen to part of a lecture in an architecture class.** 🎧 CH4_4C

Architecture

One Central Park © SAKARET

12 What aspect of building design does the professor mainly discuss?

    Ⓐ How to make buildings more efficient

    Ⓑ The best types of materials to use on buildings

    Ⓒ Creative ways to utilize greenery

    Ⓓ How to use the environment in the design process

13 Why does the professor mention urban heat island?

- Ⓐ To note how architects can account for it in the design process
- Ⓑ To state that it is the largest problem in urban design facing architects
- Ⓒ To provide examples of how it can harm the environment
- Ⓓ To claim that greenery can do little to combat its negative effects

14 What are low-impact materials?

- Ⓐ Inexpensive materials
- Ⓑ Toxic materials
- Ⓒ Recycled materials
- Ⓓ Synthetic materials

15 What is the professor's opinion of One Central Park?

- Ⓐ Its design is something architects should strive to imitate.
- Ⓑ It protects the environment in a creative manner.
- Ⓒ It is a beautiful building yet was too costly to make.
- Ⓓ It is an example of an ineffectively designed building.

16 Listen again to part of the lecture. Then answer the question.

What does the professor mean when he says this:

- Ⓐ Most buildings are not planned or designed well.
- Ⓑ It takes a long time to plan a building properly.
- Ⓒ Buildings must be planned properly to be efficient.
- Ⓓ Efficient building designs should always be emphasized.

17 Listen again to part of the lecture. Then answer the question.

What does the student imply when she says this:

- Ⓐ Most recycled materials are capable of being used in the construction process.
- Ⓑ She thinks that recycled materials can be strengthened through various ways.
- Ⓒ The high cost of recycled materials makes them hard to use on some buildings.
- Ⓓ She is against using recycled materials in the construction of buildings.

[1-5] **Listen to part of a conversation between a student and an Archaeology Department employee.** 🎧 CH4_4D

1 What problem does the student have?

Ⓐ She forgot to complete a work assignment for the man.

Ⓑ She feels that she is not being paid well enough at her job.

Ⓒ She has a conflict between her work and school schedules.

Ⓓ She is not working enough hours to pay for her tuition.

2 What is the student's opinion of Professor Marino?

Ⓐ She likes the comments that he makes on the work she submits.

Ⓑ She believes he is the most creative professor in the department.

Ⓒ She feels that he has a good teaching style which students enjoy.

Ⓓ She thinks that he will teach her well in a genre that she likes.

3 What can be inferred about the student?

    Ⓐ She is a new employee in the Archaeology Department.

    Ⓑ She does not want to lose any of her work hours.

    Ⓒ She is currently in her second year at school.

    Ⓓ She believes that Chad will accept the offer she makes.

4 What does the man imply about Gretel and Peter?

    Ⓐ They are enrolled in a class with the student.

    Ⓑ They applied to work for him but were rejected.

    Ⓒ They are employed in the Archaeology Department.

    Ⓓ They are not able to change their working hours.

5 What does the man offer to do for the student?

    Ⓐ Give her a heavier work schedule next semester

    Ⓑ Try to convince Chad to assist her

    Ⓒ Allow her to come to work late on Fridays

    Ⓓ Recommend her for a job in another office

[6-11] Listen to part of a lecture in an urban development class. 🎧 CH4_4E

Urban
Development

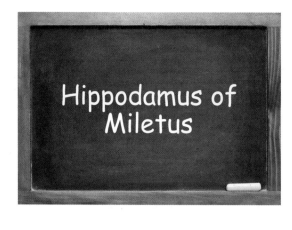

Hippodamus of
Miletus

6 What aspect of Hippodamus does the professor mainly discuss?

ⓐ His influence on Aristotle

ⓑ His beliefs on city life

ⓒ His contributions to urban planning

ⓓ His effect on the Roman Empire

7 How did Hippodamus propose to rebuild the city of Miletus?

  Ⓐ By adding a port to it so that ships could sail there

  Ⓑ By reconstructing it based on a grid pattern

  Ⓒ By putting the temples and the marketplace in the city center

  Ⓓ By building a large wall extending all around it

8 What does the professor imply about Hippodamus?

  Ⓐ He played a major role in the creation of the agora.

  Ⓑ He wrote several works on the art of urban planning.

  Ⓒ He helped design Athens after it was burned by the Persians.

  Ⓓ He was captured by the Persian Empire during a battle.

9 Why does the professor mention Alexander the Great?

  Ⓐ To argue that he knew more about urban planning than Hippodamus

  Ⓑ To point out that he personally studied under Hippodamus

  Ⓒ To say that he employed Hippodamus to design the city of Alexandria

  Ⓓ To state that he constructed a city using Hippodamus's ideas

10 According to the professor, what did Hippodamus think an ideal city was?

Click on 2 answers.

  1 A place that placed free men into various groups

  2 A place that did not permit any slaves within it

  3 A place that had the land divided into three parts

  4 A place that had around 50,000 free men in it

11 How does the professor organize the information about Hippodamus's philosophy of city life that he presents to the class?

  Ⓐ He explains how Hippodamus came to have the various thoughts on cities he developed.

  Ⓑ He points out the aspects of Hippodamus's ideas that he agrees and disagrees with.

  Ⓒ He describes Hippodamus's thoughts and then compares some with those of Aristotle.

  Ⓓ He lists Hippodamus's main ideas and then gives examples of how they were implemented.

◼ Vocabulary Review

A Complete each sentence with the appropriate word from the box.

hub	standard	verbal	forgo	elaborate

1 The officials hope the city becomes a manufacturing _____ for the entire country.

2 There are _____ designs on many of the columns in this building.

3 I plan to _____ my last year of graduate school in order to find a job.

4 Charles's _____ skills make him an outstanding public speaker.

5 The new employees were given the _____ speech by the CEO.

B Complete each sentence with the correct answer.

1 All of the **residents** of this city _____.

a. move around   b. live here

2 An **estimate** of a final price is basically just _____.

a. a guess   b. an exact price

3 People thought that Tom was _____ due to his **eccentric** behavior.

a. sick   b. strange

4 All citizens should _____ and **comply** with the orders they are given.

a. listen carefully   b. obey the law

5 Thanks to his _____, Jeff has a lot of **expertise** in his field.

a. knowledge   b. hard work

6 She decided to **contemplate** her future by _____ for a while.

a. forgetting about it   b. thinking about it

7 The fog was so **dense** that it was difficult to _____.

a. find it   b. see through it

8 Employees can earn _____ money if they feel like working **extra** hours.

a. more   b. less

9 If you do not _____, you will not be able to **concentrate** at all.

a. focus your mind   b. study very hard

10 Animals that live **solitary** lives are frequently _____.

a. with others   b. alone

Chapter **05**

Understanding Function

Question Type | Understanding Function

◢ About the Question

Understanding Function questions focus on your ability to understand the underlying meaning of what the speakers are saying in the talk. You are asked to infer the meaning of a phrase or sentence said by a person in the talk. Or you are asked to determine why a speaker brings up a particular topic or discusses some matter. These questions appear after both lectures and conversations.

Recognizing Understanding Function questions:

1   Some Understanding Function questions ask about what the speaker is inferring. These are often replay questions. They may appear like this:

  ● What does the professor imply when he says this: (replay)

  ● What can be inferred from the professor's response to the student? (replay)

2   Other Understanding Function questions ask about the purpose of a statement or a topic in the talk. These may be regular questions or replay questions. They may appear like this:

  ● What is the purpose of the woman's response? (replay)

  ● Why does the student say this: (replay)

  ● Why does the professor ask the student about his grades?

  ● Why does the man tell the student about the library?

Helpful hints for answering the questions correctly:

● Do not think about the literal meaning of what is being said. Instead, try to read between the lines to determine the real meaning by understanding what people are implying. Think about what the effect of a particular statement is on the listener.

● When professors interact with students in lectures, pay close attention to what is being said. This dialog is often used for replay questions.

● While replay questions ask about one sentence in particular, there are usually three or four sentences excerpted for them. Listen carefully to all of the sentences since they can provide context clues that will enable you to find the correct answer.

HELP   NEXT   OK   VOLUME

Why does the professor tell the students about the Battle of Actium?

- (A) To let them know the details of an important battle in history
- (B) To compare the fighting in it with that at the Battle of Lepanto
- (C) To give details of the movements of the ships in the battle
- (D) To explain the actions of Marc Antony and Cleopatra

| Script | Listen to part of a lecture in a history class.

M Professor: All right, uh, so what happened next was one of the most pivotal battles in the entire history of the West. And when I say it was pivotal, I'm not overemphasizing this in the least bit. I would argue that the Battle of Actium was one of the top ten battles in Western history. In fact, hmm . . . it might even be in the top five. Why is that . . . ? It's simple. You see, if that battle had gone another way, the Roman Empire itself may never have come to be. Or, uh, it would have taken a much different course than the one it eventually took.

So, uh, now that I've got you anticipating this battle, let me cover it. Oh, you should know that this wasn't a land battle but was a sea battle. There wouldn't be another sea battle as influential as Actium until centuries later when the Battle of Lepanto was fought. We'll be discussing Lepanto much later in this class by the way. Anyway, the Roman forces of Octavian faced off against Roman ships belonging to Marc Antony combined with Egyptian forces led by Cleopatra. The battle itself took place on September 2, 31 B.C.

The fighting lasted throughout the day. One reason was that both sides were relatively evenly matched. Basically, Romans were fighting against Romans, so each side was familiar with the tactics employed by the other. The turning point came when, for some inexplicable reason, Cleopatra suddenly left the fight and departed with around sixty of her ships. That turned the tide of the battle, so Octavian's forces began winning. Facing defeat, Marc Antony hastily retreated as well. Octavian, with a major assist from Marcus Vipsanius Agrippa, won the battle when the remainder of Marc Antony's forces, disheartened by the fleeing of their leader, surrendered to Octavian's men. A week later, Marc Antony's army in Egypt surrendered, thereby leaving Octavian as easily the most powerful man in Rome.

| Answer Explanation |

Choice (A) is the correct answer. At the beginning of the lecture, the professor comments, "I would argue that the Battle of Actium was one of the top ten battles in Western history." He further emphasizes how important the battle was, so he tells them about it to let them know the details regarding what happened.

Practice with **Short Passages**

A   **Listen to part of a conversation between a student and a professor.** 🎧 CH5_2A

1   Why does the professor tell the student about the reading material?

   Ⓐ To let him know what the class homework assignment is

   Ⓑ To provide him with some information that will help him

   Ⓒ To give him the names of authors he should read for his thesis

   Ⓓ To answer his question about the most famous Byzantine scholars

2   Listen again to part of the conversation. Then answer the question.
   What can be inferred from the professor's response to the student? 🎧

   Ⓐ She is going to teach her third class of the day very soon.

   Ⓑ She would like the student to email his questions to her.

   Ⓒ She believes that the information she taught was easy to understand.

   Ⓓ She does not have enough time to comply with the student's request.

Vocabulary

☐ **call roll:** to take attendance out loud

☐ **crusade:** a holy war

☐ **rehash:** to go over again; to recap

☐ **index:** a listing of the pages in a book where important names, places, and ideas are found

Listen to part of a conversation between a student and a student employment center employee. CH5_2B

1   Why does the man tell the student about the paper he prepared?

  Ⓐ To encourage her to use it to make her résumé better later

  Ⓑ To ask her to fill in all of the blanks and to return it to him

  Ⓒ To get her to use the tips on it when she goes to interviews

  Ⓓ To say that it contains all the corrections he made to her résumé

2   Listen again to part of the conversation. Then answer the question.

  Why does the man say this: 🎧

  Ⓐ To praise the student for the insight she made

  Ⓑ To tell the student she should have a more positive attitude

  Ⓒ To express his disagreement with the student's opinion

  Ⓓ To emphasize the difficulty the student will have in getting hired

Vocabulary

☐ **secure:** to obtain

☐ **toss:** to throw

☐ **worthwhile:** noteworthy; meaningful

☐ **concise:** short; brief

C | **Listen to part of a lecture in a physics class.** 🎧 CH5_2C

1 Why does the professor tell the students about tungsten filament?

   Ⓐ To state that it does not react well with inert gases like argon

   Ⓑ To point out that it was used in Thomas Edison's first light bulb

   Ⓒ To mention that it provides light while not getting particularly hot

   Ⓓ To emphasize the advantages that it has over carbon filament

2 Listen again to part of the lecture. Then answer the question.

  Why does the professor say this: 🎧

   Ⓐ To describe the difference between carbon and tungsten

   Ⓑ To correct a speaking mistake that he just made

   Ⓒ To acknowledge that the student's observation is correct

   Ⓓ To let the students know the topic is important

Vocabulary

☐ **phenomenon:** something that happens; an event

☐ **harness:** to capture and then utilize

☐ **inert:** having little or no ability to react

☐ **principle:** a fundamental law

D · Listen to part of a lecture in an art history class. 🎧 CH5_2D

1 Listen again to part of the lecture. Then answer the question.
What does the professor imply when he says this: 🎧

 Ⓐ He believes that Vermeer actually painted both paintings.

 Ⓑ Sweerts most likely copied Vermeer's painting after it was done.

 Ⓒ Both Vermeer and Sweerts employed similar painting styles.

 Ⓓ Some people consider Sweerts to be a better artist than Vermeer.

2 Listen again to part of the lecture. Then answer the question.
What is the purpose of the professor's response? 🎧

 Ⓐ To cast doubt upon the suggestion that the student makes

 Ⓑ To express his praise for the student's insight

 Ⓒ To state that the student is most likely correct in her opinion

 Ⓓ To argue that the answer to the question will never be known

Vocabulary

☐ **exaggerated:** overdone; overstated

☐ **grotesque:** laughable; outrageous

☐ **speculate:** to give thought to something; to hypothesize

☐ **patron:** a person who funds an artist

A **Listen to part of a conversation between a student and a professor.** 🎧 CH5_3A

✎ NOTE-TAKING

Vocabulary

- ☐ **approve:** to agree with; to think rightly of
- ☐ **switch:** to change
- ☐ **vaguely:** slightly; somewhat
- ☐ **avoid:** to keep away from

1   What problem does the student have?

- (A) She cannot register for some classes she wants to take.
- (B) She has not taken any foreign language classes.
- (C) She will not be able to graduate in only four years.
- (D) She is not getting good enough grades to keep her scholarship.

2   What was the student's major before she changed it?

← Detail Question

- (A) History
- (B) Literature
- (C) Art History
- (D) Physics

3   What can be inferred about the professor?

← Making Inferences Question

- (A) She teaches in the university's History Department.
- (B) She taught the student in a previous semester.
- (C) She is the advisor for many students at the university.
- (D) She feels the student has not thought about the future enough.

4   Listen again to part of the conversation. Then answer the question. What does the student imply when she says this: 🎧

← Understanding Function Question

- (A) She intends to improve her grades during her last two years of school.
- (B) She would prefer not to stay at the school for an extra year.
- (C) She is going to change her major to an easier subject.
- (D) She has already made plans to attend summer school this year.

Dictation

Listen to the following sentences and fill in the blanks.

❶ However, there's one thing you definitely _____ _____ _____ _____ _____ .

❷ _____ _____ _____ _____ I switched majors this semester.

❸ So _____ _____ you _____ _____ _____ take three classes during three of the next four semesters.

Listen to part of a lecture in a biology class. 🎧 CH5_3B

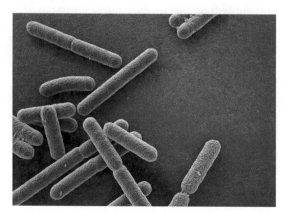

✎ NOTE-TAKING

| Vocabulary |

☐ **profound:** deep; vital

☐ **dormant:** inactive

☐ **photosynthesis:** the process through which plants use the sun and water to create energy for themselves

☐ **hydrothermal:** relating to or made by hot water

1 What is the main topic of the lecture?

← Gist-Content Question

    Ⓐ Bacteria that live in unique places on the Earth

    Ⓑ How bacteria can survive in extreme environments

    Ⓒ Why bacteria may actually exist on other planets

    Ⓓ The reasons bacteria are so important to all life

2 Why does the professor mention *E. coli*?

← Understanding Organization Question

    Ⓐ To respond to an inquiry made by a student

    Ⓑ To point out that doctors know how to treat it

    Ⓒ To claim that it does not always sicken people

    Ⓓ To argue that it is less harmful than some bacteria

3 Based on the information in the lecture, indicate which survival method the statements refer to.

← Connecting Content Question

	Forming Biofilms	Consuming Unusual Food Sources	Going Dormant
1 Was used by bacteria that processed oil in the Gulf of Mexico			
2 Requires the coming together of massive amounts of bacteria			
3 Is utilized by bacteria near hydrothermal vents			
4 Enables bacteria to remove waste matter more easily			

4 Listen again to part of the lecture. Then answer the question.

What does the professor imply when she says this: 🎧

← Understanding Function Question

    Ⓐ There are more bacteria than any other life forms on the Earth.

    Ⓑ Humans are unable to live in most of the places bacteria are found.

    Ⓒ Bacteria are able to adapt to the environments they live in.

    Ⓓ The only place where bacteria do not live is the upper atmosphere.

Dictation

Listen to the following sentences and fill in the blanks.

❶ I'm not _____ in the _____ _____ .

❷ _____ _____ _____ *E. coli* and other similar bad bacteria?

❸ It _____ _____ that there was a tremendous increase in bacteria blooms all around the oil platform.

[1-5] **Listen to part of a conversation between a student and an admissions office employee.** 🎧 CH5_4A

1 Why does the student visit the admissions office?

   Ⓐ To turn in his timesheet to the woman

   Ⓑ To conduct an interview for a position

   Ⓒ To learn how to become a tour guide

   Ⓓ To discuss his work schedule with the woman

2 According to the woman, what qualification does a tour guide need?

   Ⓐ Prior knowledge of every building on campus

   Ⓑ Outstanding academic performance

   Ⓒ Strong positive feelings toward the school

   Ⓓ Enough free time to conduct several tours a day

3   Why does the woman tell the student about the booklet?

    (A) To let him know how he can become familiar with the school's facilities

    (B) To indicate where he needs to record all of the hours that he works

    (C) To say that it contains the information that he needs to be a good guide

    (D) To ask him to write his class schedule on an empty page in it

4   What is the woman's attitude toward the student?

    (A) She is very impressed with him.

    (B) She thinks he would be an average employee.

    (C) She believes he is not very outgoing.

    (D) She is not pleased with his attitude.

5   What will the woman probably do next?

    (A) Show the student around the office

    (B) Give the student his work schedule

    (C) Speak with her boss

    (D) Send a text message

[6-11] **Listen to part of a lecture in a geology class.** 🎧 CH5_4B

Geology

6 What is the lecture mainly about?

Ⓐ The benefits of using modern technology instead of prospecting

Ⓑ The methods geologists use to find valuable minerals

Ⓒ The most likely places to find precious metals and gemstones

Ⓓ The professor's experiences finding precious metals

7 What comparison does the professor make between gold and copper?

Ⓐ Where they are often discovered

Ⓑ How they are used by people

Ⓒ What their relative values are

Ⓓ How easily they may be found

8 According to the professor, how do geologists use high-tech tools to find minerals?

Click on 2 answers.

1 By taking both radar and sonar images of the ground
2 By examining images that are taken by satellites
3 By using helicopters to detect minerals in outcroppings
4 By employing magnetic aerial surveys

9 Why does the professor tell the class about the work she did as a geologist?

Ⓐ To explain how she used to look for minerals
Ⓑ To talk about one of her greatest successes
Ⓒ To prove that high-tech equipment is not foolproof
Ⓓ To question the value of relying on past knowledge and lore

10 What will the professor probably do next?

Ⓐ Show the students a short video
Ⓑ Present some mineral samples to the students
Ⓒ Continue lecturing to the students
Ⓓ Assign homework and let the students go

11 Listen again to part of the lecture. Then answer the question.

What does the professor mean when she says this:

Ⓐ Finding valuable minerals is harder than it appears.
Ⓑ Her team searched in places that had been investigated before.
Ⓒ She did not make much money while working as a geologist.
Ⓓ Most of her team's searches were unsuccessful.

Marine Biology

fish aggregating
devices

12 What aspect of fish aggregating devices does the professor mainly discuss?

Ⓐ The manner in which they are used to attract and catch fish

Ⓑ The problems that they present to ocean marine life

Ⓒ The laws that people are trying to pass to have them banned

Ⓓ The areas of the oceans where most of them are placed

13 According to the professor, why is it believed that fish gather around fish aggregating devices?

Click on 2 answers.

☐1 The places where the devices are located have ample supplies of food.

☐2 They can use the devices to hide from larger predators.

☐3 The devices look unique and therefore provide stimulus for the fish.

☐4 Some devices make sounds that attract fish to them.

14 Why does the professor explain what fish aggregating devices look like?

(A) To make sure that the students do not get confused

(B) To answer a question asked by one of the students

(C) To point out that the picture in the textbook is misleading

(D) To emphasize some of the important parts of the devices

15 What can be inferred about manmade fish aggregating devices?

(A) They can be used multiple times to catch fish.

(B) They often have nets attached to them.

(C) They work best when they are close to shore.

(D) They can cause some ships to sink if there are collisions.

16 Why does the professor mention overfishing?

(A) To explain why he wants fish aggregating devices banned

(B) To say that environmentalists ignore that aspect of fish aggregating devices

(C) To name a big problem with fish aggregating devices

(D) To claim it is not as big an issue as some people say it is

17 Listen again to part of the lecture. Then answer the question.

What can be inferred about the professor's response to the student?

(A) Fish aggregating devices are used mostly by people in just a few countries.

(B) The laws regarding fish aggregating devices differ from country to country.

(C) He supports the passing of laws regulating fish aggregating devices.

(D) There is an ongoing effort to standardize the laws on fish aggregating devices.

[1-5] **Listen to part of a conversation between a student and a professor.** 🎧 CH5_4D

1 Why does the professor ask to see the student?

    Ⓐ To discuss some work that he would like for her to do

    Ⓑ To talk about her current performance in his class

    Ⓒ To inquire about her plans for after graduation

    Ⓓ To determine how she enjoys the class he is teaching

2 What does the professor imply about the student?

    Ⓐ She hopes to apply to graduate school at the school.

    Ⓑ She failed to submit the first assignment on time.

    Ⓒ She is in either her junior or senior year of school.

    Ⓓ She plans to graduate from school with a double major.

3   What is the professor's opinion of the student?

    Ⓐ She has plenty of experience teaching other students.

    Ⓑ She should work harder to be awarded a scholarship.

    Ⓒ She does not have an overly favorable opinion of herself.

    Ⓓ She ought to attend some study sessions to learn better.

4   What will the professor probably do next?

    Ⓐ Let the student go to have lunch with her friend

    Ⓑ Give the student a copy of her new schedule

    Ⓒ Provide the student with some topics she must discuss

    Ⓓ Tell the student how much money she will earn

5   Listen again to part of the conversation. Then answer the question.

    What does the professor imply when he says this:

    Ⓐ The student got the highest grade he has ever given in one class.

    Ⓑ Some Biology professors told the student to go to speak with him.

    Ⓒ He is currently the chairman of the Biology Department.

    Ⓓ The student has previously taken several Biology classes.

[6-11] **Listen to part of a lecture in an architecture class.** 🎧 CH5_4E

Architecture

6 What aspect of urban design does the professor mainly discuss?

    Ⓐ The shapes of individual sections of cities

    Ⓑ How to design cities based upon terrain

    Ⓒ The appearances of post-automobile cities

    Ⓓ The process of creating a planned city

7 Why does the professor tell the students to look at their textbooks?

    Ⓐ To have them see a picture of how Washington, D.C. was designed

    Ⓑ To get them to look at the results of a survey

    Ⓒ To show them some pictures of cities with rivers in them

    Ⓓ To let them see maps of various urban centers

8 What comparison does the professor make between Manhattan and Staten Island?

Ⓐ The reasons their blocks are irregular

Ⓑ The sizes of their blocks

Ⓒ The number of blocks each has

Ⓓ The lengths of their blocks

9 Based on the information in the lecture, indicate which type of city the statements refer to.

Click in the correct box for each statement.

	Pre-Automobile City	Post-Automobile City
① May have a large number of freeways		
② Tends to have streets that wind in various directions		
③ Has streets that are wider than those in the other type		
④ Is the main type of city found in Asia		

10 According to the professor, how can the terrain affect the design of a city?

Ⓐ The blocks may have to be much larger in some places than in others.

Ⓑ Some blocks may have larger numbers of bridges and tunnels.

Ⓒ The manner in which the blocks are laid out may be interrupted.

Ⓓ Streets may have to wind much more than normal in some parts of the city.

11 Listen again to part of the lecture. Then answer the question.

What is the purpose of the professor's response?

Ⓐ To indicate to the student that his line of thinking is wrong

Ⓑ To apologize for having made the student confused

Ⓒ To clarify a statement that she previously made

Ⓓ To propose a new theory that should simplify the topic

◪ Vocabulary Review

A Complete each sentence with the appropriate word from the box.

determine	principles	subsequently	nuisances	rehash

1 Students should understand the _____ of physics when studying it.

2 You must _____ what the most important feature is.

3 Jonathan discovered a cure for the disease; _____, he became famous.

4 It is not necessary to _____ the events that happened a while ago.

5 Mosquitoes and other pests are considered _____ by people.

B Complete each sentence with the correct answer.

1 **Dormant** volcanoes are said to be _____ by geologists.

a. inactive   b. extinct

2 Lisa is an **outstanding** student who almost always _____.

a. does many activities   b. gets high grades

3 Dana was asked to give a _____ speech that was very **concise**.

a. humorous   b. short

4 Receiving **unanimous** support, Jenny got votes from _____.

a. more than half of the people   b. everyone in attendance

5 One _____ that people are **speculating** on is that a new element has been discovered.

a. hypothesis   b. feature

6 Something **vital** to a country's security is considered _____.

a. very important   b. of little use

7 Anyone who _____ the mayor's opinion should vote to **approve** the building of the park.

a. understands   b. agrees with

8 Try to **visualize** your future by imagining what it _____ in your mind.

a. looks like   b. feels like

9 Some of Eric's _____ are considered quite **profound** by experts.

a. random ideas   b. deep thoughts

10 People who **congregate** at the town plaza _____.

a. gather there   b. avoid it

Chapter **06**

Understanding Attitude

Question Type | Understanding Attitude

◢ About the Question

Understanding Attitude questions focus on your ability to recognize the attitudes or opinions of speakers. You are asked to recognize how speakers feel about particular topics, to determine if speakers like or dislike something, or to understand why speakers are experiencing particular emotions. You are also asked to recognize speakers' opinions regarding various topics. These questions appear after both lectures and conversations.

Recognizing Understanding Attitude questions:

1 Some Understanding Attitude questions ask about speakers' feelings. These may be regular questions or replay questions. They may appear like this:

- What is the professor's attitude toward X?

- What is the professor's opinion of X?

- What does the woman mean when she says this: (replay)

2 Other Understanding Attitude questions ask about speakers' opinions. These may be regular questions or replay questions. They may appear like this:

- What can be inferred about the student?

- What can be inferred about the student when she says this: (replay)

- What does the professor imply about the student's paper?

Helpful hints for answering the questions correctly:

- The tone of voice that a speaker uses can be helpful in finding the correct answer.

- When speakers give their opinions on topics, pay close attention. Be sure to differentiate between the facts and opinions of speakers.

- You may need to read between the lines for these questions. The literal meanings of sentences may not be their actual meanings.

- When there are replay questions, pay close attention to all of the excerpted sentences rather than only the sentence that the question asks about. The excerpted sentences provide context clues and hints that can help you find the correct answer.

Listen again to part of the conversation. Then answer the question.
What can be inferred about the student when she says this:

(A) She borrowed some books from the library a week ago.

(B) She has not checked out any books in more than a year.

(C) She has returned some library books late this semester.

(D) She intends to return all of her overdue books soon.

| Script | Listen to part of a conversation between a student and a librarian.

W Student: Good evening. I'd like to check out all of these books, please.

M Librarian: Sure thing. Could I please see your student ID card? I need it so that I can check out your books.

W: Of course. I've got it, um . . . It's here somewhere . . . Aha, here it is.

M: Thank you very much. Okay, let me scan the ID onto the computer, and then . . . Hmm . . . I'm afraid I can't check any books out to you at this moment, Ms. Serrano.

W: Huh? What's the problem? That's my ID card, and I'm enrolled at the school this semester.

M: Yes, but you owe $15.25 in library fines, so you aren't permitted to check out any more books until you pay the fines.

W: Library fines? But I thought we don't have to pay off any library fines until the semester is over.

M: That's correct, but the problem is that you incurred some of these fines during the summer term. Technically, that counts as a different semester, so that's why you can't have the books. If you pay the money you owe from summer now though, you'll be able to borrow them.

W: Ah, sure. I have some money on me now. What's the total amount I owe?

M: It's $15.25. And you can pay either with cash or a check.

| Answer Explanation |

Choice ©️ is the correct answer. When the student says, "I thought we don't have to pay off any library fines until the semester is over," she is implying the she realizes that she owes money to the library for fines that she incurred this semester. Therefore, she is implying that she has returned some library books late this semester.

A

Listen to part of a conversation between a student and a housing office employee.

🎧 CH6_2A

1 What can be inferred about the student?

Ⓐ He has a bad habit of losing his personal items.

Ⓑ He is embarrassed about how he lost his key.

Ⓒ He is not telling the woman the complete truth.

Ⓓ He lost his room key for the second time this semester.

2 Listen again to part of the conversation. Then answer the question.

What does the student mean when he says this:

Ⓐ He does not have very much cash with him at the moment.

Ⓑ The school should not charge students for replacement keys.

Ⓒ He does not mind waiting for a while to get a new key.

Ⓓ The price of the replacement key is very expensive.

Vocabulary

☐ **silly:** foolish

☐ **head:** to go to

☐ **unfortunate:** unlucky

☐ **acceptable:** okay; permissible

B | Listen to part of a conversation between a student and a professor. 🎧 CH6_2B

1 What is the student's opinion of the museum curator?

   (A) His actions are beneficial to local teachers and students.

   (B) He ought to have more of the museum's artifacts on display.

   (C) He needs to reduce the price of admission at the museum.

   (D) His understanding of the past is not as good as it should be.

2 Listen again to part of the conversation. Then answer the question.
   What can be inferred about the professor when he says this: 🎧

   (A) He expects the student to be impressed by the museum.

   (B) He believes the student will do well on the test this week.

   (C) He wants the student to be prepared for the field trip.

   (D) He thinks the student should visit the museum every semester.

Vocabulary

☐ **treat:** a pleasure

☐ **bypass:** to go by; to skip

☐ **scholar:** an academic; a person who studies something in depth

☐ **astounded:** amazed; very surprised

Listen to part of a lecture in an anthropology class. 🎧 CH6_2C

1 What is the student's attitude toward the professor?

    Ⓐ He demands that she provide evidence to support her statements.

    Ⓑ He is skeptical toward the claims that she makes.

    Ⓒ He wants to believe what she says but cannot.

    Ⓓ He feels like she is not providing enough information.

2 Listen again to part of the lecture. Then answer the question.

  What can be inferred about the professor when she says this: 🎧

    Ⓐ She thinks most anthropologists who are studying the past are doing so improperly.

    Ⓑ She feels textbooks written in modern times are filled with incorrect conclusions.

    Ⓒ She believes it is possible for some anthropologists to do their jobs poorly.

    Ⓓ It is likely that she has made several mistakes regarding her interpretations.

| Vocabulary |

☐ **onset:** a beginning; a start

☐ **generalization:** a simplification; a sweeping statement about someone or something

☐ **forage:** to search for food

☐ **positive:** sure

D Listen to part of a lecture in an environmental science class. 🎧 CH6_2D

1 What is the professor's opinion of sound pollution in the water?

   Ⓐ It is not a serious issue that people need to worry about.

   Ⓑ The likelihood of it being a major problem in the future is high.

   Ⓒ There should be laws that ban the creation of it.

   Ⓓ It is causing harm to a wide variety of marine creatures.

2 Listen again to part of the lecture. Then answer the question.

   What does the professor mean when he says this: 🎧

   Ⓐ Nobody is really sure how much harm sound pollution is causing in the oceans.

   Ⓑ Sound pollution in the oceans is more dangerous than oil and gas drilling.

   Ⓒ Pollution and oil and gas drilling are starting to cause big problems in the oceans.

   Ⓓ The oceans are being damaged by sound pollution as well as by oil and gas drilling.

Vocabulary

☐ **dissipate:** to disappear slowly; to dissolve; to go away

☐ **slam:** to hit very hard

☐ **pulse:** a throbbing or beating sensation

☐ **navigate:** to steer; to find one's way in the water

A

Listen to part of a conversation between a student and a student services office employee. 🎧 CH6_3A

✏️ NOTE-TAKING

Vocabulary

☐ **fall ill:** to become sick

☐ **drop by:** to visit

☐ **dedicated:** devoted; enthusiastic

☐ **screen:** to show a movie or video

1 Why does the student visit the student services office?

← Gist-Purpose Question

   Ⓐ He has an appointment with an employee there.

   Ⓑ He is attempting to start a new university club.

   Ⓒ He needs to borrow a projector from the office.

   Ⓓ He received a phone call requesting that he visit.

2 What is the student's opinion of Ms. Anderson?

← Understanding Attitude Question

   Ⓐ He is amused by her comments.

   Ⓑ He thinks she works harder than everyone else.

   Ⓒ He is impressed with her actions.

   Ⓓ He dislikes her attitude toward students.

3 What will the student probably do next?

← Making Inferences Question

   Ⓐ Speak with some club members

   Ⓑ Select a room to reserve

   Ⓒ Make a call to Ms. Anderson

   Ⓓ Leave the office to go to class

4 Listen again to part of the conversation. Then answer the question.
What can be inferred about the student when he says this: 🎧

← Understanding Attitude Question

   Ⓐ He is in a hurry to get a room reserved.

   Ⓑ He hopes to get a specific room to screen a movie in.

   Ⓒ He has never reserved a room for the movie club.

   Ⓓ He has not yet attended a movie club meeting this semester.

Dictation

Listen to the following sentences and fill in the blanks.

❶ She _____ _____ she's pretty _____ to her job.

❷ _____ _____ _____ _____ I asked you the question.

❸ _____ _____ _____ describe each room to you, and then you can tell me _____ _____ _____ _____ ?

B Listen to part of a lecture in a marine biology class. 🎧 CH6_3B

✏ NOTE-TAKING

1 How is the lecture organized?

← Understanding Organization Question

   Ⓐ The professor compares and contrasts aspects of different whales.

   Ⓑ The professor focuses on explaining how toothed whales use sound.

   Ⓒ The professor shows how sound can hurt toothed and baleen whales.

   Ⓓ The professor describes a problem whales have and then provides a solution.

2 Based on the information in the lecture, indicate which type of whale the statements refer to.

← Connecting Content Question

	Toothed Whale	Baleen Whale
1 Produces sound to help it navigate in the water		
2 Makes sound in a higher frequency range than the other		
3 Has a larynx sac enabling it to make sounds		
4 Uses some sounds to identify the other members of its pod		

3 What will the professor probably do next?

← Making Inferences Question

   Ⓐ Dismiss the students from the class

   Ⓑ Play a recording for the students

   Ⓒ Have the students watch a video

   Ⓓ Continue lecturing on whales to the students

4 Listen again to part of the lecture. Then answer the question.

What can be inferred about the professor when she says this: 🎧

← Understanding Attitude Question

   Ⓐ She does not know the answer to the student's question.

   Ⓑ She dislikes being interrupted in the middle of her lecture.

   Ⓒ She does not want to discuss the answer to the student's question.

   Ⓓ She dislikes the way that the student phrased his question.

Dictation

Listen to the following sentences and fill in the blanks.

❶ _____ _____ whales produce sound _____ _____ the species.

❷ _____ _____ baleen whales, they produce sound in a _____ _____ .

❸ I think now is a _____ _____ _____ _____ some whale sounds for you _____ _____ _____ _____ appreciate their beauty.

[1-5] **Listen to part of a conversation between a student and a professor.** 🎧 CH6_4A

1 Why did the professor ask to see the student?

- (A) To encourage her to study harder for the final exam
- (B) To question her about her recent performance in class
- (C) To talk about her doing an extra-credit assignment
- (D) To suggest that she drop his class and take another one

2 What advice does the professor give the student?

Click on 2 answers.

- ☐1 To ask her advisor for some assistance
- ☐2 To talk with the dean of students about her problems
- ☐3 To join one of the study groups in the class
- ☐4 To start submitting her homework in class

3 What can be inferred about Professor Kenmore?

    Ⓐ She has taught at the university for several years.

    Ⓑ She is on good terms with Professor Lewis.

    Ⓒ She teaches the student in one of her classes.

    Ⓓ She is already involved in solving the student's problems.

4 What is the professor's attitude toward the student?

    Ⓐ He considers the student to be overly dramatic.

    Ⓑ He believes that the student is doing her best.

    Ⓒ He shows a great amount of concern for the student's well-being.

    Ⓓ He is uninterested in any of the student's personal problems.

5 Listen again to part of the conversation. Then answer the question.

    What does the student mean when she says this:

    Ⓐ She is going to visit Professor Kenmore after lunch.

    Ⓑ She intends to complete her overdue assignment.

    Ⓒ She is in favor of doing what the professor suggests.

    Ⓓ She hopes that the professor can solve her problem.

[6-11]   Listen to part of a lecture in a physiology class. 🎧 CH6_4B

Physiology

6   What is the lecture mainly about?

Ⓐ Some possible causes of aging

Ⓑ The effects of aging on health

Ⓒ When people begin to age

Ⓓ How aging affects people's appearances

7   According to the professor, what age-related problems can genes cause some groups of people?

Click on 2 answers.

1. The onset of various diseases

2. Graying hair

3. Baldness

4. The loss of strength in bones

8   What is the likely outcome of a person with the BRCA1 gene?

   Ⓐ The person may develop poor vision.

   Ⓑ The person may get a type of cancer.

   Ⓒ The person may suffer from dementia.

   Ⓓ The person may suffer the loss of hair.

9   What is the professor's opinion of research on the FOXO3A gene?

   Ⓐ He considers it mostly a waste of time.

   Ⓑ He thinks that it has produced beneficial results.

   Ⓒ He hopes the scientists doing it are successful.

   Ⓓ He believes it will discover no connection with aging.

10   Based on the information in the lecture, indicate which cause of aging the statements refer to.

Click in the correct box for each statement.

	Gene Theory	Reactive Oxygen Theory
1 Is also known as the free radical theory		
2 May affect people who belong to the same family		
3 Pertains to the loss of electrons in some molecules in the body		
4 May be responsible for plaque building up in people's arteries		

11   Why does the professor discuss the food industry?

   Ⓐ To say that its proponents believe eating well can overcome problems from bad genes

   Ⓑ To cover its relationship with the reactive oxygen theory

   Ⓒ To point out that many of its claims regarding aging have been proven false

   Ⓓ To react to a question that is asked by a student

[12-17] **Listen to part of a lecture in a performing arts class.** 🎧 CH6_4C

Performing Arts

12 What aspect of the theater does the professor mainly discuss?

- Ⓐ Roman influences on it
- Ⓑ Some of its popular actors
- Ⓒ Its origins and early years
- Ⓓ Famous Greek playwrights

13 Why does the professor discuss Thespis?

- Ⓐ To cover his contributions to the development of theater
- Ⓑ To name some of the awards that he won in ancient times
- Ⓒ To talk about some of the plays that he authored
- Ⓓ To compare his works with those of Aeschylus and Euripides

14 In the lecture, the professor talks about the development of theater in ancient Greece. Put the steps in the correct order.

Drag each sentence to the space where it belongs.

1	
2	
3	
4	

Ⓐ Theatrical performances were held at festivals for gods.

Ⓑ Comedies were performed at some festivals.

Ⓒ Singers and dancers became members of the chorus.

Ⓓ Aeschylus added another actor to staged performances.

15 According to the professor, how was Roman theater different from Greek theater?

Click on 2 answers.

1 The Romans had four or more actors on stage at once.

2 The Romans liked comedies more than tragedies.

3 The Romans let women perform in their plays.

4 The Romans did not make any use of the chorus.

16 What is the professor's opinion of miracle plays?

Ⓐ They were less important than other medieval performances.

Ⓑ They were inferior in quality to Greek and Roman plays.

Ⓒ They were more creative than plays performed in the Renaissance.

Ⓓ They were the forerunners of modern plays in the twentieth century.

17 Listen again to part of the lecture. Then answer the question.

What does the professor mean when she says this:

Ⓐ There were more performances in churches after Rome fell.

Ⓑ Theatrical performances were very prominent in Rome.

Ⓒ Most Christian churches put on seasonal staged performances.

Ⓓ The Christian church disliked theatrical performances.

[1-5] **Listen to part of a conversation between a student and a librarian.** 🎧 CH6_4D

1   What problem does the student have?

    (A) He is unable to use the library's computer system.

    (B) He cannot remember the titles of some books he needs.

    (C) He does not know how to start a research project.

    (D) He forgot to bring money to use the copy machines.

2   What is the student's opinion of the librarian?

    (A) He believes she needs to suggest some more solutions.

    (B) He thinks she should assist him more with his research.

    (C) He is happy with the interlibrary loan assistance she provides.

    (D) He is impressed with her knowledge of books.

3   Why does the librarian explain about interlibrary loan?

    (A) To suggest a free alternative to buying e-books

    (B) To mention that using it can be extremely slow

    (C) To name some schools which participate in it

    (D) To suggest it as the only way to get the necessary books

4   What will the librarian probably do next?

    (A) Search for some books on the library's computer system

    (B) Point out where the copy machines in the library are

    (C) Take the student to the front desk to check out some books

    (D) Show the student where some books are located

5   Listen again to part of the conversation. Then answer the question.

    What does the librarian imply when she says this:

    (A) She is not sure where in the library the book is located.

    (B) The student cannot borrow the book they are discussing.

    (C) Somebody has already checked out the book the student needs.

    (D) The book the student wants is not currently in the library.

[6-11] Listen to part of a lecture in an environmental science class. 🎧 CH6_4E

Environmental Science

plastics

6 What is the lecture mainly about?

   (A) The development of plastics over time

   (B) The most important natural plastics

   (C) The uses people have for plastics

   (D) The inventors responsible for making plastics

7   Why does the professor mention pasta noodles?

   Ⓐ To explain that the way to make them is similar to the way to make polymers
   Ⓑ To point out that the resin secreted from rubber trees resembles them
   Ⓒ To make a comparison while explaining why plastics can take many forms
   Ⓓ To describe what happens to rubber when it is undergoing the vulcanization process

8   What is the professor's opinion of Alexander Parkes?

   Ⓐ His scientific skills were better than his business skills.
   Ⓑ He should be better known because of his accomplishments.
   Ⓒ His work on polymers was the basis for all modern plastics.
   Ⓓ He should have become rich from his invention of Parkesine.

9   What breakthrough was Leo Baekeland responsible for?

   Ⓐ Developing plastic that could be dissolved easily
   Ⓑ Making the first plastic from petrochemicals
   Ⓒ Creating the first commercially successful form of polyester
   Ⓓ Using plant cellulose to make plastic for the first time

10   What was a likely outcome of plastics becoming so strong?

   Ⓐ They became harder to make since the process required precision.
   Ⓑ They started being used more as containers than other types of materials.
   Ⓒ They got more expensive due to the higher quality of materials that were used in them.
   Ⓓ They were able to be used in a wider variety of industries, including construction.

11   According to the professor, what is the importance of the bacterium that was discovered by Japanese researchers?

   Ⓐ It may be used to help break down plastics very quickly.
   Ⓑ It has the ability to enhance the strength of plastics.
   Ⓒ It will be useful with regard to the production of PET.
   Ⓓ It weakens plastic and allows it to be reshaped easily.

◼ Vocabulary Review

A   Complete each sentence with the appropriate word from the box.

esoteric	surmise	astounded	emit	malleable

1   The experts were _____ by the results of the survey.

2   Lucy studies _____ topics that few people know anything about.

3   Stars like the sun _____ radiation all the time.

4   You should be able to _____ that there is not much time left.

5   Gold is highly _____ because it is so soft.

B   Complete each sentence with the correct answer.

1   The teacher is fairly **lax** and _____ checks the students' homework.

   a. constantly   b. rarely

2   The truck **slammed** into the wall and hit it _____.

   a. very hard   b. gently

3   The singer's **dedicated** followers were so _____ him that they bought all of his albums.

   a. aware of   b. devoted to

4   The building is **deteriorating** rapidly and will likely _____ within months.

   a. become more valuable   b. collapse

5   **Subjective** opinions are ones that are _____ to people.

   a. personal   b. unbiased

6   When a pandemic _____, people call it the **onset** of the disease.

   a. comes to an end   b. gets its start

7   The **breakthrough** was considered the greatest _____ of the century.

   a. discovery   b. announcement

8   When the **revival** of that art style took place, _____ became interested in it.

   a. almost nobody   b. many people

9   The children were acting **silly** and therefore behaved in a _____ manner.

   a. foolish   b. severe

10 Everything **integral** to the project is _____ for it to work properly.

   a. expensive   b. necessary

Chapter **07**

Understanding
Organization

Question Type | Understanding Organization

◢ About the Question

Understanding Organization questions focus on your ability to determine how a talk is organized. You are asked to notice how the professor organizes the lecture or presents certain information to the class. Or you may be asked to determine how specific information relates to the lecture as a whole. These questions almost always appear after lectures.

Recognizing Understanding Organization questions:

1 Some Understanding Organization questions ask how the material in the professor's lecture is organized. They may appear like this:

- How does the professor organize the information about X that he presents to the class?

- How is the discussion organized?

2 Other Understanding Organization questions ask about the information that is presented in the lecture. They may appear like this:

- Why does the professor discuss X?

- Why does the professor mention X?

Helpful hints for answering the questions correctly:

- Consider how the professor organizes the lecture. Common ways are by using chronological order, by providing causes and effects, by comparing and contrasting, by categorizing, by describing problems and solutions, by giving examples, and by using sequence.

- The professor may explain the purpose of the lecture at its beginning or end. Pay close attention to these parts of the lecture.

- When the professor talks about something not related to the main topic of the lecture, consider why that happened.

- For specific facts, think about the professor's purpose in mentioning them.

Why does the professor discuss the catfish?

Ⓐ To point out that it is a carnivore

Ⓑ To explain how it acts in winter

Ⓒ To claim that it is a common aquarium fish

Ⓓ To say that it usually consumes vegetation

| Script | Listen to part of a lecture in a zoology class.

M Professor: Now that we've covered the fish living in the upper and middle levels of lakes and rivers, we need to get to the lower level. Uh, and by that, I'm referring to the fish that live at the very bottoms of lakes and rivers.

W Student: Don't we call those fish bottom feeders, Professor Burgess? My father has a big aquarium, and that's what he calls the fish in the tank that always stay down there.

M: Yes, that's a term which is used. However, it's more commonly used by aquarium owners than it is with biologists. Nevertheless, we all understand what the term means, so feel free to employ it.

All right . . . What are some fish that live at the bottoms of lakes and rivers? Among them are carp, bream, bass, sturgeon, and, of course, the catfish, which is probably the best known of all, er, bottom feeders.

Many of these fish have some characteristics in common, among them the ability to bury themselves in the mud at the bottom of their lake or river. Why would they do that . . . ? Well, when cold temperatures come, these fish often become dormant, so their bodily functions slow down, and then they bury themselves in the mud to keep warm during the winter months. There was a study during which researchers monitored some catfish that had been tagged. Basically, during winter, those catfish moved very little, uh, except for on the rare occasions that they needed to feed.

Oh, and one thing you should keep in mind is that not all bottom feeders consume vegetation, which is often the case for the fish that are kept in aquariums. Owners of aquariums typically purchase those fish to help get rid of algae in their tanks. But, uh, while some bottom feeders in lakes and rivers do consume vegetation, a large number of them, such as bass and sturgeon, are carnivores.

| Answer Explanation |

Choice Ⓑ is the correct answer. The professor tells the students, "There was a study during which researchers monitored some catfish that had been tagged. Basically, during winter, those catfish moved very little, uh, except for on the rare occasions that they needed to feed." In describing the actions of the fish, he is explaining how the catfish acts in winter.

A | Listen to part of a lecture in an art class. 🎧 CH7_2A

1 Why does the professor mention Ansel Adams?

(A) To point out his relationship with the Photographic Society of London

(B) To name him as one of the world's most famous photographers

(C) To suggest that the pictures he took could be considered art

(D) To state that he never thought of the pictures he took as art

2 How is the lecture organized?

(A) The professor explains why photography is art and then talks about why it is not art.

(B) The professor gives the opinions of photographers regarding whether photography is art.

(C) The professor focuses on the development of photography as an art form in the 1800s.

(D) The professor talks about how her opinions on photography as art changed over time.

Vocabulary

☐ **enhance:** to improve; to make better

☐ **beholder:** a person who is looking at something

☐ **bent:** an inclination

☐ **perilously:** dangerously

Listen to part of a lecture in an environmental science class. 🎧 CH7_2B

1   Why does the professor discuss the National Weather Service?

   (A) To criticize it for failing to gather enough data at times

   (B) To cover its role in the collection of weather data

   (C) To describe some flaws in its collection methods

   (D) To compare its work with that of other nations' weather services

2   How does the professor organize the information about weather data collection that he presents to the class?

   (A) By talking about the equipment according to how advanced it is

   (B) By providing examples of the various tools used in the process

   (C) By giving the students a short history of data collection methods

   (D) By describing the methods in their order of importance

Vocabulary

☐ **syllabus:** a paper describing the contents of a course

☐ **precipitation:** rain, snow, or any other form of water that falls to the ground

☐ **accurate:** correct

☐ **aloft:** in the air

Listen to part of a lecture in an anthropology class. 🎧 CH7_2C

1 Why does the professor mention the Korowai tribe?

    Ⓐ To note how its members construct their homes

    Ⓑ To say that the tribe lives near Port Moresby

    Ⓒ To state that its members hunt on the coast

    Ⓓ To describe the diet that the tribe usually eats

2 Why does the professor discuss cannibalism?

    Ⓐ To point out that only a few tribes ever engaged in it

    Ⓑ To respond to a question asked by a student

    Ⓒ To state that it is no longer practiced in New Guinea

    Ⓓ To speak strongly against the practicing of it

Vocabulary

☐ **dense:** thick

☐ **astonish:** to shock; to surprise

☐ **hut:** a crude dwelling

☐ **subsistence:** survival

Listen to part of a lecture in a zoology class. 🎧 CH7_2D

1   Why does the professor discuss butterflies?

 Ⓐ To give an example of holometabolous metamorphosis

 Ⓑ To compare their life cycles with those of grasshoppers

 Ⓒ To respond to an inquiry made by one of the students

 Ⓓ To correct a mistake that appears in the textbook

2   How is the lecture organized?

 Ⓐ The professor lectures while showing video clips of each type of metamorphosis.

 Ⓑ The professor compares and contrasts two types of metamorphosis.

 Ⓒ The professor describes the life cycles of several types of insects.

 Ⓓ The professor explains each type of metamorphosis in detail.

Vocabulary

☐ **virtually:** practically; nearly

☐ **miniature:** very small; tiny

☐ **habitat:** the place where an organism lives

☐ **burst from:** to explode from; to come out from suddenly

A

Listen to part of a lecture in a zoology class. 🎧 CH7_3A

✏ NOTE-TAKING

Vocabulary

☐ **extinct:** no longer alive on the Earth

☐ **adherent:** a believer; a supporter

☐ **recede:** to move backward

☐ **isolation:** the state of being alone

1 What aspect of megafauna does the professor mainly discuss?

← Gist-Content Question

- (A) The places on the Earth where they thrived
- (B) The primary reasons that they went extinct
- (C) The methods humans used to hunt them
- (D) The ways that climate change affected their lives

2 According to the professor, where did the changing climate negatively affect some megafauna? (Choose 2 answers.)

← Detail Question

- (A) In parts of New Zealand
- (B) In parts of North Africa
- (C) In tundra in the Northern Hemisphere
- (D) In glacial regions in Europe

3 What does the professor imply about human hunters?

← Making Inferences Question

- (A) They were able successfully to hunt animals much larger than themselves.
- (B) They preferred to hunt megafauna by having many men work together.
- (C) They killed megafauna slowly over time since the animals were so large.
- (D) They improved their hunting methods since some megafauna were hard to kill.

4 Why does the professor discuss the moa?

← Understanding Organization Question

- (A) To compare its extinction with that of the mammoth
- (B) To show how climate change caused its numbers to decrease
- (C) To give an example of a megafauna killed by human hunting
- (D) To claim that it was the most recent megafauna to go extinct

Dictation

Listen to the following sentences and fill in the blanks.

❶ The _____ megafauna _____ _____ the group of animals which are larger than humans are.

❷ We do, _____, have many theories, _____ _____ _____ have more adherents than _____ _____.

❸ So _____ _____ _____ the moa went extinct _____ _____ human hunting.

Listen to part of a lecture in an archaeology class. 🎧 CH7_3B

✎ NOTE-TAKING

Vocabulary

☐ **assimilate:** to integrate; to become one with the dominant culture or people

☐ **veritable:** absolute

☐ **warrior:** a great fighter

☐ **prevail:** to win; to triumph

1 According to the professor, where have many Celtic Briton artifacts been found?

← Detail Question

- (A) Around the Thames River
- (B) On the European mainland
- (C) At ancient hill forts
- (D) At the sites of old palaces

2 What comparison does the professor make between the Desborough Mirror and the Battersea Shield?

← Connecting Content Question

- (A) The way the La Tène culture influenced them
- (B) The nature of the people who owned them
- (C) The material that each of them is made of
- (D) The place where each one was excavated

3 How is the lecture organized?

← Understanding Organization Question

- (A) The professor provides a chronological history of the Celtic Briton people.
- (B) The professor focuses on the European influences on the Celtic Britons.
- (C) The professor covers the reasons that the Celtic Briton culture went into decline.
- (D) The professor mostly describes Celtic Briton artifacts that have been found.

4 Listen again to part of the lecture. Then answer the question.

What can be inferred from the professor's response to the student?

← Understanding Function Question

- (A) The matter they are talking about is fully covered in the textbook.
- (B) The professor intends to talk about the topic more in her lecture.
- (C) The professor is going to have a group discussion in a few minutes.
- (D) There is no definite answer to the question that the student asked.

Dictation

Listen to the following sentences and fill in the blanks.

❶ It also _____ us some _____ _____ the higher levels of culture of the Celtic people.

❷ A _____ _____ _____ is that the more loosely organized Celtic people preferred open warfare.

❸ _____ _____ _____ _____ a few images of swords that have been excavated in England.

[1-5] **Listen to part of a conversation between a student and a career center employee.** 🎧 CH7_4A

1 Why does the student visit the career center?

Click on 2 answers.

1. To register for a workshop that will be held there
2. To request some assistance with his résumé
3. To report a problem with the career center's webpage
4. To get advice on some positions he is applying for

2 What does the woman give the student?

Ⓐ Her business card
Ⓑ A brochure
Ⓒ A registration sheet
Ⓓ A list of available jobs

3 Why does the woman explain about the workshop?

    Ⓐ To inform the student that he has no need for it

    Ⓑ To emphasize it is for sophomores and juniors

    Ⓒ To point out that it will be held twice this semester

    Ⓓ To respond to the student's inquiry about it

4 What does the woman imply about the workshop?

    Ⓐ It has been held before in previous years.

    Ⓑ She is going to be one of the instructors at it.

    Ⓒ Students can sign up for it at the career center.

    Ⓓ Attendees must pay a small fee to attend it.

5 What does the woman offer to do for the student?

    Ⓐ Help him shorten his résumé to one page

    Ⓑ Give him some advice on his portfolio

    Ⓒ Rewrite his cover letters for his job applications

    Ⓓ Give him one of the remaining spots in the workshop

[6-11]   **Listen to part of a lecture in an anthropology class.** 🎧 CH7_4B

Anthropology

6   How does the professor organize the information about the Towie Stone that she presents to the class?

Ⓐ By showing pictures and then pointing out aspects of the stone
Ⓑ By providing an in-depth description of the features of the stone
Ⓒ By drawing a diagram on the board and then lecturing about it
Ⓓ By reproducing the designs on the stone and talking about their importance

7   According to the professor, how were most of the carved stone balls found?

Ⓐ Researchers on organized digs found them.
Ⓑ People walking along beaches discovered them.
Ⓒ Farmers working in their fields discovered them.
Ⓓ Archaeologists searching old battlefields found them.

8   Why does the professor explain the five Platonic solids?

   (A) To compare their appearances with those of the carved stone balls

   (B) To claim that Stone Age people discovered them before the Greeks did

   (C) To say that the carved stone balls only resemble the three smallest ones

   (D) To talk about their importance to the field of mathematics

9   In the lecture, the professor describes a number of facts about the carved stone balls. Indicate whether each of the following is a fact or not.

Click in the correct box for each statement.

	Fact	Not a Fact
1 Many of them have knobs that are sticking out from the stones.		
2 The stones have been found exclusively in Scotland.		
3 It is speculated that the stones were used by fishermen.		
4 The stones might have been used to measure the weight of food or other items.		

10 What can be inferred about the professor?

   (A) She lectures on the history of mathematics some semesters.

   (B) She is not sure what the purpose of the carved stone balls was.

   (C) She saw the Towie Stone in person on a trip to Scotland.

   (D) She believes that the carved stone balls were status symbols.

11 Listen again to part of the lecture. Then answer the question.

   What does the professor mean when she says this:

   (A) She thinks that more is going to be learned about Stone Age cultures.

   (B) Less is known about the Stone Age than any other time in human history.

   (C) It is important to learn more about the Stone Age to fill in gaps in our knowledge.

   (D) There is much that is not known about the Stone Age at the present time.

[12-17] **Listen to part of a lecture in an education class.** CH7_4C

Education

Black Mountain College

12 What is the lecture mainly about?

(A) The teaching style at Black Mountain College

(B) The students who attended Black Mountain College

(C) The achievements of the Black Mountain College faculty

(D) The history of Black Mountain College

13 Why does the professor tell the students about John Dewey?

   Ⓐ To describe the main achievements in his life

   Ⓑ To say that he helped establish Black Mountain College

   Ⓒ To focus on his importance in library science

   Ⓓ To explain his influence on Black Mountain College

14 Who was John Andrew Rice?

   Ⓐ A Black Mountain College donor

   Ⓑ One of the founders of Black Mountain College

   Ⓒ The most accomplished professor at Black Mountain College

   Ⓓ A graduate of Black Mountain College

15 What does the professor imply about the Bauhaus School?

   Ⓐ It was founded in the United States.

   Ⓑ It had a great effect on Black Mountain College.

   Ⓒ Its creator was Josef Albers.

   Ⓓ It was supported by many fascists in Europe.

16 Why does the professor mention Albert Einstein?

   Ⓐ To describe how his work influenced students at Black Mountain College

   Ⓑ To compare him with Buckminster Fuller

   Ⓒ To say that he taught at Black Mountain College

   Ⓓ To cite him as a supporter of Black Mountain College

17 Listen again to part of the lecture. Then answer the question.

Why does the student say this:

   Ⓐ To give some advice

   Ⓑ To offer an opinion

   Ⓒ To respond to a question

   Ⓓ To make an inquiry

[1-5] **Listen to part of a conversation between a student and a professor.** 🎧 CH7_4D

1   What problem does the student have?

   Ⓐ Some materials that she ordered did not arrive.

   Ⓑ A work of art that she was making developed a crack.

   Ⓒ She dropped a vase that she made and broke it.

   Ⓓ Her grade is one of the lowest in the entire class.

2   According to the professor, what can happen to clay in dry conditions?

   Ⓐ It can become bone dry in about a week.

   Ⓑ It may develop cracks while being sculpted.

   Ⓒ It may become too thin to put in a kiln.

   Ⓓ It can be difficult to be glazed and painted.

3 Why does the professor explain his grading policy to the student?

    Ⓐ To advise the student to create another vase very quickly

    Ⓑ To point out that the student needs a high grade on her final exam

    Ⓒ To mention that the student is in danger of failing his class

    Ⓓ To suggest to the student that she should not turn in her project late

4 What is the professor's attitude toward the student?

    Ⓐ He is willing to give her extra time to finish her work.

    Ⓑ He has no interest in suggesting a solution.

    Ⓒ He believes she is the cause of her problem.

    Ⓓ He is unconcerned about her need to do well in his class.

5 Listen again to part of the conversation. Then answer the question.

What does the student imply when she says this:

    Ⓐ Sculpting is something she wants to learn more about.

    Ⓑ Her class studied sculpting earlier in the semester.

    Ⓒ She can make mosaics much better than she can make sculptures.

    Ⓓ The sculpture that she created in class got a high grade.

Listen to part of a lecture in a zoology class. 🎧 CH7_4E

Zoology

a trilobite fossil and an artist's rendition

6   What aspect of trilobites does the professor mainly discuss?

   Ⓐ Their unique features

   Ⓑ Their connections to other arthropods

   Ⓒ Their physical characteristics

   Ⓓ Their eventual extinction

7   According to the professor, how did trilobites manage to survive several extinction events?

    (A) Their great amount of diversity always let some species live.

    (B) They lived deep enough underwater to avoid most problems on the Earth.

    (C) Their small sizes allowed them to endure when food was scarce.

    (D) They had bodies which were able to survive during the toughest conditions.

8   How does the professor organize the information about the bodies of trilobites that he presents to the class?

    (A) By focusing exclusively on the three body parts trilobites have

    (B) By comparing the bodies of trilobites with those of other arthropods

    (C) By showing slides to the students as he provides explanations

    (D) By having the students look at pictures in their books while he lectures

9   Why does the professor tell the students about the eyes of trilobites?

    (A) To describe the main parts that comprised their complex eyes

    (B) To point out that their great eyesight made them excellent hunters

    (C) To explain why most of them had to live deep beneath the surface

    (D) To show how much variety there was between trilobite species

10 What does the professor imply about trilobite fossils?

    (A) Complete ones containing all body parts are rare.

    (B) Most of them are found deep under the water.

    (C) They are considered prized possessions by scientists.

    (D) The largest ones are those which are most commonly found.

11 Why does the professor mention the Permian Extinction Event?

    (A) To emphasize that new species of animals arose after it

    (B) To point out that trilobites managed to survive it

    (C) To associate it with the disappearance of trilobites

    (D) To explain the precise reason that it took place

■ Vocabulary Review

A Complete each sentence with the appropriate word from the box.

similarities	scavenge	dismal	burst from	beholder

1 It is often said that beauty is in the eye of the _____.

2 Vultures _____ the bodies of dead animals and eat them for food.

3 It is easy to notice the _____ between the two men.

4 A flock of birds suddenly _____ the bushes when they sensed danger.

5 Nobody felt like going outside because of the _____ weather yesterday.

B Complete each sentence with the correct answer.

1 The eagle's **keen** eyesight allows it to _____ see tiny animals from far away.

   a. clearly   b. occasionally

2 We expected to **prevail** in the game, and we managed to _____ by more than five points.

   a. lose   b. win

3 Some of the **pointers** that Alice gave Jeff were very good _____ on improving his work.

   a. roles   b. tips

4 The **dense** jungle is so _____ that it is difficult to walk through it.

   a. thick   b. dangerous

5 The _____ made by the government with regard to economic **reform** worked very well.

   a. announcements   b. changes

6 **Precipitation** is expected this weekend, so there is a good chance it will _____.

   a. rain   b. be sunny

7 The archaeologists plan to _____ the artifacts tomorrow in order to **unearth** them.

   a. dig up   b. discover

8 An **adherent** of the president, Greg _____ the country's leader any way that he can.

   a. opposes   b. supports

9 The teacher always **deducts** from late work by _____ several points from students.

   a. considering   b. taking away

10 Immigrants are expected to **assimilate** into the culture and to _____ the natives.

   a. study with   b. become one with

164

Chapter 08

Connecting Content

■ About the Question

Connecting Content questions focus on your ability to recognize how ideas or topics in the talk relate to one another. You are asked to notice what their connections are. These connections may be stated overtly, or you may have to infer them. These questions usually appear in talks where different ideas, people, places, themes, or objects are discussed. These questions almost always appear after lectures.

Recognizing Connecting Content questions:

1   Many Connecting Content questions appear as charts or tables. They have four sentences or phrases, and you must match them with various themes, ideas, causes, effects, problems, solutions, objects, or individuals. They may appear like this:

- Based on the information in the conversation, indicate which . . . the statements refer to.

	X	Y
1 [statement]		
2 [statement]		
3 [statement]		
4 [statement]		

2   Other Connecting Content questions ask you to make inferences based on the relationships mentioned in the talk. They may appear like this:

- What is the likely outcome of doing procedure X before procedure Y?
- What can be inferred about X?
- What does the professor imply about X?
- What comparison does the professor make between X and Y?

Helpful hints for answering the questions correctly:

- When a professor discusses multiple individuals, themes, places, ideas, or objects in a lecture, it is likely that a chart question will appear. Pay attention to the important details the professor mentions.

- Pay close attention when a professor makes comparisons in a lecture.

- Think about possible future results of events or actions that the professor describes. You may sometimes need to predict a future result, come to a conclusion, or determine the effect of some cause.

Which comparison does the professor make between 51 Pegasi b and Kepler 438b?

Ⓐ The size of each planet

Ⓑ The surface temperatures of the planets

Ⓒ The distance from the Earth of each planet

Ⓓ The amount of liquid water on the planets

| Script | Listen to part of a lecture in an astronomy class.

W Professor: In recent years, one of the most exciting events in the field of astronomy is the confirmation that exoplanets exist. By exoplanet, um, I'm referring to planets orbiting stars other than our sun. That means they exist in different solar systems. While I assume most of you take it for granted that exoplanets exist, that most assuredly was not the case until a couple of decades ago. There was a lively debate in the profession as to whether our solar system was the only one to have planets. Obviously, now that we've discovered thousands of exoplanets, we know there are, um, in all likelihood, billions of them in the Milky Way Galaxy alone.

What are these exoplanets like? Well, they vary. Let me tell you about two of them so that you'll get an idea regarding their characteristics. In 1995, the exoplanet 51 Pegasi b was discovered orbiting the star 51 Pegasi. It's located fifty light years from our solar system and orbits a star similar to the sun. It's called a "hot Jupiter" by astronomers. I'll explain more about that in a moment, so hold your questions regarding it, please. Interestingly, 51 Pegasi b is closer to its star than Mercury is to the sun. As a result, it takes only four days to complete a single orbit. Its surface temperatures are likely in excess of 1,000 degrees Celsius, so surely no life as we know it can survive there.

But there are exoplanets that may have earthlike conditions, so they might be able to support life. The exoplanet Kepler 438b is a rocky planet slightly larger than the Earth and orbits the star Kepler 438. Its orbit is within the habitable zone of its star, which means that there may be liquid water on the planet's surface. Unfortunately, it's 470 light years away from us, so nobody will be visiting it for quite some time.

| **Answer Explanation** |

Choice Ⓒ is the correct answer. About 51 Pegasi b, the professor states, "It's located fifty light years from our solar system and orbits a star similar to the sun." Regarding Kepler 438b, she comments, "It's 470 light years away from us." So she compares the distance from the Earth of each planet.

A Listen to part of a conversation between a student and a professor. 🎧 CH8_2A

1 What is the likely outcome of the student going to France for the summer?

    (A) She will be obligated to take summer school the next year.

    (B) She will have to get a part-time job during the fall semester.

    (C) She will change one of her majors to Archaeology.

    (D) She will take an intensive course in French before she leaves.

2 Based on the information in the conversation, indicate which summer activity the statements refer to.

	Visiting France	Staying at School
1 The student will get to work with Professor Hamilton.		
2 The student will be able to earn some money.		
3 The student will have to spend a lot of money.		
4 The student will spend some time with her friends.		

Vocabulary

☐ **excavate:** to dig up from the ground

☐ **relic:** an item from a past culture

☐ **hands-on:** practical; applied

☐ **elective:** a course a student does not have to take but chooses to

Listen to part of a lecture in a sociology class. 🎧 CH8_2B

1 What can be inferred about suburbs?

    (A) More people drive personal vehicles in them than take the bus.

    (B) Their residents earn more money than city dwellers do.

    (C) Large numbers of city residents travel by train to them daily.

    (D) They appeal more to younger people than to people in their forties and fifties.

2 Based on the information in the lecture, indicate which place the statements refer to.

	Suburbs	Cities
1 Have large numbers of green areas		
2 Have extensive public transportation networks		
3 Have few homes in their central areas		
4 Have population densities that change throughout the day		

Vocabulary

☐ **urban:** relating to a city

☐ **dominate:** to rule over; to control

☐ **dweller:** a person who lives in a certain place

☐ **metropolis:** a large city

C | Listen to part of a lecture in a biology class. 🎧 CH8_2C

1 **What comparison does the professor make between the bullhorn acacia and the cattle egret?**

Ⓐ The countries around the world where they can be found

Ⓑ The harm that they can cause to their symbiotic partners

Ⓒ The benefits they gain from their symbiotic relationships

Ⓓ The amount of time that they spend in symbiotic relationships

2 **Based on the information in the lecture, indicate which type of symbiosis the statements refer to.**

	Mutualism	Commensalism	Parasitism
1 Can result in a host suffering some kind of damage or injury			
2 Is the type of relationship the cattle egret and the cow have			
3 Does not result in any benefits or harm to one of the partners			
4 Is the type of relationship the bullhorn acacia and ants have			

Vocabulary

☐ **interaction:** the relationship between two or more things

☐ **illustrate:** to show

☐ **thorn:** a sharp, short branch sticking out on a plant

☐ **herbivore:** an animal that only eats vegetation

170

Listen to part of a lecture in a physiology class. 🎧 CH8_2D

1 What is the likely outcome of a person getting a large amount of stage 4 sleep?

    Ⓐ The person will have many vivid dreams.

    Ⓑ The person will wake up well rested.

    Ⓒ The person will need less REM sleep.

    Ⓓ The person will have an increased heart rate.

2 What comparison does the professor make between stage 2 sleep and REM sleep?

    Ⓐ How slowly a person breathes

    Ⓑ How much a person dreams

    Ⓒ How fast the heart beats

    Ⓓ How much the eyes move

Vocabulary

☐ **surroundings:** the area around a certain place

☐ **burst:** a spurt; a sudden increase

☐ **restorative:** providing energy or healing

☐ **rigid:** stiff; unmoving

A ☐ **Listen to part of a conversation between a student and a student activities office employee.** 🎧 CH8_3A

✏ NOTE-TAKING

....

....

....

....

....

....

....

....

Vocabulary

☐ **extracurricular:** additional; extra

☐ **turn down:** to reject; to say no to

☐ **fade away:** to disappear slowly

☐ **intramural:** inside a college or university

172

1 Why does the student visit the student activities office?

← Gist-Purpose Question

    Ⓐ To inquire about some extracurricular activities

    Ⓑ To find out when a special event will be held

    Ⓒ To ask why a club no longer exists at the school

    Ⓓ To sign up to become a member of the photography club

2 What is the likely outcome of the student advertising in the school paper?

← Connecting Content Question

    Ⓐ The school will be convinced to allow more clubs on campus.

    Ⓑ The photography club will attract more members.

    Ⓒ He will find some students who are interested in playing basketball.

    Ⓓ The cycling club will be restarted during a later semester.

3 What is the student's opinion of the soccer league?

← Understanding Attitude Question

    Ⓐ He does not want to sign up for it.

    Ⓑ He would join it if he were more athletic.

    Ⓒ He is interested in learning more about it.

    Ⓓ He thinks it is more popular than the basketball league.

4 Listen again to part of the conversation. Then answer the question.
What does the student activities office employee mean when he says this:

← Understanding Function Question

🎧

    Ⓐ The student cannot register for any clubs.

    Ⓑ He is concerned about the student's problem.

    Ⓒ The meeting the student wants to attend was canceled.

    Ⓓ The campus center contains no information the student wants.

Dictation

Listen to the following sentences and fill in the blanks.

❶ Is this where I'm _____ to go to _____ _____ _____ some extracurricular activities?

❷ _____ _____ _____ _____ which activities you're interested in doing?

❸ _____ _____ _____ I could start up a cycling club this semester?

Listen to part of a lecture in a biology class. 🎧 CH8_3B

✏ NOTE-TAKING

| Vocabulary |

☐ **plethora:** a large amount

☐ **gunk:** slime; grease; filth

☐ **strand:** a long string

☐ **devise:** to come up with; to think of

1 Why does the professor explain extracellular polymeric substances?

← Understanding Organization Question

    Ⓐ To describe the process through which bacteria create biofilm

    Ⓑ To talk about the way that biofilm can acquire water and nutrients

    Ⓒ To mention what helps keep biofilm from being destroyed

    Ⓓ To state that scientists are currently conducting research on them

2 In the lecture, the professor explains the process in which biofilm is created. Put the steps in the correct order.

← Connecting Content Question

    Ⓐ Nutrients and water are acquired.

    Ⓑ Bacteria produce EPS strands.

    Ⓒ Substances other than bacteria join together.

    Ⓓ Bacteria become connected to one another.

3 What comparison does the professor make between bacteria and biofilm?

← Connecting Content Question

    Ⓐ The amount of nutrients that they consume

    Ⓑ Their resistance to various modern medicines

    Ⓒ Their ability to survive in hostile environments

    Ⓓ The number of them living in human bodies

4 Listen again to part of the lecture. Then answer the question.
What does the professor mean when he says this: 🎧

← Understanding Attitude Question

    Ⓐ It is possible for many bacteria to unite to become biofilm.

    Ⓑ Bacteria are more commonly found than biofilm is.

    Ⓒ The most dangerous biofilm is able to change forms.

    Ⓓ Many types of biofilm exist in all sorts of places.

Dictation

Listen to the following sentences and fill in the blanks.

❶ Biofilm is bacteria, and it's all around us in a _____ _____ _____ .

❷ These sugary strands _____ _____ extracellular polymeric substances, _____ EPS, _____
_____ .

❸ But the _____ _____ _____ _____ since biofilm can also be beneficial.

[1-5] Listen to part of a conversation between a student and a professor. CH8_4A

1   What are the speakers mainly discussing?

    (A) A volleyball tournament that the student competed in

    (B) The information the student needs to study for a test

    (C) An extra assignment the student can complete for a class

    (D) The student's need to take an exam at an alternative time

2   What comparison does the student make between the exams for Professor Dawson and Professor Allston?

    (A) Where she has to go to take them

    (B) What she needs to study for them

    (C) When she is going to take them

    (D) How difficult they are going to be

3 What can be inferred about the student?

    Ⓐ She intends to work on her papers while she is at the tournament.

    Ⓑ She has not spoken with her other professors about her problem.

    Ⓒ She is going to quit the volleyball team after this semester.

    Ⓓ She is taking the professor's class as one of her elective courses.

4 In the conversation, the student and professor describe a number of facts about the exam for the professor's class. Indicate whether each of the following is a fact or not.

Click in the correct box for each statement.

	Fact	Not a Fact
☐1 The students are supposed to take it during their regular class time.		
☐2 The students can choose to take the exam or submit a paper.		
☐3 The material will cover only what the class has learned in the past two weeks.		
☐4 The exam should take the students around two hours to complete.		

5 Listen again to part of the conversation. Then answer the question.

Why does the professor say this:

    Ⓐ To indicate that she is unwilling to go along with the student's suggestion

    Ⓑ To express her displeasure with the scheduling of the tournament

    Ⓒ To tell the student that she will not receive any special treatment

    Ⓓ To encourage the student to focus more on her studies than on sports

[6-11] **Listen to part of a lecture in a history class.** 🎧 CH8_4B

History

6   What aspect of the Wars of the Roses does the professor mainly discuss?

    Ⓐ The major battles that took place during it

    Ⓑ Its connection with the Hundred Years' War

    Ⓒ The manner in which it arrived at its conclusion

    Ⓓ The main events that led to it breaking out

7   What does the professor imply about Richard of York?

    Ⓐ His actions were opposed by most of the English people.

    Ⓑ He was more of a warrior than Henry VI was.

    Ⓒ He never married during his entire life.

    Ⓓ He suffered an injury while fighting in France.

8   What is the professor's attitude toward the advisors of Henry VI?

    Ⓐ They tried their best to help their country.

    Ⓑ Their actions were the primary cause of the start of hostilities.

    Ⓒ Their advice often proved to be poor.

    Ⓓ The manner in which they acted was wrong.

9   What happened at the First Battle of St. Albans?

    Ⓐ Henry VI was captured during the fighting.

    Ⓑ Richard of York's forces won the fight.

    Ⓒ Henry VI fled to France after the battle ended.

    Ⓓ Richard of York was crowned king of England on the battlefield.

10   Based on the information in the lecture, indicate which noble house the statements refer to.

Click in the correct box for each statement.

	House of York	House of Lancaster
1 Had possession of the English throne at the start of the Wars of the Roses		
2 Had one of its leaders want to resume fighting the French after the Hundred Years' War ended		
3 Initiated hostilities during the Wars of the Roses		
4 Was led by a person who suffered mental problems		

11   Listen again to part of the lecture. Then answer the question.

What does the professor imply when she says this:

    Ⓐ Edward III was a better king than Henry VI was.

    Ⓑ Richard of York was close to Edward III.

    Ⓒ Henry VI and Richard of York were closely related to each other.

    Ⓓ She expects the students to know who Edward III was.

[12-17] Listen to part of a lecture in a physics class. CH8_4C

Physics

12 Why does the professor tell the students to look at his desk?

    Ⓐ To show them some balls that are sitting on it

    Ⓑ To get them to look at some papers he has

    Ⓒ To have them watch an experiment he will do

    Ⓓ To point out the model car that is resting on it

13 According to the professor, what kind of force is friction?

    Ⓐ A balanced force

    Ⓑ An unbalanced force

    Ⓒ A net force

    Ⓓ A gravitational force

14 Based on the information in the lecture, indicate which of the laws of motion the statements refer to.

Click in the correct box for each statement.

	First Law of Motion	Second Law of Motion	Third Law of Motion
1 Uses the terms force, mass, and acceleration			
2 Explains why a book on a desk does not move			
3 Says that there is an equal and opposite reaction for every action			
4 Explains why it is harder to push a large iron ball than a small one			

15 How does the professor organize the information about the laws of motion that he presents to the class?

Ⓐ He provides examples to describe each of them individually.

Ⓑ He covers them in the order that Isaac Newton discovered them.

Ⓒ He talks about them according to their order of importance.

Ⓓ He shows video clips demonstrating how each one works.

16 What will the professor probably do next?

Ⓐ Talk about Isaac Newton's life

Ⓑ Answer the student's question

Ⓒ Give the class a short break

Ⓓ Repeat his explanation of the third law of motion

17 Listen again to part of the lecture. Then answer the question.

What can be inferred about the professor when he says this:

Ⓐ He will review the material he covers at the end of his lecture.

Ⓑ He enjoys asking students questions while he speaks.

Ⓒ He believes the students will easily understand the material he covers.

Ⓓ He dislikes being interrupted while he is lecturing.

[1-5] **Listen to part of a conversation between a student and a professor.** 🎧 CH8_4D

1 What are the speakers mainly discussing?

    Ⓐ The courses the student is currently enrolled in

    Ⓑ The student's desire to do a senior project

    Ⓒ An ancient dig site in Ethiopia

    Ⓓ The topic that the student wants to research

2 What can be inferred about the student?

    Ⓐ He took Anthropology 11 and 17 with the professor.

    Ⓑ He is planning to declare a double major next semester.

    Ⓒ He has not taken enough Business Administration classes to graduate.

    Ⓓ He intends to take two Anthropology classes during his senior year.

3 What does the student imply about Professor Porter?

Ⓐ He is a professor in the Anthropology Department.

Ⓑ He is the student's Business Administration academic advisor.

Ⓒ He is guiding the student in an independent study course.

Ⓓ He is teaching a class on ancient Ethiopia.

4 Why does the professor encourage the student to get a minor in Anthropology?

Click on 2 answers.

1 To improve the overall quality of his résumé

2 To get acknowledgment for the classes he has taken in the subject

3 To be able to apply to graduate schools in that field

4 To qualify to do a senior project in Anthropology

5 Why does the student tell the professor to wait for his response to her suggestion?

Ⓐ He needs to take the hours he works at his part-time job into account.

Ⓑ He would like to have a discussion with his academic advisor.

Ⓒ He is not sure when the classes he wants to take will be offered.

Ⓓ He has to think of a topic that he is interested in researching first.

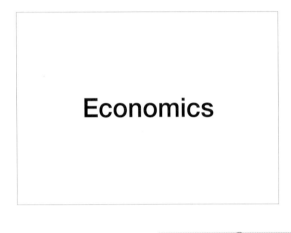

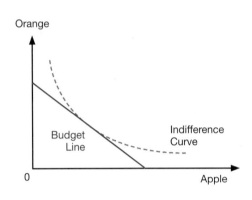

6 Why does the professor discuss Adam Smith?

  Ⓐ To argue that his economic ideas had too many flaws

  Ⓑ To name the titles of some of the books he wrote

  Ⓒ To describe his thoughts on rational consumers

  Ⓓ To state that he is considered the father of modern economics

7 Why does the professor tell the students to open their textbooks?

  Ⓐ To show them some pictures of Adam Smith

  Ⓑ To have them look at a graph printed in it

  Ⓒ To encourage them to read a short passage

  Ⓓ To get them to see some economic statistics

8   What does the budget line do?

   Ⓐ Helps economists compare individuals' and groups' purchasing power

   Ⓑ Runs parallel to the indifference curve line

   Ⓒ Lets people see how satisfied consumers are with their purchases

   Ⓓ Shows how much of a certain item a person can afford to buy

9   Based on the information in the lecture, indicate which type of consumer the statements refer to.

   Click in the correct box for each statement.

	Rational Consumer	Irrational Consumer
1 Can be influenced by brand loyalty		
2 Was once considered the basis for economic theory		
3 May make purchases based on past choices		
4 Often seeks to buy items for the best prices		

10 What can be inferred about the use of psychology in advertisements?

   Ⓐ Advertisements have been using it for hundreds of years.

   Ⓑ It is effective at getting irrational consumers to make purchases.

   Ⓒ There are very few people who are affected by it.

   Ⓓ It is more effective in television ads than in print ads.

11 What will the professor probably do next?

   Ⓐ Talk to the students about their final exam

   Ⓑ Allow the students to ask him some questions

   Ⓒ Have some students give their presentations

   Ⓓ Give a quiz on the day's material to the students

■ Vocabulary Review

A Complete each sentence with the appropriate word from the box.

| devise | metropolis | sentiment | surroundings | simultaneously |

1 The _____ in this neighborhood are mostly forests and lakes.

2 There is a lot of negative _____ toward the government due to the new law.

3 More than ten million people live in this _____ in Asia.

4 Nobody was sure who won the race since the two men finished _____.

5 The team is trying to _____ a new way to conduct the experiment.

B Complete each sentence with the correct answer.

1 The **dispute** between the two sides was _____ that lasted several months.

   a. a negotiation   b. an argument

2 Dr. Watkins **illustrated** his point by _____ several graphics to the audience.

   a. designing   b. showing

3 **Rational** thinking will usually result in _____ solution to a problem.

   a. an emotional   b. a logical

4 Do not **interfere** with the attendees by doing anything that could _____ them.

   a. bother   b. approach

5 The sun began to **fade away** as it slowly _____ beneath the horizon.

   a. appeared from   b. disappeared

6 If you **qualify** for the event, you will be allowed to _____ it.

   a. participate in   b. watch

7 The two roads _____ and **intersect** in the area around Western Park.

   a. meet each other   b. branch off from each other

8 There are a **plethora** of solutions, including _____ suggested by Mr. Duncan.

   a. a couple   b. many

9 Any **external** influences from _____ individuals are not allowed in the contest.

   a. influential   b. outside

10 The teacher's **hands-on** style allows him to provide _____ training for his students.

   a. practical   b. extra

Actual Test

Listening Section Directions

This section measures your ability to understand conversations and lectures in English.

The Listening section is divided into separately timed parts. In each part, you will listen to 1 conversation and 1or 2 lectures. You will hear each conversation or lecture only one time.

After each conversation or lecture, you will answer some questions about it. The questions typically ask about the main idea and supporting details. Some questions ask about a speaker's purpose or attitude. Answer the questions based on what is stated or implied by the speakers.

You may take notes while you listen. You may use your notes to help you answer the questions. Your notes will not be scored.

If you need to change the volume while you listen, click on the **VOLUME ICON** at the top of the screen.

In some questions, you will see this icon: 🎧 This means that you will hear, but not see, part of the question.

Some of the questions have special directions. These directions appear in a gray box on the screen.

Most questions are worth 1 point. If a question is worth more than 1 point, it will have special directions that indicate how many points you can receive.

A clock at the top of the screen will show you how much time is remaining. The clock will not count down while you are listening. The clock will count down only while you are answering the questions.

AT01

1 Why does the student visit the professor?

    Ⓐ To ask about a presentation that he must give soon

    Ⓑ To discuss an assignment that he is working on

    Ⓒ To review a lecture that the professor previously gave

    Ⓓ To inquire about some material that will be covered on an exam

2 According to the student, why did he change the topic of his paper?

Click on 2 answers.

    ☐1 His previous topic was too difficult for him.

    ☐2 He found the first topic to be uninteresting.

    ☐3 He could not get enough information on the previous topic.

    ☐4 Another student is also writing about the first topic.

3 Why does the professor tell the student about Dr. Austin Fletcher?

    Ⓐ To indicate that she knows him as well as his research

    Ⓑ To point out that they are currently working together

    Ⓒ To tell the student she can help him get an interview with Dr. Fletcher

    Ⓓ To mention that she thinks Dr. Fletcher's work is not credible

4   What will the professor probably do next?

    Ⓐ Suggest some reading material for the student

    Ⓑ Ask the student for some of his sources

    Ⓒ Get in touch with one of her colleagues

    Ⓓ Read the paper that the student just submitted

5   Listen again to part of the conversation. Then answer the question.

What does the professor mean when she says this:

    Ⓐ The student ought to be more optimistic about the research that he has already conducted.

    Ⓑ She does not believe that the student has done enough work on his class project.

    Ⓒ There is a great deal more work for the student to do before she will feel less pessimistic.

    Ⓓ Her attitude toward the student's work has changed for the better during their conversation.

AT02

English
Literature

6 What is the main topic of the lecture?

    Ⓐ Examples of plays claimed to have been written by Shakespeare

    Ⓑ How Shakespeare's writing style is different from that of other writers

    Ⓒ Eighteenth-century plays considered to be Shakespearean in style

    Ⓓ The lives of William Henry Ireland and Lewis Theobald

7 According to the professor, what did William Henry Ireland do after staging his play?

    Ⓐ He retired from the theater and went into the publishing industry.

    Ⓑ He tried to get financing to stage it elsewhere.

    Ⓒ He announced that he had really written it.

    Ⓓ He got reviewers to compare it with Shakespeare's works.

8 Based on the information in the lecture, indicate which play the statements refer to.

Click in the correct box for each statement.

	Vortigern and Rowena	*Double Falsehood*
1 Was based on the Shakespearean work *The History of Cardenio*		
2 Was actually written by William Henry Ireland		
3 Is believed to be very similar to a work written by Shakespeare		
4 Was staged only a single time		

9 How is the lecture organized?

Ⓐ The professor separately discusses two different plays written in the eighteenth century.

Ⓑ The professor compares the works of Shakespeare, William Henry Ireland, and Lewis Theobald.

Ⓒ The professor discusses the plots of both *Vortigern and Rowena* and *Double Falsehood* in detail.

Ⓓ The professor focuses on the manner in which two different plays were written.

10 What is the professor's opinion of *Double Falsehood*?

Ⓐ It was an outstanding work of original playwriting.

Ⓑ It was directly influenced by a lost work of Shakespeare.

Ⓒ It was really written by John Fletcher.

Ⓓ It was a fraud created by Lewis Theobald.

11 Listen again to part of the lecture. Then answer the question.

What is the purpose of the student's response?

Ⓐ To bring up another fact

Ⓑ To dispute a statement

Ⓒ To express his surprise

Ⓓ To question a result

AT03

Zoology

gliding animals

12 What is the lecture mainly about?

    (A) How gliding animals and flying animals differ

    (B) Why some gliding animals evolved to become flying ones

    (C) How various gliding animals can move through the air

    (D) Where on the planet most gliding animals can be found

13 What comparison does the professor make between flying frogs and flying snakes?

    (A) The forms of the body parts permitting them to glide

    (B) The manner in which they use their gliding ability

    (C) The areas from which they tend to begin gliding

    (D) The sizes of the special membranes on their bodies

14 According to the professor, what do the tailfins of flying fish do?

    (A) Allow them to achieve flight

    (B) Help them move faster above the water

    (C) Make their bodies more aerodynamic

    (D) Enable them to leap higher in the air

15 Why does the professor mention the flying squirrel?

    Ⓐ To give an example of a gliding animal that does not live in the tropics

    Ⓑ To talk about how evolution enabled it to become a gliding animal

    Ⓒ To describe the unique structure of the membranes on its feet

    Ⓓ To point out that it is arguably the best known of all gliding animals

16 Why does the professor tell the students about the evolution of gliding animals?

    Ⓐ To explain how bats are different from flying snakes

    Ⓑ To provide a response to a question regarding that matter

    Ⓒ To change the topic to one that he is more interested in

    Ⓓ To describe his own beliefs on how gliding animals evolved

17 In the lecture, the professor describes a number of facts about gliding animals. Indicate whether each of the following is a fact or not.

Click in the correct box for each statement.

	Fact	Not a Fact
① They are incapable of sustaining true flight.		
② They have a variety of body structures enabling them to glide.		
③ There are more gliding animals that are predators than are prey animals.		
④ Many of them evolved in a similar manner as the bat.		

AT04

1 Why does the student visit the Registrar's office?

    Ⓐ To find out what his grades for the semester are

    Ⓑ To learn when he will receive his diploma

    Ⓒ To obtain some copies of official documents

    Ⓓ To inquire about how he can apply for a job

2 What does the woman give the student?

    Ⓐ A copy of his transcript

    Ⓑ His diploma

    Ⓒ A form to fill out

    Ⓓ A receipt

3 What can be inferred about the student?

    Ⓐ He will visit the Registrar's office again at another time.

    Ⓑ He intends to transfer to another university.

    Ⓒ He is worried about not being able to graduate on time.

    Ⓓ He believes it will be difficult to find a job after graduating.

4 What is the student's opinion of the woman?

Ⓐ He finds her attitude condescending.

Ⓑ He appreciates her knowledge of her job.

Ⓒ He is thankful for her giving him a discount.

Ⓓ He is pleased with her helpfulness.

5 Listen again to part of the conversation. Then answer the question.

What can be inferred from the woman's response to the student?

Ⓐ The student's transcripts are not ready yet.

Ⓑ The student needs to come up with another idea.

Ⓒ The student ought to explain his plan one more time.

Ⓓ The student is applying for jobs late in the year.

AT05

Physics

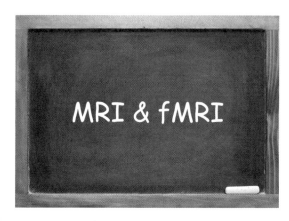

6 What is the main topic of the lecture?

    Ⓐ Why doctors prefer using MRI technology to fMRI technology

    Ⓑ The differences between CAT scans and MRI scans

    Ⓒ The manner in which some types of scanning technology work

    Ⓓ Which types of scanning technology are best for certain body parts

7 What does the professor imply about MRI and fMRI technologies?

    Ⓐ They enable doctors to avoid doing surgery on some patients.

    Ⓑ The expense of using them is too high for many patients.

    Ⓒ Both of them cause much less harm to the body than X-rays do.

    Ⓓ Only doctors with specialized training can utilize them.

8 What is the likely outcome of a person doing an activity while having an fMRI scan done?

    Ⓐ The patient's motor reflexes will be affected by the fMRI machine.

    Ⓑ The blood vessels in the patient's brain will begin to constrict.

    Ⓒ The brain of the patient may not receive enough oxygen.

    Ⓓ The doctor will learn which part of the patient's brain is being used.

9 Based on the information in the lecture, indicate which type of technology the statements refer to.

Click in the correct box for each statement.

	MRI	fMRI
☐1 Is used by some doctors to study patients with mental issues		
☐2 Focuses on the body's anatomical structure		
☐3 May be utilized to detect cancerous tumors in the body		
☐4 Is the less commonly used of the two		

10 How is the lecture organized?

Ⓐ The professor only discusses the differences between the two types of technology.

Ⓑ The professor compares MRI and fMRI technologies with CAT scan technology.

Ⓒ The professor covers MRI and fMRI technologies from the point of view of a doctor.

Ⓓ The professor focuses on each type of technology independent of the other.

11 Listen again to part of the lecture. Then answer the question.

Why does the professor say this: 🎧

Ⓐ To encourage the student to answer the professor's question

Ⓑ To ask the student to clarify her previous statement

Ⓒ To indicate that the student has given the correct answer

Ⓓ To point out that the student understands the material well

1   What are the speakers mainly discussing?

    (A) The student's decision to have a second major

    (B) The student's need to find a new academic advisor

    (C) The student's schedule for summer school

    (D) The student's need to obtain financial aid for school

2   What does the professor tell the student she should expect to do to achieve her goal?

Click on 2 answers.

    1 Improve the quality of the work she does

    2 Take classes during the summer term

    3 Pay closer attention to her professors' lectures

    4 Enroll in as many classes as possible each semester

3   What can be inferred about the student?

    (A) She is going to give up her dream of studying abroad.

    (B) She intends to find a new advisor during her junior year.

    (C) She is unsatisfied with the work she is doing in her major.

    (D) She is currently enrolled in one of the professor's classes.

4 Listen again to part of the conversation. Then answer the question.

Why does the professor say this:

(A) To show her support for the student's decision

(B) To confirm what the student just indicated to her

(C) To encourage the student to think more deeply

(D) To ask the student to justify her decision

5 Listen again to part of the conversation. Then answer the question.

What can be inferred about the professor when she says this:

(A) She expects the student to come up with a better plan.

(B) She wants the student to give her some documentation.

(C) She is satisfied with the student's response.

(D) She prefers that the student not work part time.

AT07

History

the Peasants' Revolt

6 Why does the professor explain the effects of the Black Death?

    (A) To discuss the main reason that the Peasants' Revolt happened

    (B) To emphasize how many people it killed all throughout England

    (C) To blame it for starting the Hundred Years' War against France

    (D) To point out how it made the peasants' lives worse than before

7 What resulted from the passing of the Statute of Laborers?

Click on 2 answers.

    [1] Lords and landowners were given permission to enslave some of their peasants.

    [2] The wages that peasants were allowed to receive were lowered.

    [3] Peasants were not permitted to marry people in other social classes.

    [4] Peasants were banned from moving to other places to look for work.

8 What is the professor's attitude toward the peasants who rebelled in the Peasants' Revolt?

    (A) He understands what caused them to fight back against the government.

    (B) He disagrees with the violence that many of them resorted to.

    (C) He supports their wish to improve their social status by rebelling.

    (D) He dislikes that they did not attempt to use diplomacy before they rebelled.

9 According to the professor, how did the English government try to pay for the Hundred Years' War?

   Ⓐ By having peasants provide free labor for the government

   Ⓑ By instituting a poll tax for all adults to pay

   Ⓒ By increasing tariffs on goods imported to England

   Ⓓ By requiring all landowners to pay property taxes

10 What does the professor imply about Wat Tyler?

   Ⓐ He had fought as a knight in the Hundred Years' War.

   Ⓑ He was a distant relative of King Richard II.

   Ⓒ He was one of the men involved in the initial revolt.

   Ⓓ He was an influential person amongst the rebelling peasants.

11 How does the professor organize the information about the Peasants' Revolt that he presents to the class?

   Ⓐ By examining the revolt from the point of view of the nobility

   Ⓑ By discussing the events in chronological order

   Ⓒ By focusing on the major individuals involved in it

   Ⓓ By covering the effects of the revolt and then its causes

Authors

Michael A. Putlack
- MA in History, Tufts University, Medford, MA, USA
- Expert test developer of TOEFL, TOEIC, and TEPS
- Main author of the Darakwon *How to Master Skills for the TOEFL® iBT* series and *TOEFL® MAP* series

Stephen Poirier
- Candidate for PhD in History, University of Western Ontario, Canada
- Certificate of Professional Technical Writing, Carleton University, Canada
- Co-author of the Darakwon *How to Master Skills for the TOEFL® iBT* series and *TOEFL® MAP* series

Maximilian Tolochko
- BA in History and Education, University of Oklahoma, USA
- MS in Procurement and Contract Management, Florida Institute of Technology, USA
- Co-author of the Darakwon *TOEFL® MAP* series

Decoding the TOEFL® iBT
LISTENING Advanced NEW TOEFL® EDITION

Publisher Chung Kyudo
Editor Kim Minju
Authors Michael A. Putlack, Stephen Poirier, Maximilian Tolochko
Proofreader Michael A. Putlack
Designers Koo Soojung, Park Sunyoung

First published in November 2020
By Darakwon, Inc.
Darakwon Bldg., 211, Munbal-ro, Paju-si, Gyeonggi-do 10881
Republic of Korea
Tel: 82-2-736-2031 (Ext. 250)
Fax: 82-2-732-2037

ISBN 978-89-277-0885-8 14740
        978-89-277-0875-9 14740 (set)

www.darakwon.co.kr

Photo Credits
p. 92 SAKARET / Shutterstock.com
https://www.shutterstock.com/ko/image-photo/sydneynsw-australia-november-11-2018-one-1241796475

Components Student Book / Answer Book
11 10 9 8 7 6 5   24 25 26 27 28

Decoding the TOEFL® iBT

Answers
Scripts
Explanations

Advanced

LISTENING

Decoding the TOEFL® iBT

Advanced

LISTENING

Answers
Scripts
Explanations

A

Answers   1 ⓓ   2 ⓑ

| Script |

Listen to part of a conversation between a student and a professor.

W Student: Hi, Professor Watkins. I read your e-mail after my biology class ended, so I got here as quickly as I could. What do you need to chat with me about?

M Professor: Hi, Jane. Thanks for coming so quickly. I just got something in today's mail that I think you might be interested in.

W: Yeah? What is it?

M: Did you know there's going to be a conference on nanotechnology in Dallas this summer?

W: No, I had no idea.

M: Neither did I. Apparently, it's the first time this conference is going to be held, and the organizers haven't done a stellar job of letting people know about it. That's why I got a brochure for it today despite the fact that it's going to be held two months from now.

W: That's considered slow?

M: Yes, it is. In fact, it's quite problematic. You see, people need to know when a special event is going to be held at least six months in advance. That way, they can, uh, arrange their schedules and make plans to attend it. Regarding this conference, I'd totally love to go to it, but I'm scheduled to teach classes this summer, and it's right in the middle of the summer semester.

W: That's too bad.

M: It sure is. However, while I can't go, you can. You're still planning on working here in my lab this summer, aren't you?

W: That's correct. But, uh, I don't have enough money to fly to Dallas. And there's no way I could afford a hotel and everything else. I appreciate the thought, Professor Watkins, but I don't see how I could go.

M: Actually, it's pretty easy. You may not be aware of this, but the department has money set aside in the budget to help deserving students pay for trips such as this. If your application is approved, the school will cover your airfare and hotel fee and also provide you with a per diem to pay for your food and transportation costs. Oh, and it will take care of your registration fee for the conference as well.

W: That's incredible. I had no idea. How do I get one of these applications?

M: I thought you'd never ask. I've got one for you right here. Shall we fill it out together?

Answer Explanations

1 ⓓ About the conference in the summer, the professor says, "In fact, it's quite problematic. You see, people need to know when a special event is going to be held at least six months in advance. That way, they can, uh, arrange their schedules and make plans to attend it. Regarding this conference, I'd totally love to go to it, but I'm scheduled to teach classes this summer, and it's right in the middle of the summer semester."

2 ⓑ The speakers are mostly talking about a conference which will be held for the first time.

B

Answers   1 ⓐ   2 ⓑ

| Script |

Listen to part of a conversation between a student and a Chemistry Department office employee.

M1 Student: Excuse me, but I was told by the lab instructor that I need to come here to speak with someone in the office.

M2 Chemistry Department Office Employee: Sure. Does your problem have something to do with Chemistry 105?

M1: Yes, that's right. Uh . . . how did you know that?

M2: I'm sorry to say that there's a big problem concerning this class. For some reason, the Registrar's office allowed way too many students to enroll in the class. There are only supposed to be fifty slots for this class, but more than 200 students signed up for it.

M1: Okay, so, uh, what's going to happen? I mean, uh, I enrolled in the class and attended the first lecture this morning. The lecture hall was packed, but it was pretty big, so I didn't think much of it. But when I got to the lab, there wasn't any room at all. The lab instructor checked my name on a list and told me I needed to come to this office.

M2: All right . . . Why don't you give me your name, please?

M1: I'm Marcus Peterson.

M2: Okay . . . let me check . . . Ah, I found it. Hmm . . . It appears as though you were one of the last people to enroll in the course.

M1: What does that mean?

M2: It means that you'll be permitted to remain in the class, but you will not be able to take the lab option.

M1: Uh . . . But I have to take the lab. I'm a Chemistry major, so I need to take the lab for this class. Otherwise, it won't count as one of the core courses for my major.

M2: Yes, I understand. In that case, you're just going to have to take the class next semester or during summer school.

M1: Next semester? But I need to take the class now. And what if the same thing happens next semester?

M2: Actually, that's guaranteed not to happen. Anyone like you who can't take the lab option this semester will be automatically enrolled in it next semester. So you won't have to worry about any problems next semester.

M1: I guess that's better than nothing. But are you sure there's no way for me to take the lab option this semester?

M2: I regret to say this, but unless the school opens another lab class, there's absolutely nothing you can do.

Answer Explanations

1 Ⓐ The student's problem is that the school will not let him take a lab class that he already signed up for.

2 Ⓑ The speakers are mostly talking about a problem with a class that is in the Chemistry Department.

C

Answers 1 Ⓑ 2 Ⓐ

| Script |

Listen to part of a lecture in an astronomy class.

M Professor: I'd like to continue our discussion of magnetic fields by moving away from the Earth and heading to the moon. Figuratively speaking, of course. At present, the moon doesn't have a magnetic field, but there's strong evidence it had one in the past, uh, perhaps billions of years ago. Obviously, the question we astronomers have is this: What happened to that magnetic field to make it disappear . . . ?

W Student: How do we know that the moon once had a magnetic field? I mean, uh, that's not something which was discovered with a telescope, right?

M: Indeed not. We know this thanks to the moon landings. Before we landed on the moon in the late 1960s, we had no evidence that the moon had ever had a magnetic field. But some of the moon rocks the *Apollo 11* astronauts brought to the Earth with them at the completion of their mission were discovered to be magnetic. Let me tell you that that discovery came as quite a shock to NASA scientists. Since then, various theories as to why the rocks are magnetic have been proposed, but two seem, in my opinion, to be the closest to what really happened.

First, however, let me remind you about what I mentioned regarding magnetic fields a few moments ago. Remember that inside the Earth, electric currents come from the movement of fluids in the core. It's those superheated moving liquid metals, uh, iron and nickel for the most part, that comprise the outer core and give the Earth its magnetic field.

W: Does the moon also have a moving core like the Earth does?

M: Hmm . . . The evidence suggests that it doesn't have a moving liquid core any longer, but it may have had one in the past. Most celestial bodies in the solar system fall into one of two categories. They're either large and have a multilayered structure or are so small that they're merely solid objects, such as asteroids, which are basically made of rock. As for the moon . . . well, it may fit somewhere between those two types of celestial bodies. It's small but may have been large enough at its creation to have developed a simplistic, yet multilayered, structure with a moving metal core. If that's true—and numerous sophisticated computer simulations suggest that it is— then that's what created the moon's magnetic field billions of years ago. Ah, this probably happened between 4.25 and 3.56 billion years ago, which is approximately one billion years after the moon formed. Interestingly, the evidence and computer simulations both suggest that the moon's magnetic field was even stronger than the Earth's magnetic field presently is.

What about the second theory . . . ? The moon, as you surely know, is heavily cratered. The second theory posits that heavy impacts on the moon's surface from a bombardment of meteoroids caused the moon's internal material to be stirred up. Essentially, the moon's interior became heated, which caused it to liquefy, and then it formed an electric dynamo that produced a magnetic field for a while.

The problem with both theories is that nobody knows when exactly the moon stopped producing its magnetic field. The reason why, however, is fairly certain: As the moon aged, its inner core likely cooled to the point that it was no longer a moving fluid. Instead, it became solidified and therefore stopped producing electricity, which naturally caused its magnetic field to disappear. As for the impact theory, astronomers believe that the rate of impacts grew less or stopped altogether, which enabled the inner material to cool, so the magnetic field was no longer produced.

Answer Explanations

1 Ⓑ The professor spends most of the lecture talking about why the moon might have developed a magnetic field in the past.

2 Ⓐ About the *Apollo 11* mission, the professor focuses on the importance of the moon rocks the astronauts brought back in stating, "But some of the moon rocks the *Apollo 11* astronauts brought to the Earth with them at the completion of their mission were discovered to be magnetic. Let me tell you that that discovery came as

quite a shock to NASA scientists."

D

| Script |

Listen to part of a lecture in an art history class.

W Professor: The still life is a basic form of painting taught to most budding artists, yet it's often considered a low form of art since it's fairly simplistic and easy to do. But, in fact, for hundreds of years, it has been a popular art style for buyers. Before I get into the history of the still life and go into detail on some of the more famous paintings in the genre, I'd like to tell you what it's all about.

As you can see here on the screen . . . a still-life work of art is typically a basic, colorful painting . . . showing a simple background with various everyday objects in the foreground . . . These objects frequently have a botanical nature and may feature arrangements of fruits . . . or flowers . . . Other still lifes feature household objects like this one here . . . and this one here . . . Food, as you can see . . . is another common still-life subject. In the past, dead animals . . . such as freshly caught fish . . . or birds killed by hunters . . . were common subjects. Some still lifes from the past had religious themes . . . but this is rather rare today.

Still-life techniques vary, but there are some common themes. Bright colors are normal . . . and so are realistic depictions of the objects being painted. That means there's no Cubism or Surrealism in a still life. Most of them are set in interior locations such as kitchens . . . or sitting rooms . . . Other common objects displayed in still lifes are Chinese porcelain . . . kitchen cutlery . . . and other cooking implements . . . glasses . . . silverware . . . and other common household objects. People rarely appear in still lifes, but it's not entirely unknown. See here . . . and here . . .

Historically, the still life is one of the oldest forms of art. Still lifes have been found on the walls of the ruins of Pompeii, the ancient Roman city that was covered by volcanic ash . . . They have also been found in ancient Egyptian . . . and Greek ruins . . . In more modern times, the art form came to prominence in Northwestern Europe during the Renaissance . . . It became popular in both the Netherlands . . . and later in Italy . . . As the people of the Netherlands grew rich from trading and the other businesses they engaged in, they started demanding artwork. Still lifes were appreciated by the Dutch people because the paintings could be displayed in their domiciles to give their homes a more natural feel. The discovery of the properties of oil paints further increased the popularity of still lifes. The reason is that oil paintings have more vibrant colors and allow for greater depth and realism, all of which are hallmarks of the still-life art form.

M Student: Weren't religious-themed paintings more prominent during that time though?

W: True, but there was a gradual move away from religious works during the Renaissance. And for the most part, the religious works were painted either for churches or the powerful and wealthy families that lived during that time. For the less wealthy and, uh, those who simply wanted a bit of the natural world hanging on their walls, a still life was ideal. And even the great artists of the day such as Leonardo da Vinci tried their hand at still lifes. Nowadays, practically everyone who has ever painted a picture has attempted to make a still life.

Answer Explanations

1 Ⓐ The professor focuses on the still life, which is a popular painting genre.

2 Ⓑ Regarding the Renaissance, the professor mainly talks about which types of artwork became popular during that period when she notes, "True, but there was a gradual move away from religious works during the Renaissance. And for the most part, the religious works were painted either for churches or the powerful and wealthy families that lived during that time. For the less wealthy and, uh, those who simply wanted a bit of the natural world hanging on their walls, a still life was ideal. And even the great artists of the day such as Leonardo da Vinci tried their hand at still lifes."

Practice with Long Passages   p. 18

A

| Script |

Listen to part of a conversation between a student and a professor.

W1 Student: Good afternoon, Professor Hamilton. That was a good class we had this morning. I learned quite a bit in it.

W2 Professor: I'm glad you enjoyed it, Karen. It's one of my favorite lectures to give each semester.

W1: So, uh, you mentioned that you wanted to see me sometime soon. This is the first break I've had since breakfast all day, so I thought I'd drop by your office right now. Do you happen to have some time to speak with me?

W2: Yes, Karen, I do. There's something I'd like to converse with you about. So, uh, why don't you have a seat right there, please?

W1: Sure, Professor.

W2: Thanks. I'm curious . . . What's your schedule like for the rest of the semester? 🎧4 Do you have a lot of work to do?

W1: Hmm . . . I'm not particularly busy right now. I mean, uh, I'm taking five classes. **But I'm not doing a part-time job this term, so I've got a bit more time than I have had in previous semesters.**

W2: That's good to hear. So . . . Would you be interested in participating in an extracurricular activity? You don't happen to be involved in one now, do you?

W1: No, I don't. I had considered joining a couple of clubs at the start of the semester, but they didn't seem particularly interesting when I went to the first meetings. What exactly do you have in mind?

W2: Well, it's not a club, but I'm leading several students who are going to give a dance performance this semester. Unfortunately, a couple of individuals had to drop out recently. One of them got injured while the other had, uh, some personal issues. We need a couple of replacement dancers, or else we won't be able to put on the performance. I know you enjoy dancing, so I thought I'd ask you to join our dance troupe.

W1: That sounds interesting. What kind of dancing is it?

W2: It's a combination of modern and classical.

W1: Oh . . . I don't really know much about classical dance. I probably wouldn't do that well, so are you sure you want me?

W2: Don't worry about your lack of experience. First, um, this isn't a professional group. Anyway, I can teach you the steps, and I think you'll find that it's both a lot of fun and great exercise. The other students are very nice. In fact, um, you probably already know a couple of them.

W1: You know, uh, I think I might. Is Amy Campbell in the troupe?

W2: Yes, she is. So, uh, what do you think?

W1: Okay. I'll give it a shot. When is the next practice session?

W2: It's tomorrow at 6:30 in the evening in room 103 in Robertson Hall. Thanks a lot, Karen. I'm looking forward to seeing you there.

W1: And I'm looking forward to attending. This sounds like it could be fun.

Answer Explanations

1　Ⓑ The speakers are mostly talking about the dance troupe that the professor would like the student to be a part of.

2　Ⓓ The professor tells the student, "The other had, uh, some personal issues. We need a couple of replacement dancers, or else we won't be able to put on the performance."

3　Ⓐ The student indicates that she is eager to join the group when she says, "And I'm looking forward to

attending. This sounds like it could be fun."

4　Ⓓ The student implies that she has worked part time in other semesters when she mentions that since she is not doing a part-time job this term, she has "got a bit more time than I have had in previous semesters."

Dictation

1　There's something I'd like to <u>converse with you about</u>.

2　<u>Would you be interested</u> in participating in an extracurricular activity?

3　We need a couple of <u>replacement</u> dancers, <u>or else</u> we won't be able to put on the performance.

B

Answers

1　Ⓑ　　2　Fact: ①, ②, ④　Not a Fact: ③
3　Ⓓ　　4　Ⓓ

| Script |

Listen to part of a lecture in a history class.

M Professor: The Vikings were among history's greatest seafarers, yet much of what the majority of people know about them comes from portrayals in movies and on television programs, which often show them at their worst, uh, invading lands and making war on people. In fact, there are numerous misconceptions about the Vikings in our modern culture. For instance, hmm . . . They're typically regarded solely as raiders who pillaged, looted, and caused other types of mayhem. 🎧4 The Vikings are shown as wild, hairy, unshaven, and unclean men. They're pictured as a united group of people under a single leader. And, uh, finally, they're regularly shown only sailing their boats near coastlines. **Well, uh, I'd like to disabuse you of all these notions right now.**

First, let me talk about their reputation for violence and wildness. Yes, it's true that the Vikings attacked other lands, stole, and killed. But they didn't do these activities all the time; uh, they only did them when opportunities presented themselves. For the most part, the Vikings were farmers, fishermen, and traders, just like most other Europeans were. And how about the way they're commonly portrayed on TV and in movies—you know, as hairy, unclean beasts . . . ? Well, that's far from the truth. The Vikings were among the few Europeans of their time to bathe regularly. At least once a week, almost every Viking enjoyed a hot bath. Compare that to most Europeans, who bathed once a year, um, if ever.

Now, uh, as to the notion that the Vikings were a single people, that's false as well. The word "Viking" itself was used by the Norse people to describe their seafarers who went on long voyages, so it was not a word they employed to describe themselves as a whole. In addition, the Vikings consisted of many clans of people scattered throughout Scandinavia. These clans resided mostly near the coast, and their lives were centered on small villages. In each region, they formed strong clans based mainly on family ties and allegiance to a strong leader, their chieftain. The clans had complex relationships with one another. They were at peace sometimes but went to war on other occasions. While large groups of Vikings might assemble to go to war or to go on long sea voyages, in no sense should we ever consider the Vikings to have been united in something resembling a modern nation-state.

W Student: But didn't the Vikings form large armies to invade places such as England and, uh, parts of France?

M: Well . . . they most assuredly did attack, invade, and establish permanent colonies in other lands, but they never had anything remotely resembling large armies, especially by modern standards. The Vikings mostly used, uh, I guess we'd call them raiding parties. They consisted of as little as a few dozen men to maybe several hundred or a few thousand men at the most. In the majority of instances, they raided for a few days and then departed unless they were interested in founding colonies in some lands.

And that brings us to the last myth about them, which concerns their seafaring abilities. The Vikings were without a doubt the best seafarers of the Middle Ages. They had excellent longships and knew about latitude, which meant they could sail east or west in a straight line. Using their navigational abilities, they spread out across the Atlantic Ocean. They discovered Iceland and Greenland and colonized both places. The colony in Greenland eventually failed, but the one in Iceland didn't, and the people of Iceland today are the descendants of those Viking seafarers. The Vikings also got to North America and set up a small colony there, but it failed after a few years. In Europe, the Vikings sailed as far south as Sicily in the Mediterranean Sea, and they even sent trading ships up the great rivers of Russia, where they eventually settled as well.

Answer Explanations

1 Ⓑ The professor focuses on discussing some misconceptions that people have about the Vikings in modern times.

2 Fact: ①, ②, ④ Not a Fact: ③
About the Vikings, the professor remarks, "The Vikings were among the few Europeans of their time to bathe regularly. At least once a week, almost every Viking enjoyed a hot bath. Compare that to most Europeans, who bathed once a year, um, if ever." He adds, "While large groups of Vikings might assemble to go to war or to go on long sea voyages, in no sense should we ever consider the Vikings to have been united in something resembling a modern nation-state." He also comments, "Using their navigational abilities, they spread out across the Atlantic Ocean," and, "In Europe, the Vikings sailed

as far south as Sicily in the Mediterranean Sea." However, Viking armies were not large with tens of thousands of men. Instead, he points out, "They consisted of as little as a few dozen men to maybe several hundred or a few thousand men at the most."

3 Ⓓ The professor organizes his lecture by talking about specific aspects of the Vikings one by one.

4 Ⓓ When the professor tells the class, "I'd like to disabuse you of all these notions right now," he is saying that he is going to correct the students so that they no longer have any misconceptions about the Vikings.

Dictation

1 In fact, there are numerous misconceptions about the Vikings in our modern culture.

2 Well, that's far from the truth.

3 Now, uh, as to the notion that the Vikings were a single people, that's false as well.

iBT Practice Test   p. 22

Answers

PART 1

1 Ⓒ	2 Ⓐ	3 Fact: ②, ④ Not a Fact: ①, ③
4 Ⓑ	5 Ⓓ	6 Ⓑ	7 Ⓐ	8 Ⓑ
9 ①, ④	10 Ⓑ	11 Ⓒ	12 Ⓑ

13 Fact: ①, ③ Not a Fact: ②, ④

| 14 Ⓓ | 15 Ⓐ | 16 Ⓑ | 17 Ⓓ |

PART 2

| 1 Ⓐ | 2 Ⓒ | 3 Ⓐ | 4 ①, ③ | 5 Ⓓ |
| 6 Ⓑ | 7 Ⓐ | 8 Ⓓ | 9 Ⓒ |

10 Natural Lighting: ①, ②, ④ Artificial Lighting: ③

11 Ⓓ

PART 1

Conversation [1–5]

| Script |

Listen to part of a conversation between a student and a café manager.

W Student: Hi. The cashier over there told me that you're the manager of this place. Is that correct?

M Café Manager: Yes, that's right. I'm Bryan Caldwell. What can I do for you?

W: My name is Julie Summers, and I'm here because I've got a request I'd like to make. You know that midterm exams are coming up, right?

M: Yes, I'm aware of that.

W: Well, uh, it would be great if you could extend the opening hours of this café during the exam period. I mean, uh, you close at ten every night, but it would be awesome if you could remain open until midnight, uh, or maybe even later than that.

M: Why would you like us to stay open later during the exam period? What time does the library close?

W: The library stays open until one AM, but, uh, in my opinion, this is the best place on campus to study. I mean, uh, there simply isn't any place better to be when I'm preparing for an exam.

M: Seriously? What makes you say that?

W: Well, uh, there are several reasons. To begin with, take a look at the chairs here.

M: The chairs?

W: Yes, the chairs. The chairs are so comfortable. They're so much nicer than the hard chairs the school library has. Whenever I come here to study, I can curl up with a good book for a couple of hours. I have a need to be comfortable when I study, and the chairs here make me feel great.

M: Yeah, I've noticed you here at least three times a week during the past month. And when you come, you seem to stay here for a couple of hours.

W: Oh, you've noticed me. That's cool. I try to come here every chance I get. Oh, yeah, and another reason I like this place has to do with the food. For starters, I can eat and drink here, but I can't do that at the library. I simply must have something to snack on while I'm studying.

M: I can understand that. I used to do the same thing when I was a student studying for tests in the past.

W: In addition, this place doesn't sell junk food like the café at the campus center does. Instead, everything here is healthy and nutritious.

M: Thanks for saying that. I worked hard to improve the quality of the food that's served here, and I'm pleased someone has finally realized that.

W: Wow, so you're the person responsible? Thanks a lot. So, uh, anyway, what do you think of my suggestion? Would it be possible to extend the hours here for the next couple of weeks?

M: You know, uh, I personally love your idea, and I appreciate the pleasant things you said about the café, but I can't accommodate your request.

W: Huh? Why not?

M: It's simply not practical from a business standpoint. Remaining open for more hours would require me to pay my employees more money. The school also insists that students working late at night receive higher wages, so I'd be paying much more than minimum wage.

W: Oh . . . I wasn't aware of that.

M: Yeah, and this place barely makes a profit. If we stayed open later, we'd practically be guaranteed to lose money. Unless you can bring in a whole bunch of new customers every night, then our hours simply aren't going to expand.

Answer Explanations

1 **Gist-Content Question**

Ⓒ The speakers are mostly talking about the request that the student makes that the man keep the café open longer.

2 **Connecting Content Question**

Ⓐ About the café, the student says, "I mean, uh, you close at ten every night." And she also says, "The library stays open until one AM."

3 **Detail Question**

Fact: ②, ④ Not a Fact: ①, ③

About the café, the student says, "The chairs are so comfortable. They're so much nicer than the hard chairs the school library has." She also notes, "Everything here is healthy and nutritious." However, the café closes at ten, not midnight, and it is not located in the university's student center.

4 **Understanding Function Question**

Ⓑ In rejecting the student's request, the man comments, "It's simply not practical from a business standpoint. Remaining open for more hours would require me to pay my employees more money. The school also insists that students working late at night receive higher wages, so I'd be paying much more than minimum wage."

5 **Making Inferences Question**

Ⓓ The man remarks, "Unless you can bring in a whole bunch of new customers every night, then our hours simply aren't going to expand." In saying that, he implies that the café could stay open later if more people visited it.

Lecture #1 [6–11]

| Script |

Listen to part of a lecture in a zoology class.

W Professor: Okay, uh, that's all I want to say about the hermit crab. Now, uh, I believe we've got a few more minutes until we're done, so let me cover one more animal before we finish up. We need to discuss one of the more unique species of marine life . . . the horseshoe crab. It's among the world's oldest living species as it dates back to roughly 450 million years ago, making it older than the dinosaurs. There are four species of horseshoe crab, three of which live in Asia and one in North America.

Here's a picture of the upper side of the horseshoe crab . . . You can see that it has a hard outer exoskeleton and a long tail with, uh, with some spiny protrusions on its shell. Here's the underside . . . Notice there are ten legs visible. In the center of the legs here . . . is its mouth. The crab uses its legs to walk, to swim, and to pull food toward its mouth. Although its long tail appears dangerous, it isn't. The tail's main function is to help flip the crab over if it winds up on its back. Now, uh, look at its eyes here . . . The horseshoe crab has nine eyes. Some are in pairs . . . and some are by themselves . . . They're used to let it see straight ahead and also to provide it with vision around its body to warn it of approaching danger. Zoologists believe some eyes let the crab see moonlight, which is important for mating.

This picture here . . . shows a male and a female side by side. The female is about one third bigger than the male. A female horseshoe crab grows to be around forty-five centimeters long while a male can be about thirty-five centimeters.

M1 Student: 🎧11 They don't really look like crabs.

W: **You can say that again.** However, they're similar to other species of crustaceans, so that's why they're classified as crabs. But, in actuality, the horseshoe crab has many similarities to arachnids, the family of animals which spiders belong to.

Moving on . . . What about the life span and mating habits of the horseshoe crab . . . ? It lives for around twenty years but doesn't begin mating until it's approximately ten. Mating begins in late spring and early summer during periods when there are new and full moons. Mating takes place on beaches at night. First, the males go ashore and then wait for the females. When the females reach the shore, they release pheromones that attract the males. The pheromones are chemical signals indicating that the females are ready to mate. After mating, each female lays tens of thousands of fertilized eggs. The female crabs dig small holes in the sand and deposit their eggs in them. That, by the way, is the only role parents play in the lives of their progeny.

The vast majority of the eggs never hatch but instead become food for birds and reptiles. In addition, the eggs that do hatch into small larvae often become food, and those crabs which manage to reach the water are often consumed by fish. But don't worry since hundreds of thousands of horseshoe crabs mate each year, and millions of eggs are laid, so many survive. Interestingly, horseshoe crab eggs and larvae are such important food sources for so many animals that marine biologists consider the horseshoe crab a keystone species. In other words, if it were suddenly to vanish, its disappearance would have a drastic effect on many other species.

M2 Student: I heard it's important in the medical industry.

W: That's correct. It's important due to its unique blood. While humans and most other animals rely on hemoglobin to transport oxygen through their bodies, the horseshoe crab has hemocyanin, which is like copper.

It makes the crab's blood blue in color rather than red. Its blood also has special antibody properties. The crab doesn't have white blood cells to fight infections like we do but instead has amebocytes, which are used to make a substance called limulus amebocyte lysate. This term is usually shortened to LAL, which I'll use. LAL has special properties, among them being that it coagulates in the presence of bacteria. This makes it the perfect material to use for a test that can check for bacteria. Since the 1970s, LAL tests have been used in hospitals to test for harmful bacteria on medical instruments. The test only works on instruments that have come in contact with blood or other human bodily fluids, so it's useful because it enables medical instruments to be employed repeatedly on different patients without doctors having to worry about spreading an infection from one patient to another. Unfortunately, breeding and raising horseshoe crabs in captivity is rather difficult, so the blood needed for LAL tests is often taken from crabs in the wild. The process doesn't usually kill the crabs as people merely draw blood from them and then release them back into the water.

Okay, I think that's all we have time for. Please don't forget to submit your term papers next Monday before class starts.

Answer Explanations

6 Gist-Content Question

Ⓑ The professor spends most of her time describing the characteristics of the horseshoe crab.

7 Understanding Organization Question

Ⓐ While talking about the body of the horseshoe crab, the professor states, "Here's a picture of the upper side of the horseshoe crab." She then points out various features of the crab while she shows pictures to the class.

8 Detail Question

Ⓑ The professor declares, "Interestingly, horseshoe crab eggs and larvae are such important food sources for so many animals that marine biologists consider the horseshoe crab a keystone species. In other words, if it were suddenly to vanish, its disappearance would have a drastic effect on many other species."

9 Detail Question

[1], [4] The professor states, "It makes the crab's blood blue in color rather than red." Then, she adds, "The crab doesn't have white blood cells to fight infections like we do but instead has amebocytes, which are used to make a substance called limulus amebocyte lysate. This term is usually shortened to LAL, which I'll use. LAL has special properties, among them being that it coagulates in the presence of bacteria. This makes it the perfect material to use for a test that can check for bacteria."

10 Making Inferences Question

Ⓑ At the beginning of the lecture, the professor mentions, "Now, uh, I believe we've got a few more minutes until we're done, so let me cover one more animal before we finish up." And at the end of the talk, the professor says, "Okay, I think that's all we have time for. Please don't forget to submit your term papers next Monday before class starts." So she will probably dismiss the students for the day next.

11 Understanding Function Question

Ⓒ When the professor responds, "You can say that again," to the student's comment that the horseshoe crabs do not look like crabs, she is indicating that she agrees with what the student just said.

Lecture #2 [12–17]

| Script |

Listen to part of a lecture in an anthropology class.

M Professor: One of the more unique aspects of North American Native culture is the ceremony called the potlatch. It was once common among the tribes that resided in the Pacific Northwest areas in both the United States and Canada. Each tribe had its own variations on the potlatch ceremony, but I'm merely going to give you the basics on what it was all about. Please feel free to do some research on your own if you're interested in how individual tribes conducted them though. You'll find what you learn to be quite fascinating.

The potlatch was, hmm . . . well, it was a combination of many things. To begin with, it was a ceremony usually held to celebrate events such as births, marriages, and funerals. It involved feasting, gift giving, dancing, singing, and sometimes even theatrical performances. It could last for a single day or for several, and it could involve only one tribe or many. The ceremony was often utilized as an occasion for a tribal leader to express his strength, uh, that is, to demonstrate his superiority among his people and also to show other tribes how powerful or great he was. Another function of the potlatch was to settle disputes within a tribe or between tribes. It served, you see, as a meeting place for people to air their disputes and for the chief or tribal elders to settle them. As for what kinds of disputes between tribes were commonly settled, they tended to involve fishing and hunting rights in different lands.

The main characteristic of the potlatch was the chief's giving away of gifts to his people and others. The nature of these gifts varied over time. In pre-Columbian times, the gifts were predominantly food, wooden carvings, canoes, copper, and slaves. Yes, slavery was actually quite common for Native American tribes. The slaves were often people from other tribes who had been captured during wars. Among his own people, a chief could also bestow titles, thereby giving ranks to people in the tribe, which would increase their prestige among their own people. After the arrival of Europeans in North America, new gift

items, including firearms, textiles, and metal products, were frequently given at potlatches.

🎧17 Oftentimes, when the chief of a tribe reached old age and had collected an impressive amount of wealth, he would hold a potlatch and give most of it away to show his generosity to his people as he entered the final years of his life. **And, um, in what may seem a bit peculiar to us, the chief would destroy some of his possessions.** This was almost always done by burning them in a bonfire. If you're curious why, the reason was that the chief wanted to show his people that he was so superior that material possessions meant, uh, they meant nothing to him. It was also intended to instruct his people that they shouldn't become too attached to material things since they served no purpose after death. During a potlatch, something of a contest between two tribal chiefs tended to occur. The chief who invited the other tribe would give away gifts or destroy them and then challenge the other chief to do the same. If the invited chief refused to give away or destroy an equal amount of items as the host, he and his people would lose face and be regarded as less powerful.

W Student: I'm sorry, but I don't get it. How would doing that prove who is more powerful?

M: It has to do with the psyche of the native people. Don't try to explain their actions by ascribing our values to them. Sure, it seems, uh, odd to us for someone to give away or destroy his wealth. But to them, prestige was all about being the most generous with gifts at a potlatch. It was a point of pride to be the most generous. Some tribes would take years to amass great amounts of wealth solely to give it away or destroy it eventually. Interestingly enough, some anthropologists believe one reason for the endemic warfare between tribes was the need to capture slaves in order to give them away at a potlatch.

When Americans and Canadians arrived in the Pacific Northwest in strength in the nineteenth century, they sadly regarded this beautiful event as primitive. To the natives, it was a normal part of their lives, but it was a cause of trouble to the American and Canadian governments. In their minds, in addition to causing warfare and slavery, the potlatch ceremony itself was regarded as wasteful. Basically, the giving away or destroying of gifts was contrary to their sense of property ownership and wealth accumulation. It was also perceived as the cause of jealousy and resentment as one or more tribes were always deemed more powerful than the others. The governments further believed that the potlatch would prevent natives from assimilating into the new order. To settle this problem, the Canadian government banned the potlatch ceremony in 1884. Resistance and changing attitudes resulted in the ban being lifted in 1951, so the potlatch fortunately remains a part of tribal life today. However, today, it's mostly a feast rather than an elaborate gift-giving and prestige ceremony.

12 Gist-Content Question

Ⓑ The professor focuses on the role of gifts in the potlatch while she discusses it.

13 Detail Question

Fact: ①, ③ Not a Fact: ②, ④

About the potlatch, the professor comments, "To begin with, it was a ceremony usually held to celebrate events such as births, marriages, and funerals." He also says, "Another function of the potlatch was to settle disputes within a tribe or between tribes. It served, you see, as a meeting place for people to air their disputes and for the chief or tribal elders to settle them. As for what kinds of disputes between tribes were commonly settled, the professor says, "They tended to involve fishing and hunting rights in different lands." However, he also states, "It could last for a single day or for several, and it could involve only one tribe or many," and he adds that only the chief gave presents.

14 Connecting Content Question

Ⓓ The professor says, "The nature of these gifts varied over time. In pre-Columbian times, the gifts were predominantly food, wooden carvings, canoes, copper, and slaves. Yes, slavery was actually quite common for Native American tribes. The slaves were often people from other tribes who had been captured during wars. Among his own people, a chief could also bestow titles, thereby giving ranks to people in the tribe, which would increase their prestige among their own people. After the arrival of Europeans in North America, new gift items, including firearms, textiles, and metal products, were frequently given at potlatches." So he compares the gifts that were given away during potlatches.

15 Detail Question

Ⓐ The professor notes, "Interestingly enough, some anthropologists believe one reason for the endemic warfare between tribes was the need to capture slaves in order to give them away at a potlatch."

16 Understanding Attitude Question

Ⓑ The professor states, "When Americans and Canadians arrived in the Pacific Northwest in strength in the nineteenth century, they sadly regarded this beautiful event as primitive."

17 Understanding Function Question

Ⓓ In stating, "In what may seem a bit peculiar to us, the chief would destroy some of his possessions," the professor implies that most modern-day people do not destroy the things that they own.

PART 2

Conversation [1–5]

| Script |

Listen to part of a conversation between a student and a professor.

W Professor: Do you have any more questions about your term paper, Jason?

M Student: No, ma'am. Thanks for answering my questions. I'm sorry I was absent from class yesterday when you told everyone about it. I was quite unwell, so I was at the doctor's office at that time. Um, do you need me to provide a note from the doctor so that my absence from class is excused?

W: Yes, Jason, according to school policy, you need to do that. You've got two weeks to submit it, so it's not too urgent, but I suggest doing it in the next day or two simply because it might otherwise slip your mind.

M: I'm going to head over to the clinic after my last class finishes today.

W: That's good. I can get the note from you in class tomorrow then.

M: Perfect. Now, uh, do you mind if I ask a couple of questions about yesterday's lecture? I borrowed my friend's class notes, but I'm afraid I don't understand everything he wrote down.

W: Which part of the lecture are you referring to? The talk about liverworts, hornworts, or mosses?

M: Mosses. Everything he wrote about liverworts and hornworts was fine, but I think he, uh, he started losing focus when you discussed mosses. He only took a few notes about them, and they weren't particularly clear.

W: Okay. What would you like to know about them?

M: Are there really mosses that can be tens of centimeters tall? I was under the impression that mosses are short and fuzzy and don't grow very high.

W: For the most part, you're correct. The majority of species of mosses—there are about 12,000 species by the way—the majority of mosses are small and only reach one or two centimeters in height.

M: But some others?

W: The world's largest moss grows in New Zealand. It can be more than thirty centimeters high.

M: Wow, that's impressive. I had thought Jeff was kidding when he wrote that in his notebook. I guess he was serious.

W: Yes, I mentioned that to the class mostly as a curiosity. It's quite unusual, so it's not too terribly important.

M: That's good to know. Okay. Uh, how do mosses get water? They don't have roots, right? So they can't absorb water from the ground.

W: You're correct in that they don't have roots. Basically, they absorb water like a sponge, so that means mosses can only grow in two types of places. The first is near sources of water such as streams, rivers, creeks, lakes, or ponds. The second is in places where there is plenty of fog. If mosses don't get enough water, they'll simply dry up and die.

M: Is that why mosses grow so closely together? To enable them to absorb as much water as possible?

W: That's a good question, Jason. I didn't mention that in class, so I'll assume you came up with it by yourself. You're correct. By growing so closely together, the individual moss plants can absorb enough water to survive.

M: Great. Thanks. Okay, I think that's everything. If I come up with any more questions, I'll visit your office later this week during your office hours.

W: My door is always open, Jason. You can drop by to ask questions whenever I'm available.

Answer Explanations

1 Gist-Content Question

Ⓐ The student asks the professor, "Now, uh, do you mind if I ask a couple of questions about yesterday's lecture? I borrowed my friend's class notes, but I'm afraid I don't understand everything he wrote down." Then, they spend the rest of the conversation discussing the student's questions.

2 Detail Question

Ⓒ The student remarks, "I'm sorry I was absent from class yesterday when you told everyone about it. I was quite unwell, so I was at the doctor's office at that time."

3 Understanding Function Question

Ⓐ Regarding the student's question about the height of mosses, he explains, "I had thought Jeff was kidding when he wrote that in his notebook. I guess he was serious."

4 Detail Question

① , ③ The professor tells the student, "Mosses can only grow in two types of places. The first is near sources of water such as streams, rivers, creeks, lakes, or ponds. The second is in places where there is plenty of fog."

5 Understanding Attitude Question

Ⓓ At the end of the conversation, the professor comments, "You can drop by to ask questions whenever I'm available."

Lecture [6-11]

| Script |

Listen to part of a lecture in an architecture class.

W Professor: There are two kinds of lighting for buildings: natural and artificial. Natural lighting comes from natural sources such as the sun, the moon, and the stars. Artificial lighting comes from manmade sources, some of which are fire, candles, gas lamps, and electric lights. Electric lights include incandescent lights, fluorescent lights, and light-emitted diodes, which are often called LED light sources. There are advantages and disadvantages to both types of light when using them to illuminate buildings.

Let's start with natural light. The main advantage of it is that it's free, so nobody has to pay for it since it's available to everyone. There's one other major advantage. Studies have showed that people feel better and work better in buildings that utilize more natural light. One of the main benefits of more natural light in buildings is that people get more sleep and feel better each day. Those individuals who spend lots of time in buildings relying mostly upon artificial light have more trouble falling asleep. One recent study concluded that more natural light in buildings mimicked people's need for a regulated day-night pattern, which affects the circadian rhythms that control sleep.

However, there are some disadvantages to natural light. First, it isn't always available. When it's cloudy, there are reduced levels of natural light, and at night, the moon and the stars produce much less natural light than the sun does during the day. In addition, at certain latitudes in the far north and south, there's less direct sunlight. In the north, buildings need southward-facing windows to capture the most sunlight. Studies have also showed that having plenty of glass windows in a building may capture more natural light, but this drives up energy costs. Too much natural sunlight in summer can cause heat levels to rise inside buildings, which, in turn, increases air-conditioning usage and electricity bills. Likewise, in winter, too many large glass windows make people feel colder even though the building may have an adequate heat source. So people increase the heat, which increases energy costs. To sum up, more glass windows means more natural light and healthier workers, but it can increase electricity bills. Ah, I nearly forgot. Because people use more electricity, that can deplete natural resources in places that rely on oil, gas, or coal for heating.

M Student: Is it possible for buildings to have total natural lighting during the daytime?

W: Not quite. Even in buildings with plenty of windows, artificial light is still necessary. One study claimed that every building needs at least ten to twenty percent of its lighting to be artificial, uh, even during the day.

The greatest advantage of artificial lighting is that it can be controlled. Flip a switch, and there it is, ready whenever we want it, which makes it convenient. It's also clean and safe. That wasn't always the case, especially in the past before electricity when the only sources of artificial light at night were fires, candles, and gas lamps. All three were not very clean and were potential fire hazards. Then came the incandescent light bulb, which changed history. Buildings lit up by electric light could be open all day and night, which led to changes in work habits. This had detrimental health effects on those workers who had to be inside buildings with total artificial lighting at night. As I mentioned earlier, people need a balance in their sleep patterns to remain healthy and happy.

After the incandescent light bulb came the fluorescent light bulb. It lasts longer, is more energy efficient, and gives off less heat. But there are some health concerns. For example, the flickering of fluorescent light bulbs can bother people with conditions such as epilepsy. These bulbs also contain mercury, a toxic substance. There is the issue of employee morale for those individuals who work in buildings with fluorescent light bulbs, too. Many people feel that places illuminated by them are cold, depersonalized environments with no connection to the real world.

Last, but not least, are light-emitting diodes, LED light sources. LED light bulbs are more energy efficient and last much longer than both incandescent and fluorescent light bulbs. This helps lower electricity usage and reduces harmful emissions. LEDs are more efficient at directional lighting, which is used for desk lamps and light track systems on ceilings. They can focus light on small spaces, so this feature is useful since it reduces the amount of artificial lighting by having it only where it's required. Unfortunately, there are a few drawbacks to LEDs. They tend to be more expensive than other types of light systems. They have high levels of blue light, and overexposure to it can cause some eye problems. Despite these issues, LED light systems are the lights of the future as they're being used in the designs of new buildings and being installed in older ones.

Answer Explanations

6 Gist-Content Question

Ⓑ In her lecture, the professor focuses mainly on the different types of light used to illuminate buildings.

7 Detail Organization Question

Ⓐ The professor tells the class, "Studies have also showed that having plenty of glass windows in a building may capture more natural light, but this drives up energy costs. Too much natural sunlight in summer can cause heat levels to rise inside buildings, which, in turn, increases air-conditioning usage and electricity bills. Likewise, in winter, too many large glass windows make people feel colder even though the building may have an adequate heat source."

8 Making Inferences Question

Ⓓ The professor notes, "That wasn't always the case, especially in the past before electricity when the only sources of artificial light at night were fires, candles, and gas lamps. All three were not very clean and were

potential fire hazards." Since they were potential fire hazards, it can be inferred that the sources of artificial light in the past before electricity occasionally caused some buildings to burn down.

9 Connecting Content Question

Ⓒ About incandescent light bulbs, the professor points out, "Then came the incandescent light bulb, which changed history. Buildings lit up by electric light could be open all day and night, which led to changes in work habits. This had detrimental health effects on those workers who had to be inside buildings with total artificial lighting at night. As I mentioned earlier, people need a balance in their sleep patterns to remain healthy and happy." Regarding fluorescent light bulbs, she remarks, "But there are some health concerns. For example, the flickering of fluorescent light bulbs can bother people with conditions such as epilepsy. These bulbs also contain mercury, a toxic substance." So she compares the ways that both types of light bulbs can affect people's health.

10 Connecting Content Question

Natural Lighting: ①, ②, ④   Artificial Lighting: ③

Regarding natural lighting, the professor says, "One recent study concluded that more natural light in buildings mimicked people's need for a regulated day-night pattern, which affects the circadian rhythms that control sleep," and, "Even in buildings with plenty of windows, artificial light is still necessary. One study claimed that every building needs at least ten to twenty percent of its lighting to be artificial, uh, even during the day." She also notes, "One of the main benefits of more natural light in buildings is that people get more sleep and feel better each day." As for artificial lighting, the professor states, "LEDs are more efficient at directional lighting, which is used for desk lamps and light track systems on ceilings. They can focus light on small spaces, so this feature is useful since it reduces the amount of artificial lighting by having it only where it's required."

10 Understanding Organization Question

Ⓓ During the lecture, the professor first talks about natural light, and then she switches to discussing artificial light.

Vocabulary Review

Answers

A
| 1 reside | 2 voyage | 3 budding |
| 4 prestige | 5 drop by | |

B
| 1 a | 2 a | 3 b | 4 b | 5 a |
| 6 a | 7 b | 8 a | 9 b | 10 b |

Practice with Short Passages
p. 36

A

Answers   1 Ⓐ   2 Ⓒ

| Script |

Listen to part of a conversation between a student and a student center employee.

M1 Student: Pardon me, but I wonder if you can help me out. I'm having a problem with something.

M2 Student Center Employee: I'll do my best. What seems to be the problem?

M1: Well, uh, I was trying to get into the library, but the person at the front door wouldn't let me inside. He told me to turn around and go away.

M2: I'm very sorry, but the library is solely reserved for the usage of students, faculty, staff, and alumni. Since you're not a student here, then you can't get in. Why don't you use the public library downtown? I understand that it has a nice collection of books.

M1: Er . . . Actually, I am a student here.

M2: Huh? Then why didn't the person permit you to enter? Were you eating food or talking on your phone loudly as you were going in? You know you're not supposed to do either of those two things, don't you?

M1: No, uh, it wasn't that. He wouldn't let me in because I didn't have my student ID. What's up with that?

M2: Ah . . . freshman?

M1: Yes.

M2: Ever since last year, the school has made it obligatory for students to carry their IDs at all times. You can't get into most of the buildings here on campus without showing an ID card.

M1: Why do they require that? That seems kind of odd.

M2: There were some, uh, issues with nonstudents on campus during the spring semester. Some people were coming to campus, pretending to be students, and causing all sorts of problems. That's why the dean instituted the rule. It's sort of annoying, but it did solve the problems. Um, didn't they tell you this at orientation?

M1: Um . . . I sort of missed my orientation session. I just arrived on campus yesterday.

M2: Okay, I see. Well, make sure you have your ID card whenever you leave your dorm. Otherwise, you won't be able to get inside the library and most other buildings. All you need to do is show it to the person at the front door of the building you're entering.

M1: Great. Thanks for letting me know. I appreciate it.

Answer Explanations

1   Ⓐ The student goes to the student center to ask why the person at the library would not permit him to enter.

2   Ⓒ In response to the student's inquiry about why ID cards are needed to get into buildings on campus, the employee tells the student, "There were some, uh, issues with nonstudents on campus during the spring semester. Some people were coming to campus, pretending to be students, and causing all sorts of problems. That's why the dean instituted the rule. It's sort of annoying, but it did solve the problems."

B

Answers   1 Ⓒ   2 Ⓓ

| Script |

Listen to part of a conversation between a student and a professor.

M Student: Good morning, Professor Clay. I'm here for our meeting.

W Professor: Good morning, Kevin. Thanks for dropping by. Um, Kevin, you indicated last week that you would be interested in doing an independent research project next semester. Are you still considering that?

M: Yes, ma'am, I am.

W: Do you mind if I ask you why you'd like to do that?

M: Not at all. The answer is pretty simple. Next year is going to be my senior year, so I've been doing some thinking about my future. I pretty much have two options available after I graduate: I can find a job, or I can attend graduate school.

W: That's true. Do you know which of the two you're probably going to do?

M: Not yet. And that's why I'd like to do an independent research project next fall. You see, uh, I'm not really sure if graduate school is the place for me. First of all, it's rather expensive unless I manage to get a TA or an RA. Second of all, I'm not sure if I'll enjoy staying at school and doing research primarily on my own for a couple of years.

W: So that's why you want to do the research project next semester, right?

M: Precisely. I figure that I'll learn a great deal about, uh, my abilities as a researcher as well as how much I actually enjoy doing it. So, uh, is that a good reason?

W: It's a perfect reason, Kevin. College is the ideal place to find out about yourself and your interests and abilities. Personally, I think you'd make a good researcher. I guess we're going to find out soon, won't we?

M: Yes, ma'am. I guess so.

W: So do you know what you'd like to do research on?

M: Um . . . Well, since my focus is on marine biology, I think it should be something connected with it. But, uh, other than that, to be honest, I haven't given it very much thought.

W: That's fine. Most students need a bit of guidance. Here . . . This is a sheet with some possible research topics that I prepared in case any students want to do research. Do any of these strike you as interesting?

M: Hmm . . . Hold on a moment and let me read everything, please.

Answer Explanations

1 Ⓒ The student visits the professor to talk about doing an independent research project during his senior year.

2 Ⓓ The student says, "Next year is going to be my senior year, so I've been doing some thinking about my future. I pretty much have two options available after I graduate: I can find a job, or I can attend graduate school." When the professor asks if the student knows which choice he will make, he responds that he does not know yet.

C

Answers   1 Ⓑ   2 Ⓑ

| Script |

Listen to part of a conversation between a student and a dining services employee.

W Student: Excuse me, but could I speak with you about something, please?

M Dining Services Employee: Sure. What can I help you with?

W: If you don't mind, I'd like to talk about my meal plan.

M: No problem. Do you want to purchase one?

W: No, sir. Instead, I'd like to reduce the one I currently have. You see, um, before the semester started, I signed up for the meal plan that permits me to eat three meals a day at any of the school's dining halls. However, I rarely even eat in the dining halls twice a day, so I'm pretty much wasting my money.

M: Yes, that would seem to be the case. May I ask why you don't eat here that often? Is the quality or taste of the food not to your liking?

W: Oh, no. I was quite surprised when I arrived here and found that the food in the dining halls is mostly good. I love eating here, but . . .

M: But what?

W: Well, I'm not much of a morning person, and I don't

have any classes that start before eleven, so I haven't had breakfast a single time this semester.

M: What about lunch?

W: Hmm . . . I'd say I only eat lunch in the dining halls three or four times a week. The reason is that I don't always have enough time in between classes to get to the dining hall, so I often wind up simply buying a sandwich at the café in the campus center.

M: Okay, it sounds like you definitely have a meal plan that's too much for you.

W: So, uh, how do I reduce it?

M: It's a simple process. Just give me your student ID, and I can call up your information on the computer. It sounds like you need either the ten-meal-a-week plan or the fourteen-meal-a-week plan. Which of those would you prefer?

W: I think I'll go with the former. Nine or ten meals a week is about all I have time for.

Answer Explanations

1 Ⓑ The student visits the office to make a change in the meal plan that she has.

2 Ⓑ The student tells the man about her eating habits in order to point out why she does not always have her meals in the dining halls.

D

Answers   1 Ⓒ   2 Ⓐ

| Script |

Listen to part of a conversation between a student and a professor.

W Student: Hi, Professor Vinson. I got your message that you wanted to see me.

M Professor: Hi, Allison. Thanks for coming so quickly. Did you have a good vacation?

W: It was all right. I visited my parents and stayed with them the entire time. So, uh, what's going on?

M: You know, I had my first class of the semester this morning, and I was extremely surprised not to see you there. I remember you telling me last December that you intended to take my course on mercantilism. Did you decide not to sign up for it?

W: Oh, uh, yeah. I was planning to visit you soon to talk about that. I tried signing up for the class, but the person at the Registrar's office informed me that it's full. She said I couldn't get into your class unless someone happened to drop it. I couldn't believe that happened.

M: I guess my classes suddenly got popular during the last couple of weeks since my latest book came out.

W: Oh, right. Congratulations on making all the bestseller

lists. I haven't read your book yet, but I'm planning to as soon as I have some free time. I guess everything makes sense, doesn't it? Now that most students on campus know about you, they want to take your classes this semester.

M: Yeah, that's what it seems like.

W: So, uh, is there any way I can get into your class? Has anyone dropped it?

M: Nobody has done that, but it's still possible for you to enroll in the class. Even though the class limit is twenty-five students, I'm permitted to allow a couple of other students to take the course if I want. Therefore, if you're still interested in learning about mercantilism, I can sign a form for you that will permit you to sign up for it.

W: Really? You would do that for me?

M: Sure. I know you're interested in the topic, and you're a good student as well, so it's no problem at all.

W: Thanks so much. What do I need to do?

M: Go back to the Registrar's office and ask someone there for a copy of form R45-1. Bring it back here, and I'll fill everything out for you.

Answer Explanations

1 Ⓒ The professor says, "You know, I had my first class of the semester this morning, and I was extremely surprised not to see you there. I remember you telling me last December that you intended to take my course on mercantilism. Did you decide not to sign up for it?" So he wants to know why the student is not taking his class.

2 Ⓐ The student tells the professor, "I was planning to visit you soon to talk about that. I tried signing up for the class, but the person at the Registrar's office informed me that it's full. She said I couldn't get into your class unless someone happened to drop it."

Practice with Long Passages   p. 40

A

| Answers | 1 Ⓐ | 2 Ⓒ | 3 Ⓑ, Ⓓ | 4 Ⓒ |

| Script |

Listen to part of a conversation between a student and a professor.

M1 Student: Professor Gordon, um, you didn't hand back my exam in class today. Um . . . You didn't lose it, did you?

M2 Professor: Ah, come in, Randall, and have a seat. I'd like to have a word with you.

M1: Uh, sure. Okay.

M2: I didn't give you back your exam because, well . . . I didn't want you to get embarrassed in front of your friends.

M1: Uh-oh . . . That doesn't sound good.

M2: I'm afraid not. Here's your exam . . . As you can see, you didn't do very well on it.

M1: Ouch. You're right. I got a sixty-eight. Wow . . . I don't think I've gotten a score this low since, uh . . . maybe since elementary school.

M2: It happens to the best of us, Randall. Now, um, I wonder if you could tell me about your study habits. This is the third exam we've had this semester, and your grades have gone steadily downhill since the first one. Let's see . . . You got a ninety-four on the first one, an eighty-two on the second one, and now a sixty-eight on this exam. That downward trend does not indicate anything positive about your performance on our upcoming final exam.

M1: You can say that again. Well, uh, as for my study habits, I mostly just read everything that we covered in the textbook and then go over my notes several times to make sure I know everything. I guess I study for about two days prior to each exam.

M2: 🎧4 How many hours per day would you say that you study before an exam?

M1: Easily two hours in my dorm room each day. That's all I really need to learn the material.

M2: **On the contrary, your grades indicate to me that you need more than two hours of studying each day to learn the material.** I recommend that you do one of the following. First, you could simply study more when we have a test. And please don't study in your dorm room. I know students prefer doing that, but a dorm room isn't very conducive to effective studying. The library would be a much better place to go. The other option would be to join a study group.

M1: A study group? I wasn't aware that this class had a study group.

M2: There are several. I mentioned the study groups on the first day of class. Virtually every student in the class, hmm . . . I'd say about ninety percent of them . . . has joined one of the study groups, each of which is led by a graduate student. You might find that joining a study group will enable you to learn the material better, so you can therefore improve your grade.

M1: Yes, that sounds good. Uh, what do I have to do?

M2: Take this . . . There's a group meeting tonight. That sheet has the information about where and when it will be. Go there and see if it's helpful.

M1: I will. Thanks a lot, sir.

1　Ⓐ At the start of the conversation, the student remarks, "Professor Gordon, um, you didn't hand back my exam in class today. Um . . . You didn't lose it, did you?"

2　Ⓒ The professor comments, "This is the third exam we've had this semester, and your grades have gone steadily downhill since the first one. Let's see . . . You got a ninety-four on the first one, an eighty-two on the second one, and now a sixty-eight on this exam. That downward trend does not indicate anything positive about your performance on our upcoming final exam." In saying that, the professor implies that the student will not do well on the final exam.

3　Ⓑ, Ⓓ The professor advises the student, "First, you could simply study more when we have a test. And please don't study in your dorm room. I know students prefer doing that, but a dorm room isn't very conducive to effective studying. The library would be a much better place to go. The other option would be to join a study group."

4　Ⓒ When the professor begins by saying, "On the contrary," he is indicating that he disagrees with what the student told him.

Dictation

1　I didn't want <u>you to get embarrassed</u> in front of your friends.

2　I <u>wonder if you could</u> tell me about your study habits.

3　I <u>recommend that you do</u> one of the following.

B

Answers	1 Ⓒ	2 Ⓐ	3 Ⓐ, Ⓑ	4 Ⓒ

| Script |

Listen to part of a conversation between a student and a study abroad office employee.

W1 Study Abroad Office Employee: Good afternoon and welcome to the study abroad office. How may I be of service to you?

W2 Student: Hello. I just returned home from a semester abroad in Greece.

W1: Greece? You must have had a great time there. How did you enjoy it?

W2: Oh, uh, it was amazing. I'm majoring in Archaeology, so I had the opportunity to explore ancient ruins and dig sites virtually every weekend. I must say I had the time of my life there.

W1: That's good to know. It's always encouraging whenever I hear that a student had a positive experience while traveling abroad. That doesn't always happen, you know.

W2: It doesn't?

W1: 4 Not at all. Some students only manage to stay abroad for a couple of weeks before they come back home. Others have negative experiences for various reasons, such as, uh, they don't speak the language well enough, so they get frustrated, or they're not outgoing enough to head out and explore their new environment.

W2: **That's a real shame.** I would have hated to waste my time in Greece like that.

W1: I'm glad to hear you didn't. Anyway, uh, I think we got a bit sidetracked there. You're obviously not here to get information about studying abroad, so what is it that I can do to help you with today?

W2: I'm having a problem getting my grades from my school in Greece transferred here, and I'm not sure what to do. One of my friends mentioned that she had the same problem a year ago and that someone from this office was able to assist her, so I thought I should drop by.

W1: Ah, sure. We get problems like that sometimes. Now, uh, I'm curious . . . Did you attend a university in Greece that is affiliated with our school?

W2: No, I didn't. Oh, no, is that a problem?

W1: Not really. If you had gone to a school we have a relationship with, then all of your grades would automatically be accepted here. Since you didn't do that, here's what you need to do.

W2: Yes?

W1: You need to get in touch with the school in Greece and ask for one of its course catalogs. Then, you have to find the description of each course you took there and match it with a similar class that's taught here.

W2: Oh, that sounds easy.

W1: That's true, but here comes the hard part. You have to find the professor who teaches the corresponding course here and have him or her agree that the class in Greece is similar enough for you to receive credit. Uh, how many classes did you take there?

W2: Five.

W1: Okay. Here are five of the forms. Please get each professor to fill out a form for the proper class. I know this sounds a bit hard, but let me assure you that there are almost never any problems. Yes, it's a time-consuming process, but I'm positive you'll get credit for every class you took.

Answer Explanations

1　Ⓒ The student tells the employee, "I'm having a problem getting my grades from my school in Greece transferred here, and I'm not sure what to do."

2　Ⓐ The student says, "One of my friends mentioned that she had the same problem a year ago and that someone from this office was able to assist her, so I thought I should drop by."

3　Ⓐ, Ⓑ First, the employee states, "You need to get in

touch with the school in Greece and ask for one of its course catalogs. Then, you have to find the description of each course you took there and match it with a similar class that's taught here." Then, she adds, "You have to find the professor who teaches the corresponding course here and have him or her agree that the class in Greece is similar enough for you to receive credit."

4 Ⓒ When the student says, "That's a real shame," she means that it is unfortunate that some of the students who study abroad have bad times there.

Dictation

1 I would have hated to waste my time in Greece like that.

2 I'm having a problem getting my grades from my school in Greece transferred here, and I'm not sure what to do.

3 That's true, but here comes the hard part.

iBT Practice Test
p. 44

Answers

PART 1

1 Ⓑ	2 Ⓒ	3 Ⓓ	4 Ⓐ	5 Ⓐ
6 Ⓒ	7 Ⓐ	8 Ⓑ	9 Cause: ①	
Effect: ②, ③, ④	10 Ⓑ	11 Ⓒ	12 Ⓑ	
13 Ⓑ	14 ②, ③	15 Ⓓ	16 Ⓓ	17 Ⓐ

PART 2

1 Ⓒ	2 ②, ④	3 Ⓐ	4 Ⓐ	5 Ⓒ
6 Ⓐ	7 ③, ④	8 Ⓒ	9 Ⓓ	10 Ⓒ
11 Ⓒ				

PART 1

Conversation [1–5]

| Script |

Listen to part of a conversation between a student and a professor.

W Student: Hi, Professor Thompson. I'm pleased to see you're in your office right now.

M Professor: Good afternoon, Theresa. How are you doing today?

W: I'm all right. I have to visit the local healthcare facility in a few minutes so that I can do my volunteer work for our class there.

M: Are you enjoying the experience?

W: Definitely. I'd never gotten the chance to work closely with people with mental health issues until this semester. You know, uh, I was pretty apprehensive at first, but I'm starting to get used to it. I'm also glad we're required to do the volunteer work. To be honest, um, I thought it was a bit unfair to force us to do it when I first heard about the requirement, but now I'm happy I've got this opportunity.

M: I'm pleased you feel that way. But your class may be the last one that has the opportunity to do this work as the head of the Sociology Department is considering getting rid of the requirement that students in our department do volunteer work to graduate.

W: Oh, it would be terrible if he did that. It's such a valuable experience.

M: I agree, but there's not much I can do about it because I'm just a junior member of the faculty.

W: Well, maybe he'll change his mind.

M: Let's hope so.

W: Anyway, uh, I didn't come here simply to chat with you about the volunteer work. I have a minor request I'd like to make of you.

M: Of course. What can I do for you?

W: I've decided that I'd like to get a master's degree in Sociology, so I'm going to be applying to several graduate schools. As I'm sure you know, I have to submit at least two letters of recommendation to each school I apply to. And, um, I'd like for you to write one of the letters if you don't mind.

M: I most definitely don't mind. Just give me the list of schools you're applying to, and I'll write letters for them.

W: Great. Thanks so much.

M: What sort of information would you like me to focus upon in the letters?

W: Hmm . . . I'd appreciate it if you could write about the work I have done both in and out of the classroom. That will let schools know I'm not just a good student but am also doing hands-on work at the healthcare center.

M: That's smart. I'll do that. Oh, uh, why don't you have Dr. Richards at the healthcare center write a letter for you as well?

W: Dr. Richards? Uh . . . Shouldn't I just have my professors write them?

M: No, you don't always need to do that. Plus, Dr. Richards is one of the most respected people in the field of mental health care. A recommendation from him would be, quite frankly, much more valuable than one from me.

W: 🎧5 Oh . . . I had no idea.

M: Why don't you look him up on the Internet when you have some time? **You'll gain a new appreciation for the kind of man Dr. Richards is.** Plus, uh, it's always a good idea to know about the people you're working with.

W: Okay. I'll be sure to do that while I'm on the bus going there. Thanks for the advice, Professor Thompson.

1 **Gist-Purpose Question**

Ⓑ The student tells the professor, "I'd like for you to write one of the letters if you don't mind."

2 **Understanding Attitude Question**

Ⓒ The student remarks, "It's such a valuable experience."

3 **Making Inferences Question**

Ⓓ When the student expresses her disagreement with the actions of the head of the department, the professor responds, "I agree, but there's not much I can do about it because I'm just a junior member of the faculty." In saying that, he is implying that the department head's thoughts on the requirement for volunteering are wrong.

4 **Making Inferences Question**

Ⓐ The student says, "I have to visit the local healthcare facility in a few minutes so that I can do my volunteer work for our class there." Then, at the end of the conversation, she notes that she will be on the bus soon, so she will probably go to the healthcare center next.

5 **Understanding Function Question**

Ⓐ When the professor says that the student will "gain a new appreciation for the kind of man Dr. Richards is," he is implying that he respects Dr. Richards a great deal.

Lecture #1 [6-11]

| Script |

Listen to part of a lecture in a sociology class.

W Professor: During the late nineteenth century in the United States, there were a number of inventions which changed American society forever. Many of them were in the areas of communication, entertainment, industry, and transportation. In my opinion, the five most vital of these inventions were the motion picture, the automobile, the telephone, the phonograph, and the incandescent light bulb. Now, um, I don't want to go into the background regarding how these inventions came about. You can take a history of science class if you're interested in learning that. Instead, I'd prefer to look at them in turn and to examine how each one changed American society.

We shall begin with the motion picture. In order to understand the influence of motion pictures on society, you must first clearly understand what people did for entertainment in the late nineteenth century. For the most part, individuals spent time with their families when they weren't working. When they did have a holiday, which was a fairly rare event, a trip to a nearby beach or the countryside was typical, especially after train service became more widespread in the country. In addition, once the safety bicycle was invented, cycling became a common pastime. Sports, especially professional baseball, were popular, and circuses were well attended,

particularly since they were events parents could take their children to. Theater was popular and evolved into two types. There was traditional theater, in which plays and operas were staged. It was mostly attended by the well-to-do and cultured elites living in big cities. As for the masses, cheap vaudeville shows were preferred by them. These were traveling shows that went from place to place and featured a variety of performers, including singers, musicians, dancers, and comedians.

Into this mix came the motion picture. In the 1890s, movies were merely short strips of films which rarely lasted longer than a few minutes. They were mostly used to show off the wonders of the new invention. People went to places called nickelodeons, where small machines that cost them a nickel . . . uh, five cents . . . showed a short film strip. Simply the wonder of seeing people move on a small screen captured the imagination of the public and made nickelodeons extremely popular. The only problem with them was that, well, only one or two people could view a film strip at the same time.

For early filmmakers, their ideas on how to make and show motion pictures to the masses developed from the theater. Motion pictures adapted many elements from the theater, including, uh, let's see . . . paid actors, directors, and well-written scripts. Over time, motion pictures became longer and told stories that were either dramas or comedies. Moviemakers purchased theaters across the country, installed huge screens, and showed the latest movies to packed houses. By the early twentieth century, there were more than 10,000 motion picture theaters in the United States.

This had quite a few effects on American leisure and society as a whole. For one, motion pictures could be enjoyed by people of all ages and by men and women together. They could be viewed by all classes of people since they were cheap yet also entertaining. For instance, a movie theater might be filled with families, bankers, laborers, and farmers all rubbing elbows with one another while enjoying a good movie. This helped dismantle some of the barriers that existed between the social classes of the day. It did not, however, demolish them completely. Do keep that in mind. A second influence concerned the manner in which leisure changed. People began popularizing motion pictures to the point that traditional theater and vaudeville both suffered. Traditional theater never died out, and there's still an audience for it today, but attendance at plays, operas, and other similar staged events declined dramatically. As for vaudeville, it slowly disappeared. One of the reasons it vanished was that most of the famous, and best, vaudeville entertainers were lured into the motion picture industry by the higher pay. In addition, American tastes turned away from the simplicity of vaudeville acts and moved to the lure of lavish entertainment on the silver screen. So, uh, by the 1930s, vaudeville was pretty much dead.

An additional change concerned how people treated movie stars. The most popular actors, such as Charlie Chaplin, became the first movie idols. This, in turn, created the entertainment news industry. People everywhere wanted to know more about their favorite stars. Magazines and newspaper sections were dedicated to reporting the latest news from Hollywood, which was established as the motion picture capital of the country by the 1920s. People loved hearing gossip about their favorite stars, uh, much as they still do today. With the invention of sound technology for movies in the 1920s, the popularity of movies increased even more. By the 1930s, motion pictures were the most popular form of entertainment in the country.

I've got a short clip I'd like to show you now. It'll show you some images from nickelodeons, early films, and even some vaudeville shows, so I think you'll find it rather entertaining. Would somebody by the door be kind enough to turn off the lights, please?

Answer Explanations

6 Gist-Content Question

ⓒ The professor mostly talks about the way in which motion pictures affected the American people.

7 Gist-Purpose Question

ⓐ The professor tells the students about entertainment in the late 1800s to let the students know how motion pictures influenced society.

8 Detail Question

ⓑ The professor says, "People went to places called nickelodeons, where small machines that cost them a nickel . . . uh, five cents . . . showed a short film strip. Simply the wonder of seeing people move on a small screen captured the imagination of the public and made nickelodeons extremely popular."

9 Connecting Content Question

Cause: 1   Effect: 2, 3, 4

As for causes, the professor states, "They could be viewed by all classes of people since they were cheap yet also entertaining." Regarding the effects of the rise of motion pictures, the professor says, "Traditional theater never died out, and there's still an audience for it today, but attendance at plays, operas, and other similar staged events declined dramatically." She adds, "They could be viewed by all classes of people since they were cheap yet also entertaining. For instance, a movie theater might be filled with families, bankers, laborers, and farmers all rubbing elbows with one another while enjoying a good movie. This helped dismantle some of the barriers that existed between the social classes of the day." She also comments, "As for vaudeville, it slowly disappeared. One of the reasons it vanished was that most of the famous, and best, vaudeville entertainers were lured into the motion picture industry by the higher pay."

10 Understanding Organization Question

ⓑ The professor remarks, "The most popular actors, such as Charlie Chaplin, became the first movie idols."

11 Making Inferences Question

ⓒ At the end of the lecture, the professor tells the class, "I've got a short clip I'd like to show you now. It'll show you some images from nickelodeons, early films, and even some vaudeville shows, so I think you'll find it rather entertaining."

Lecture #2 [12–17]

| Script |

Listen to part of a lecture in an environmental science class.

M Professor: The scientific term we use to refer to extended periods of extreme cold is glacial epoch, but ice age is the expression people are more familiar with, so it's the one I shall use during today's lecture. To begin with, let me define what an ice age is. An ice age is a period of lower temperatures during which glaciers advance from the poles and mountain ranges to cover a significant portion of the world. What do I mean by a significant portion of the world . . . ? Well, it's estimated that, um, at their greatest extent, glacial sheets covered nearly one-third of the entire planet.

The mechanics of glacial advancement are fairly straightforward. First, what happens is that temperatures begin to decrease, uh, by as much as five to ten degrees Celsius. As a result, significant climate change occurs throughout the planet. At the Polar Regions and in mountainous areas such as the Alps and Himalayas, there's an increasing amount of snowfall, which accumulates over hundreds or thousands of years, resulting in the formation of massive glaciers. On top of that, ocean waters in the Polar Regions become frozen into permanent ice sheets. This leads to something called the albedo effect. Can anyone tell me what it is? Yes? You with your hand up.

W Student: The albedo effect refers to how anything that's white reflects heat rather than absorbing it. Since we're talking about ice sheets, I guess what you mean is that because the snow and ice which comprise those ice sheets are white in color, during an ice age, there are large parts of the Earth's surface that reflect heat and don't absorb it.

M: That's correct. I'm pleased that at least one student did the reading I assigned for this class last week. So what happens as a result of the albedo effect, um, is that a great amount of heat is lost, which further lowers temperatures, resulting in more snowfall and more frozen ocean areas.

Then, uh, the glaciers begin advancing since the weight of the ice pushes down on them, and the ocean water freezes in great amounts. Meter by meter over decades, centuries, or millennia, these gargantuan ice sheets move forward, uh, sometimes traveling thousands of kilometers away from their initial points of origin. In the past, large—or entire—parts of Greenland, Canada, Russia, Scandinavia, Britain, mainland Europe, and Central Asia were buried beneath the ice. Yes, you have a question?

W: I've heard scientists claim they know that the Earth experienced ice ages at various times in the past, but, um, how exactly do they know that?

M: 🎧17 **One way we know that has to do with how the ice sheets altered the face of the land as they advanced. For instance, they carved out valleys and lakes, ground down hills, and moved rocks—some as big as houses—great distances. It was similar changes in the land caused by small glaciers in more modern times that led to our theorizing about extensive ice ages.** The first place this was noticed was in the Alps in the eighteenth century. Since then, more evidence from around the world has helped us theorize about when ice ages happened millions of years ago.

It's currently believed that the planet has gone through five significant ice ages and that we're currently living in the last one. And, yes, I'm well aware that Manhattan and London aren't covered by glaciers. But you should know that ice ages are characterized by cycles of advances and retreats of ice sheets. The last major ice age began approximately two million years ago, and the last great advance of ice sheets was roughly 15,000 years ago. Right now, we're living during a time when the ice sheets have retreated.

W: When is the next advance going to happen?

M: Hmm . . . Let me first explain why we think ice ages happen, and then I shall answer your question. There are several theories regarding what causes ice ages. Some experts theorize that great volcanic eruptions in the past threw up so much ash that the skies darkened, dramatically decreasing temperatures. Another theory is that the atmosphere's composition changed and, uh, and allowed heat to escape from the Earth, um . . . kind of like a greenhouse with all its windows open. A third theory claims that changes in the temperatures of ocean currents caused changes leading to ice ages.

The fourth theory is one that many scientists support. It's based on the amount of heat the Earth receives from the sun based on the planet's orbit and angle on its axis. Over thousands of years, the Earth's position changes, so we go through periods where we receive more heat or less heat. This is called the Milankovitch Cycle Theory. The scientist who proposed it believed that due to the Earth's imperfect orbit around the sun and changes in the tilt of its axis, the Earth went through cycles every 21,000 to 26,000 years during which it received less solar radiation than normal. He and others considered this to be the cause of ice ages. So I'd say that means we're going to see another glacial advance in around six to eleven thousand years.

Answer Explanations

12 Gist-Content Question

Ⓑ The professor's lecture is mostly about the reasons that ice ages take place on the Earth at certain times.

13 Understanding Attitude Question

Ⓑ The professor compliments the student for her knowledge by saying, "That's correct. I'm pleased that at least one student did the reading I assigned for this class last week."

14 Detail Question

② , ③ First, the student comments, "Since we're talking about ice sheets, I guess what you mean is that because the snow and ice which comprise those ice sheets are white in color, during an ice age, there are large parts of the Earth's surface that reflect heat and don't absorb it." Then, the professor states, "So what happens as a result of the albedo effect, um, is that a great amount of heat is lost, which further lowers temperatures, resulting in more snowfall and more frozen ocean areas."

15 Gist-Purpose Question

Ⓓ The professor lectures, "The fourth theory is one that many scientists support. It's based on the amount of heat the Earth receives from the sun based on the planet's orbit and angle on its axis. Over thousands of years, the Earth's position changes, so we go through periods where we receive more heat or less heat. This is called the Milankovitch Cycle Theory. The scientist who proposed it believed that due to the Earth's imperfect orbit around the sun and changes in the tilt of its axis, the Earth went through cycles every 21,000 to 26,000 years during which it received less solar radiation than normal. He and others considered this to be the cause of ice ages. So I'd say that means we're going to see another glacial advance in around six to eleven thousand years."

16 Making Inferences Question

Ⓓ In stating, "So I'd say that means we're going to see another glacial advance in around six to eleven thousand years," after discussing the Milankovitch Cycle Theory, the professor implies that he is a supporter of it.

17 Understanding Attitude Question

Ⓐ The professor's statement means that events which happened recently were utilized to make guesses about other events that happened in the past in other ice ages.

PART 2

Conversation [1–5]

| Script |

Listen to part of a conversation between a student and a job counselor.

W Job Counselor: Good morning and welcome to my office. Please have a seat. My name is Tiffany Goodman, and I'm a job counselor here at this university.

M Student: It's a pleasure to meet you, Ms. Goodman. I'm Eric Hemingway.

W: The pleasure is all mine, Eric. Now, uh, I scheduled this meeting because it's a requirement that all first-year students speak with a job counselor. We talk about what you're considering majoring in and then go over some possible jobs you can do. That can help you prepare for the future after you graduate.

M: That makes sense.

W: Have you decided what you might major in yet, Eric?

M: Yes. I intend to major in History. I'm enrolled in two classes this semester, and I'm enjoying them thoroughly.

W: Okay. And have you thought about what you'd like to do after you graduate?

M: That's a good question. I'm considering attending graduate school, but I can't say for sure. My graduation date is a long time from now, so it's not something I'm particularly concerned about at this moment.

W: I understand. Now, uh, history is the perfect choice for a student in the liberal arts because you'll learn plenty of important skills. Obviously, you'll acquire knowledge about the past, but you'll also learn how to conduct research. Almost all history professors here require students to write at least one paper each semester.

M: Yes, both of the classes I'm taking require ten-page papers at the conclusion of the course.

W: That's excellent. You'll therefore learn how to write and how to organize your thoughts well. Those are skills many businesses require. Since you'll be obligated to make various arguments in the papers you write, you'll learn critical-thinking skills and how to debate and argue.

M: I had never really considered that, but I suppose you're correct.

W: Now, uh, as for jobs, there are plenty you can do. Many History majors at this school become teachers at middle schools and high schools.

M: That's something I have no desire to do. If I teach, I'd rather do it at the university level.

W: All right. Have you considered the law profession? A large number of lawyers majored in History.

M: I wasn't aware of that.

W: It's true. Many law schools are interested in History majors because of the skills they have which I just mentioned. Lots of History majors also attend graduate school to become librarians. That's a great profession if you're interested in reading and conducting research.

M: Okay. What else?

W: Well, writers, editors, and researchers are frequently History majors. You could also consider working as an archivist or even a tour guide.

M: 🎧5 I didn't know I would have so many options. Several of my friends immediately asked me if I was planning to become a teacher when they found out I was interested in majoring in History. **I was almost beginning to think I was making a mistake.**

W: Not at all. There are a wide range of professions you can choose from. I mean, uh, some History majors even go on to work at major companies doing various jobs. And you can always opt to double-major in another field. That would increase your options even more.

M: That's true. I am considering getting a second major in Art History as well. Would you mind telling me a bit about that major?

1 Gist-Purpose Question

ⓒ The job counselor says, "Now, uh, I scheduled this meeting because it's a requirement that all first-year students speak with a job counselor. We talk about what you're considering majoring in and then go over some possible jobs you can do. That can help you prepare for the future after you graduate."

2 Detail Question

②, ④ The job counselor states, "You'll therefore learn how to write and how to organize your thoughts well," and then she says, "Since you'll be obligated to make various arguments in the papers you write, you'll learn critical-thinking skills and how to debate and argue."

3 Understanding Attitude Question

Ⓐ When the job counselor says that many History majors become middle or high school teachers, the student responds by saying, "That's something I have no desire to do."

4 Making Inferences Question

Ⓐ At the end of the conversation, the student comments, "I am considering getting a second major in Art History as well. Would you mind telling me a bit about that major?" So the job counselor will probably respond to the student's question.

5 Understanding Function Question

ⓒ When the student says, "I was almost beginning to think I was making a mistake," with regard to his decision to become a History major, he is indicating his lack of confidence in the major he chose.

Lecture [6–11]

| Script |

Listen to part of a lecture in a zoology class.

M Professor: One of the most interesting things zoologists have learned about by observing chimpanzees in the wild is their grooming habits. Grooming is an act which involves cleaning the hair of another chimp. There are several aspects to it, the first of which is that it's a hygienic act. Grooming is also a social act and a way to gather food in the form of small insects that one chimp finds in another chimp's hair.

Chimps often groom others during periods of relaxation when they might be bored. A chimp approaches another one and presents part of its body to that chimp. Then, if the second chimp is willing, it begins to groom the first one. This is typically done in groups as multiple chimps groom one another. A chimp normally does this by using one hand to pull another chimp's hair back and then using either the free hand, its lips, or its teeth to remove foreign objects from the hair. Foreign objects include dirt, leaves, dead skin, insects, and parasites. Chimps can also groom themselves if no others are willing or able to assist them. Grooming sessions may last a few minutes or several hours.

While making other chimps clean is the primary purpose of grooming, there's more to it than just getting a nice, clean, shiny coat. Observers in the wild have noticed that when one chimp becomes stressed and agitated, other chimps often begin grooming the stressed chimp. This helps soothe the agitated chimp, calms it down, and reduces tension within the entire chimp troop. Ah, yes, a group of chimpanzees is known as a troop. Now, uh, this act has been compared to what a human mother does to soothe her upset child. In fact, one thing observers have noted is that chimp mothers often groom infant chimps when they're trying to wean the infants off mother's milk so that they can make the transition to adult food. This change is quite stressful for infants, so grooming helps them make it through the process.

Speaking of food, in some cases, grooming helps chimps find food. It's not much, but chimps often find tiny insects hiding in other chimps' hair. Observers have seen different insect-gathering behavior among different troops of chimps. In some troops, chimps use leaves to gather insects. Then, they squash the insects with the leaves and pop the insects into their mouths. Chimps in other troops simply use their bare hands. They squash the insects in their hands before consuming them while others smash the insects on their arms first.

Another key aspect of grooming is that it's reciprocal. Basically, chimps expect some kind of a reward for grooming other chimps, and they usually receive grooming in return. By maintaining this giving-and-receiving structure, chimps form strong bonds within their troops.

W Student: Does grooming have a role in the hierarchy of a chimpanzee troop?

M: Yes, but before I cover that, I'd like to discuss the hierarchy a bit. Chimpanzee troops are dominated by large males. Sometimes a single male dominates, but

it's typically a coalition of several big males. These large males use physical strength to dominate their troops. The smaller, weaker males cannot outright challenge the larger males in a fight, so they use grooming to gather the support of the other smaller males as well as the females. Basically, um, what happens is that the smaller males and the females bond through grooming. This gives the smaller males a higher standing in the troop. It allows them to form coalitions to prevent attacks by larger chimps, and it may give them more access to food and mating opportunities.

Something else regarding grooming that I'd like to mention is how chimps act when in the presence of a chimp that is higher ranked. Often, low-ranked chimps groom high-ranked chimps. But if an even higher-ranked chimp is nearby, the groomer won't, uh, groom for very long. It's believed that the reason is that the groomer believes the mid-ranked chimp being groomed will not reciprocate the act of grooming. Instead, the groomed mid-ranked chimp will soon go over to the higher-ranked chimp to groom it. So the lowest-ranked chimp, which started the grooming of the mid-ranked chimp, quickly gives up due to the belief that the grooming is a waste of time and that nothing will be gained from it.

Overall, it's clear that grooming is beneficial to a chimpanzee troop. It provides a number of advantages for chimps and has virtually no drawbacks. Okay, are there any questions . . . ?

No. Great. Now, I'd like to conclude my lecture for the day because I need to discuss something of great importance. As you are aware, it's time for midterms. Your test is going to take place next Monday. Let me give you a few hints so that you'll know what to expect on it.

6 Gist-Content Question

Ⓐ The professor mainly discusses the benefits of grooming and how chimpanzees do it.

7 Detail Question

③, ④ First, the professor notes, "While making other chimps clean is the primary purpose of grooming, there's more to it than just getting a nice, clean, shiny coat." He then adds, "Speaking of food, in some cases, grooming helps chimps find food. It's not much, but chimps often find tiny insects hiding in other chimps' hair."

8 Connecting Content Question

Ⓒ About human and chimpanzee mothers, the professor remarks, "Now, uh, this act has been compared to what a human mother does to soothe her upset child. In fact, one thing observers have noted is that chimp mothers often groom infant chimps when they're trying to wean the infants off mother's milk so that they can make the transition to adult food. This change is quite stressful for infants, so grooming helps them make it through the process." So the professor compares how they act to calm down stressed babies.

9 Gist-Purpose Question

Ⓓ The professor lectures, "The smaller, weaker males cannot outright challenge the larger males in a fight, so they use grooming to gather the support of the other smaller males as well as the females. Basically, um, what happens is that the smaller males and the females bond through grooming. This gives the smaller males a higher standing in the troop. It allows them to form coalitions to prevent attacks by larger chimps, and it may give them more access to food and mating opportunities."

10 Understanding Attitude Question

Ⓒ About grooming, the professor states, "Overall, it's clear that grooming is beneficial to a chimpanzee troop. It provides a number of advantages for chimps and has virtually no drawbacks."

11 Making Inferences Question

Ⓒ At the end of the lecture, the professor says, "Now, I'd like to conclude my lecture for the day because I need to discuss something of great importance. As you are aware, it's time for midterms. Your test is going to take place next Monday. Let me give you a few hints so that you'll know what to expect on it."

| Vocabulary Review   p. 54

Answers

A
1	obliged	2	apprehensive	3	ruins
4	lavish	5	strikes		

B
1	b	2	a	3	a	4	b	5	a
6	a	7	b	8	a	9	b	10	b

Practice with Short Passages

p. 58

A

Answers   1   Ⓒ   2   Ⓐ

| Script |

Listen to part of a conversation between a student and a student housing office employee.

M Student: Excuse me, but I need to check out of my dormitory room. Are you the person I need to speak with to do that?

W Student Housing Office Employee: I'm sorry, but did you just say that you need to check out of your dormitory room?

M: Yes, that's correct.

W: Um . . . why are you doing that? We haven't even passed the halfway point of the semester yet.

M: Well, uh, I've decided I'm going to move back home with my parents. They aren't in the best of health, so I should be at home for them in case they have any problems. As a result, I no longer need to have my dormitory room. You know, uh, I called this morning and spoke with someone here. She told me that it wouldn't be a problem and that I'd be able to check out of my room easily. I'm guessing it wasn't you with whom I spoke, right?

W: Yes, this is the first time that I've heard of this. Do you recall the woman's name?

M: Sorry, but she never mentioned it while I was speaking with her. There, uh, there aren't going to be any problems turning in my key and filling out any forms, are there? I've got a class to attend soon, and I was hoping to get this taken care of before then.

W: Er, unfortunately, I think you're going to have to come back later in the day to take care of this matter.

M: Why's that?

W: Since it's lunchtime, everyone except me is out of the office. And I, um, I only started working here on Monday, so I'm not familiar at all with the procedure. Would it be possible for you to return after your class?

M: Yeah, okay. I guess I can do that. I'll be back here around, hmm . . . around two thirty. Yeah, I can make it here by then.

W: Great. Could you let me know your name, please?

M: Sure. I'm Dylan Carter.

W: Thanks, Dylan. I'll find out who you talked with and make sure she's here at half past two. See you then.

Answer Explanations

1   Ⓒ   The student comments, "Well, uh, I've decided I'm going to move back home with my parents. They aren't in the best of health, so I should be at home for them in case they have any problems. As a result, I no longer need to have my dormitory room."

2   Ⓐ   The woman says, "Since it's lunchtime, everyone except me is out of the office. And I, um, I only started working here on Monday, so I'm not familiar at all with the procedure. Would it be possible for you to return after your class?"

B

Answers   1   Ⓑ   2   Fact: ①, ③   Not a Fact: ②, ④

| Script |

Listen to part of a conversation between a student and a professor.

M1 Professor: Good afternoon, Kevin. Do you need to speak with me about something?

M2 Student: Yes, Professor Campbell, I do. Would you happen to have a couple of minutes to spare for me?

M1: Sure. What do you want to talk to me about?

M2: It's the homework that you assigned to us in class. There's a, uh, a bit of a problem with it.

M1: A problem? But I only assigned a short reading and writing assignment. How could there possibly be something wrong with that?

M2: Er . . . I think I may have misspoken just now. There's not actually a problem with the assignment itself. But there is a problem for me concerning the due date.

M1: What is it?

M2: Well, um, we're supposed to do the reading and then submit our analysis of it by this Friday, right?

M1: That's correct.

M2: But, uh, I don't believe I can get it to you until next Monday. You see, uh, I'm a member of the school's swimming team, and we're going to have a swim meet on Friday. It's going to be held out of town—uh, in Madison—so we're leaving for the swim meet on Thursday afternoon. But we'll be back on Saturday, so I should be able to do the assignment over the weekend and then turn it in to you in class on Monday. How does that sound?

M1: I'm afraid that's an unacceptable suggestion, Kevin.

M2: Huh? Why do you say that?

M1: Kevin, today's Monday, so you have plenty of time to get the assignment done. You only need to read fifteen pages in the textbook and then write a two-page analysis of what you read. I'm pretty sure you can get it to me before you leave on Thursday.

M2: B-b-b-but . . . I've got class all day on Thursday. How will I be able to submit my paper to you?

M1: You can either have a friend drop it off with me, or you can email it. Either way will suffice.

Answer Explanations

1 Ⓑ The student says, "You see, uh, I'm a member of the school's swimming team, and we're going to have a swim meet on Friday. It's going to be held out of town— uh, in Madison—so we're leaving for the swim meet on Thursday afternoon. But we'll be back on Saturday, so I should be able to do the assignment over the weekend and then turn it in to you in class on Monday."

2 Fact: ①, ③ Not a Fact: ②, ④
It is a fact that the student's assignment is due on Friday. The professor also says, "You only need to read fifteen pages in the textbook and then write a two-page analysis of what you read," so it is true that the student must write about some pages in the book. It is not true that the assignment is worth ten points or that the professor will only accept emailed submissions.

C

Answers 1 Ⓑ 2 Ⓑ, Ⓒ

| Script |

Listen to part of a lecture in a marine biology class.

W Professor: Ever since man began sailing, there have been tales about monsters dwelling in the world's oceans and seas. Monster sightings were actually quite common in the past. Sailors, you see, are superstitious by nature, so they were quick to believe there were great beasts living in the ocean that were capable of grasping ships and pulling them and their crews beneath the surface. These creatures were often called sea serpents, but they also got more fanciful names, such as the kraken of Norse mythology. So the question is . . . did sailors truly see real monsters, or were they just, well, were they just spinning tales? And if they did see something, what explanations can we give for those sightings based upon our current knowledge of marine life? Ted, your hand is up.

M Student: They probably saw whales or, uh, maybe giant squid.

W: Hmm . . . Giant squid is a definite possibility, but I'm not so sure about whales. Actually, I'm quite confident in stating that sailors claiming to have seen a kraken had really merely observed giant squid. Here's why . . . A kraken supposedly had ten arms—just like squid—and

could grasp objects. Sailors claimed it was so big that it could grab a sailing ship with three masts and drag it to the bottom of the sea. But I'm pretty sure that was their imaginations working overtime. After all, most giant squid never grow larger than a dozen meters in length, and that includes their long tentacles. While that is pretty big, a giant squid could never drag a large vessel underwater. It might manage to sink a small rowboat, uh, but not a big ship. But, um, as for whales, I don't believe sailors would have mistaken them for sea monsters due to the fact that whales were well known to sailors. They would have recognized whales for what they were.

There's another possibility though . . . the oarfish. Sailors might have seen it and thought it was a sea serpent. Look up here on the screen . . . and you'll see why. This is a picture of an oarfish that washed ashore in California a while ago. This very long, silver-colored fish swims close to the surface when it's sick or dying and sometimes washes ashore after it dies. While this specimen isn't very long, the oarfish has been known to grow as long as eleven meters. Note its long, spiny dorsal fin . . . Notice how it runs the length of the fish's body from head to tail. And consider the fact that the oarfish rarely swims near the surface, so many sailors had never seen one before. Combine that fact with its long, snaky body and spiny dorsal fin, and you have the makings of a sea serpent.

But we have to consider one more thing: These sea serpents, monsters, krakens, or whatever you call them could be an unknown species of marine life. Remember that we discover more species of plants and animals every year. The world's oceans—and also its rainforests—are a couple of places that haven't been completely explored yet. So it's entirely possible that there are unknown and uncatalogued creatures swimming deep in the ocean and rarely coming to the surface. Some suggest that these unknown creatures may be beasts from the age of dinosaurs that were long thought to be extinct. I guess we won't know until we discover one of them.

Answer Explanations

1 Ⓑ The professor notes, "A kraken supposedly had ten arms—just like squid—and could grasp objects."

2 Ⓑ, Ⓒ The professor lectures, "Note its long, spiny dorsal fin . . . Notice how it runs the length of the fish's body from head to tail. And consider the fact that the oarfish rarely swims near the surface, so many sailors had never seen one before. Combine that fact with its long, snaky body and spiny dorsal fin, and you have the makings of a sea serpent."

D

Answers 1 Ⓓ 2 Ⓐ

Listen to part of a lecture in a chemistry class.

M Professor: Snow, as you know, is a form of precipitation. It forms when the moisture in clouds cools and makes crystal structures that we see as snowflakes. Of course, uh, this doesn't always happen since there must be the right combination of temperature and humidity for snowflakes to form. There must also be some impurities, such as dust particles, for the water to attach to and then freeze on. Each snowflake isn't the same either. Depending upon changes in the temperature and humidity as it falls, a snowflake can change its structure. Scientists theorize that there are more than 100 variables which influence how a snowflake forms. Because of that, they believe there are an infinite number of snowflake shapes, so the end result is that, well, every snowflake is unique.

But snowflakes do have one thing in common: They always start by forming a basic six-sided hexagonal structure. They have this shape on account of the way the water molecules bond to a dust particle and then freeze in a crystal lattice, uh, with the oxygen and hydrogen atoms in different molecules of water bonding to one another. Here's an image on the screen . . . This is an enlarged microscopic image of the beginning of the formation of a snowflake. At the start, it's merely a solid six-sided ice crystal like you can see here. The lattice's sides are perfectly straight. But, uh, the snowflake doesn't remain in this shape for long. Instead, as it forms, it becomes heavier and falls from the clouds. While falling, it passes through layers of air with various temperatures and amounts of humidity. These transform the ice crystal into different shapes and sizes and therefore create the snowflake's final shape.

The most common additions to ice crystals are arms of ice that grow from the central six-sided lattice. Here . . . Uh, these are twelve enlarged images of snowflakes, all of which have different shapes.

W Student: Each of them appears the same in the center. Shall I assume that's the original crystal lattice?

M: That's a good—and correct—observation. Yes, class, look at the center of each snowflake, and you'll see the original six-sided lattice, which is the same for every one of them. But as these flakes fell, water molecules attached themselves to the lattice and formed larger snowflakes. And due to variations in temperature and humidity, the literally infinite variety of combinations of these two factors, and the different number of layers of air these snowflakes passed through, they all developed different final structures.

One thing you might observe is that these pictures show perfectly formed snowflakes that are symmetrical on all sides. That's not always the case though. Oftentimes, one part of a snowflake grows larger than another part. This may occur when a sudden change in the environment

the snowflake is in happens so rapidly that it doesn't have time to affect the growth of the entire snowflake while it's falling toward the ground.

Another difference you should be aware of is the size. Not all snowflakes are the same size, but snowflakes are limited in size. The smallest ones are no more than zero point two millimeters wide while the largest are no greater than five millimeters wide. Ice crystals smaller than that are too light to fall to the ground as snow, so they remain in the air. And those bigger than five millimeters are too large, so they break up into smaller pieces as they fall to the ground.

Answer Explanations

1 Ⓓ The professor tells the students, "But snowflakes do have one thing in common: They always start by forming a basic six-sided hexagonal structure."

2 Ⓐ The professor comments, "Oftentimes, one part of a snowflake grows larger than another part. This may occur when a sudden change in the environment the snowflake is in happens so rapidly that it doesn't have time to affect the growth of the entire snowflake while it's falling toward the ground."

Practice with Long Passages   p. 62

A

Answers	1 Ⓑ	2 Ⓓ	3 Ⓐ	4 Ⓒ

| Script |

Listen to part of a conversation between a student and a librarian.

W Student: Pardon me, but are you one of the librarians here? I have a problem which I think only a librarian can help me with.

M Librarian: Hi. Uh, yes, I'm a librarian. What kind of problem do you have? Do you need a reference book or something?

W: Um, I'm not really sure. I need some books, but I'm having a bit of difficulty using the computerized search system. Do you think you can assist me for a moment?

M: Of course. Which computer are you working on?

W: This one right over here.

M: Okay, what exactly is the problem you're encountering when you're trying to find a book?

W: Well, uh, I keep inputting some different subjects, but nothing's coming up on the screen. Take a look at this . . . I'm going to type the subject now . . . scholasticism . . . but I'm getting this message from the computer. It reads

"No books available."

M: Huh . . . That can't be right. I know for a fact we have plenty of books on that particular topic. Do you happen to know the names of any specific authors? We can try searching for one of them.

W: Sure. Uh, let me consult my notes here . . . Ah, yes. Marrone is one. That's M-A-R-R-O-N-E. One of my classmates checked out a book by him from the library last month and said it was pretty good.

M: Hmm . . . Again, we just got the same message. And I'm familiar with that author and know we have no fewer than two of his books in our collection. Why don't we try to use another computer? There could be a problem with this computer.

W: All right. Nobody's using this one here, so let me type in the author's name again . . . Nope, it's the same message as before.

M: Okay, it appears as though there's a problem with the entire computerized search system. I need to contact someone to let her know about this issue so that the technicians can get to work on fixing the system.

W: Sounds good. How long will that take?

M: I've got absolutely no idea. 🎧4 Sorry, but I just don't know. It could be a quick fix, which might require an hour or so of maintenance, or it could take a lot longer. It depends on what's wrong with the system.

W: **I'm sorry, but did you just say it could take an hour to fix if it's a minor problem?**

M: Yes. That's correct.

W: Um . . . I don't have that much time to wait around, and I have to get some books as quickly as possible.

M: Well, I can take you to the place in the library's collection where the books you need are kept. But would you mind waiting a couple of minutes? I need to speak to my boss at once.

W: Sure. I'll be right here when you get back.

M: Thanks. I'll come back in a bit.

Answer Explanations

1 Ⓑ The student tells the librarian, "I need some books, but I'm having a bit of difficulty using the computerized search system."

2 Ⓓ The librarian remarks to the student, "And I'm familiar with that author and know we have no fewer than two of his books in our collection."

3 Ⓐ At the end of the conversation, the librarian states, "But would you mind waiting a couple of minutes? I need to speak to my boss at once."

4 Ⓒ The student is expressing her surprise at what the librarian says. She cannot believe that it will take an hour to fix a minor problem, so she shows how surprised she is when she says that.

B

Answers

1 Ⓒ   2 Ⓒ, Ⓓ
3 Fact: ③   Not a Fact: ①, ②, ④   4 Ⓒ

| Script |

Listen to part of a lecture in an oceanology class.

M Professor: Approximately seventy-one percent of the Earth's surface is covered by water, and the vast majority of that, uh, more than ninety-five percent, is found in the oceans. Regarded as a whole, the oceans constitute one enormous body of water surrounding all of the landmasses on the planet. However, we conveniently divide the oceans into separate parts, the three largest of which are the Pacific, Atlantic, and Indian oceans. Before we go into more detail on the oceans today, I'd like to go over how they were initially formed with you. I think you'll find it rather enlightening.

Firstly, you should be aware that there are two major theories concerning the formation of the oceans. One claims that the water came from inside the planet while the other avers that the water arrived on the Earth by external sources, by which I mean, um, comets and large asteroids hitting the planet. Let's look at the first theory now. It's related to how the Earth itself was formed. Billions of years ago, swirling masses of gas, ice, and dust formed the solar system and all its heavenly bodies. As these particles collided, they formed larger and larger masses and eventually became the planets, including the Earth. But the Earth didn't initially appear the way it does today either on its surface or in its interior. You see, uh, inside the planet, the different layers were still forming from the mass of material which had collided. As this material gradually separated into the crust, mantle, and core, a great amount of gas was released from the ground through volcanic activity. This is called outgassing, um, in case you're unaware. Well, uh, this gas helped form the first atmosphere, which included molecules of water in their gaseous forms, so they became clouds. However, the Earth was still very hot—more than 400 degrees Celsius. It was so hot that water vapor couldn't become liquid water. After millions of years, the Earth cooled enough, so the temperature fell beneath 100 degrees Celsius, and that caused the water in the clouds to fall to the surface as rain. Over a long period of time, the falling water filled in the low-lying spots and became the oceans.

The second theory posits that asteroids and large comets hit the Earth. They were partially composed of ice, which melted on the planet, became water vapor, and rose into the atmosphere. When the Earth cooled enough, the clouds released the water in them, rain fell, and the water formed the oceans.

W Student: 🎧4 Couldn't both theories be correct? I mean, um, each of them could have played a role in forming the oceans, right?

M: **That's a distinct possibility.** In fact, many scientists are starting to lean toward it. There's even a growing debate on which method contributed more water to the oceans. Personally, I believe outgassing accounted for the majority of the water on the planet. Why is that? Well, I simply feel that the huge amount of water in the oceans couldn't possibly have come from comets and asteroids. I agree with the theoretical models suggesting that eighty percent of the water came from outgassing while the rest arrived on comets and asteroids.

Now, uh, you may wonder why the Earth has such large oceans but the other planets and their moons don't. There are three main reasons. First, the Earth's location in the solar system is neither too close to the sun nor too far from it. So the planet is hot enough for water to be in a liquid state but not so hot that it turns into gas. Likewise, it's not so far away from the sun that it's so cold that the water freezes into enormous sheets of ice. A second reason is that the Earth's gravity is strong enough to prevent the water from flying off the planet's surface. Lastly, the planet has a thick atmosphere, which prevents ultraviolet radiation from burning off the water.

Answer Explanations

1 Ⓒ While talking about the formation of the solar system, the professor says, "It's related to how the Earth itself was formed." Then, he talks about how it affected the creation of the Earth.

2 Ⓒ, Ⓓ The professor states, "One claims that the water came from inside the planet while the other avers that the water arrived on the Earth by external sources, by which I mean, um, comets and large asteroids hitting the planet." He also says, "As this material gradually separated into the crust, mantle, and core, a great amount of gas was released from the ground through volcanic activity. This is called outgassing, um, in case you're unaware. Well, uh, this gas helped form the first atmosphere, which included molecules of water in their gaseous forms, so they became clouds."

3 Fact: ③ Not a Fact: ①, ②, ④
The professor mentions, "Now, uh, you may wonder why the Earth has such large oceans but the other planets and their moons don't." However, he also remarks,

"Approximately seventy-one percent of the Earth's surface is covered by water, and the vast majority of that, uh, more than ninety-five percent, is found in the oceans." So it is not true that seventy percent of the water on the planet is in the oceans. In addition, the oceans did not form right after the Earth was created, and he also points out, "Lastly, the planet has a thick atmosphere, which prevents ultraviolet radiation from burning off the water." Therefore ultraviolet radiation does not burn off any of the water in the oceans.

4 Ⓒ When the professor states, "That's a distinct possibility," it can be inferred that the professor believes that the student's theory could be correct.

Dictation

1 Before we <u>go into more detail</u> on the oceans today, I'd like to <u>go over</u> how they were initially formed with you.

2 Firstly, you should be <u>aware</u> that there are two major theories <u>concerning</u> the formation of the oceans.

3 The second theory <u>posits that</u> asteroids and large comets hit the Earth.

iBT Practice Test
p. 66

Answers

PART 1

1 ①, ③	2 Ⓑ	3 Ⓓ	4 Ⓑ	5 Ⓓ
6 Ⓐ	7 Ⓑ	8 Ⓑ	9 Ⓓ	10 Ⓐ
11 Ⓒ	12 Ⓑ	13 Ⓒ	14 Ⓓ	

15 Fact: ①, ②, ④ Not a Fact: ③ 16 ②, ③ 17 Ⓐ

PART 2

1 Ⓐ	2 Ⓓ	3 Ⓓ	4 Ⓑ	5 Ⓑ
6 Ⓒ	7 ②, ③	8 Ⓐ	9 Ⓒ	10 Ⓓ
11 Ⓑ				

PART 1

Conversation [1-5]

| Script |

Listen to part of a conversation between a student and a professor.

W1 Student: Good afternoon, Professor Hamilton. Thanks for agreeing to see me on such short notice.

W2 Professor: It's no problem, Andrea. So, uh, what can I help you with today? Do you have something to discuss regarding yesterday's lecture?

W1: Oh, no, ma'am. I didn't have any problems understanding the material you covered. I thought it was fascinating, so I went to the library and checked out some books on David Ricardo. I haven't looked at them yet, but I'm planning to do some reading this weekend.

W2: 🎧5 I'm pleased to learn my lecture inspired you to do some research of your own. I find Ricardo to be an intriguing economist. I've even published a few articles on his theories, so feel free to come here to discuss the books with me when you're finished reading them.

W1: **I'll be sure to take you up on that offer, ma'am.**

W2: Excellent.

W1: So, uh, anyway, I want to discuss a couple of things with you. The first is the final exam.

W2: What about it?

W1: I know it's not for three more weeks, but I've already started studying for it. I wonder if there are any, uh, tips you can give me for the test. I mean, uh, do I need to study all the material we've learned thus far, or should I focus exclusively on what we've studied since the midterm exam?

W2: Hmm . . . I'd say the bulk of the exam questions will be about the material we've covered since March. However, you need to be familiar with everything we've learned this semester. Having said that, spend, uh, ninety percent of your time on the information you haven't been tested on yet. Is that good enough?

W1: Yes, it is. Thanks a lot.

W2: And the other thing you need to talk about?

W1: Ah, yes. I'm planning on doing an internship this summer.

W2: Er . . . Don't you think it's a bit too late to be applying for them? Most students apply for them either in late winter or early spring.

W1: Oh, uh, I already applied, and I found out this week that two companies have offered me internships. I was hoping you could give me some advice on which of the two internships I should accept.

W2: Congratulations, Andrea. That's very well done, especially since you're only a sophomore. It's extremely impressive to get two offers in one summer. Tell me about them.

W1: The first is an internship at Philips Consulting, which is located here in the city.

W2: I'm familiar with the company. And the other one?

W1: It's for a firm in London called Wilson Financial. My, uh, father knows some people there—uh, they're colleagues of his—so he helped arrange it for me. Both are paid internships by the way.

W2: Well, not knowing the specific details, I'd recommend that you go to London as it would be a great experience to live and work in a foreign country. You'd probably get a lot more out of it than you would by staying here. And it would look good on your résumé because Wilson Financial is very well known in the business world.

W1: Hmm . . . I was leaning toward taking the Philips Consulting job, but I'll have to reconsider now.

W2: I would if I were you. Philips is a good company, but it's nothing compared to Wilson.

Answer Explanations

1 **Gist-Purpose Question**

1, 3 First, the student says, "So, uh, anyway, I want to discuss a couple of things with you. The first is the final exam." Then, in response to the professor's question about the other thing she wants to talk about, the student comments, "Ah, yes. I'm planning on doing an internship this summer."

2 **Detail Question**

Ⓑ The professor tells the student, "I'd say the bulk of the exam questions will be about the material we've covered since March. However, you need to be familiar with everything we've learned this semester. Having said that, spend, uh, ninety percent of your time on the information you haven't been tested on yet."

3 **Making Inferences Question**

Ⓓ The student remarks, "It's for a firm in London called Wilson Financial. My, uh, father knows some people there—uh, they're colleagues of his—so he helped arrange it for me." When the student says that, it can be inferred that her father works in the financial sector since he has colleagues at Wilson Financial.

4 **Understanding Attitude Question**

Ⓑ The professor proclaims, "Philips is a good company, but it's nothing compared to Wilson."

5 **Understanding Attitude Question**

Ⓓ When the student says that she'll be sure to take the professor up on her offer, she means that she will visit the professor in her office to discuss some books after she reads them.

Lecture #1 [6–11]

| **Script** |

Listen to part of a lecture in an environmental science class.

W Professor: The environments in different parts of the world are interconnected in some unusual ways. What happens in one place frequently influences what occurs in another. This may have positive or negative effects. Let me give you an example of what I'm talking about. In Africa, there's a depression . . . uh, that means it's a low area of land . . . called the Bodele Depression. You spell it B-O-D-E-L-E in case you're unaware. The Bodele Depression is in the North African nation of Chad. It has such high winds that large dust storms occur there roughly 200 days a year. And I'm not talking about simple gusts of wind either. These dust storms are so powerful that they pick up huge amounts of dust and carry it into the atmosphere. Then, the air currents in the upper atmosphere transport the dust all the way across the Atlantic Ocean and deposit it in Brazil, mostly in the Amazon Rainforest.

Now, um, you'd think that being constantly covered by large clouds of dusts would be bad for the rainforests in Brazil, wouldn't you? Remember that this is an enormous amount of dust. It's estimated that forty million tons of dust is transported from the entire Sahara region to the Amazon each year. A large part—approximately half—comes solely from the Bodele Depression. Well, uh, rather than being harmful, the dust actually provides numerous benefits for the rainforest. The reason is that it's rich in minerals which positively affect the growth of plants. Here, uh, I shall explain . . . These minerals come from the floor of the depression, which was the bottom of a sea millions of years ago. During that time, uncountable numbers of marine lifeforms died and then formed sedimentary layers of mineral-rich rocks on the seafloor. Most of the marine lifeforms were small ones called diatoms. They're a form of algae that have hard outer shells. The sedimentary rock that formed is called diatomite. As the wind blows across the Bodele Depression, it picks up eroded diatomite particles and then carries them across the Atlantic Ocean.

M Student: Excuse me, but how is the wind possibly strong enough to do that?

W: Good question. The reason has to do with the unique geography of the depression. Hold on a moment . . . Okay, there it is up on the screen. You're looking at a satellite image of the Bodele Depression. Notice the two large land formations to the north and south here . . . Now, um, notice how it narrows at its southwest end. These two large masses are high mountain formations that form a narrow valley. The depression is the floor of this valley. The mountains create a, um, a natural funnel for the wind to blow through. It's estimated that the winds reach speeds of up to fourteen meters per second, which is around fifty kilometers per hour. Those aren't hurricane-force winds, but they're still blowing rather fast. During wintertime in the Northern Hemisphere . . . uh, between the months of November and March, the winds in the Sahara blow mainly from the northeast and move in a southwesterly direction on a direct path to Brazil. The dust is therefore picked up and carried as high as three kilometers into the air. Then, it flows more than 5,000 kilometers all the way to Brazil.

Of course, um, some dust falls into the ocean, but quite a large amount still makes it to Brazil. So, uh, what are the benefits . . . ? Well, first off, you need to understand something about the Amazon Rainforest. It's a wet place with poor naturally occurring soil. Most of the nutrients and minerals in it are washed away by heavy rains. Yes?

M: Ah, I get it. The dust from the Bodele Depression is like, uh, it's like fertilizer for the soil in the Amazon.

W: Precisely. The minerals in the dust enrich the soil, which

enables plants to grow well. Some studies suggest that without the dust from the Bodele Depression, most of the area covered by the Amazon Rainforest would be like a desert—a hot, wet desert with poor soil unable to sustain life. That would have drastic consequences for the world since the Amazon region and its large biomass of plant life provide many benefits, particularly the production of oxygen and the removal of carbon dioxide from the atmosphere. On top of this are the large numbers of plants in the Amazon that have medicinal benefits and the fact that the region is home to thousands of species of mammals, birds, insects, and other animals.

The question is how long this enriching of the Amazon by African dust can continue. It's unknown how large the deposit of mineral-rich soil in the Bodele Depression is. And it's also unknown at what rate the sedimentary rock will continue to erode to provide a source of the dust. Yes, uh, it's true that other regions of the Sahara provide some of the dust that blows westward to the Amazon, but, as I already mentioned, the Bodele Depression provides more than half of it. The worry is that, one day, this source will be exhausted, and then there will be some serious consequences for both the Amazon and the rest of the world.

Answer Explanations

6 Gist-Content Question

Ⓐ Most of the lecture is about the Bodele Depression and how it affects the Amazon Rainforest.

7 Making Inferences Question

Ⓑ The professor remarks, "It has such high winds that large dust storms occur there roughly 200 days a year. And I'm not talking about simple gusts of wind either. These dust storms are so powerful that they pick up huge amounts of dust and carry it into the atmosphere." Since there is so much dust there, it can be inferred that the land is dry and that little rain falls there.

8 Detail Question

Ⓑ The professor comments, "Most of the marine lifeforms were small ones called diatoms. They're a form of algae that have hard outer shells. The sedimentary rock that formed is called diatomite."

9 Understanding Function Question

Ⓓ About the wind, the professor says, "During wintertime in the Northern Hemisphere . . . uh, between the months of November and March, the winds in the Sahara blow mainly from the northeast and move in a southwesterly direction on a direct path to Brazil. The dust is therefore picked up and carried as high as three kilometers into the air. Then, it flows more than 5,000 kilometers all the way to Brazil." So she talks about the wind to explain how it can blow so much dust to Brazil.

10 Detail Question

Ⓐ The professor points out, "The minerals in the dust

enrich the soil, which enables plants to grow well. Some studies suggest that without the dust from the Bodele Depression, most of the area covered by the Amazon Rainforest would be like a desert—a hot, wet desert with poor soil unable to sustain life."

11 Connecting Content Question

Ⓒ The professor states, "Well, first off, you need to understand something about the Amazon Rainforest. It's a wet place with poor naturally occurring soil. Most of the nutrients and minerals in it are washed away by heavy rains." Furthermore, she comments, "Some studies suggest that without the dust from the Bodele Depression, most of the area covered by the Amazon Rainforest would be like a desert—a hot, wet desert with poor soil unable to sustain life." Thus the disappearance of mineral-rich soil from the Bodele Depression would likely result in fewer plants growing in the Amazon Rainforest.

Lecture #2 [12–17]

| Script |

Listen to part of a lecture in an art history class.

W Professor: As you may or may not be aware, in ancient times, the Greeks established several colonies in the southern part of Italy just as Rome was becoming a strong power in central Italy. Ultimately, the two sides clashed, and the Greeks were forced out of Italy. Nevertheless, the Greeks influenced the Romans long after they were no longer physically present. Of course, we're interested primarily in art in this class, but the Greeks also influenced the Romans with regard to, hmm, well . . . religion, law, architecture, politics, and even warfare. If you want to find out more, I suggest enrolling in Professor Stern's history of Rome class next semester. You'll find it highly educational.

Anyway, when we talk about Roman art, we're mainly referring to sculptures, especially statues. 🎧17 The reason is that most of the surviving art pieces we have from Roman times are statues which have stood the test of time. The Romans utilized both metal and stone to make statues. Bronze and marble were their two favorite materials. **However, metal had a high reuse value in the centuries after many pieces were created, so most of the Roman statues that have survived to the present day are ones sculpted from stone.**

The Greek influence on these statues is easy to see, especially with regard to statues from the time of the Roman Republic, which happened before the Romans began moving away from Greek influence. The Romans often copied Greek statues. They did this so much that many examples of Greek statues can only be found in Roman copies since the originals have been lost over time. Statues of Greek gods and heroes were particularly popular. The Greeks strove to make their statues perfect representations of the human body, an aspect greatly admired by the Romans. The Greek style varied from the Etruscan style, which had influenced the Romans in earlier times. The Etruscans, in case you are curious, were less concerned about representing the human body accurately.

Another reason the Greeks influenced Roman art is that many of the sculptors working in Rome were from Greece. They were either hired to create art or were slaves that had been captured during Rome's numerous conquests. The Romans were so enamored by the Greek style that they shipped many works of art to Italy after conquering Greece. When the supply of original Greek statues was exhausted, the Romans founded two schools to train sculptors to make copies. One school was in Rome while the other was in Athens. There was even heavy demand for miniature replicas of Greek statues, which Romans used as decorations for their homes.

M Student: Did the Romans also copy the statues the Greeks decorated their buildings with?

W: Not that much. The Greeks made statues of people and animals but also heavily used statues of mythological figures and gods for their buildings. The Romans, on the other hand, preferred more realism. The carvings and sculptures on the Arch of Constantine and Trajan's Column mostly depict people. These people were typically Roman warriors, conquered enemies, and Roman emperors. I should point out that the two examples I just mentioned come from the empire period, when the Greek influence on Roman sculptures was waning. Around then, the Romans started making their statues even more realistic than the Greeks had. They used tricks of light and shading to make their statues seem as lifelike as possible.

The Greeks additionally influenced Roman portrait sculptures, which showed only the head or, um, the upper body and head of an individual. The Romans, just like the Greeks, started by creating realistic images of people carved in stone and metal. The Romans even imitated the Greek style of painting on irises and pupils rather than carving directly on the eyes. Perhaps you've noticed that many Greek and Roman statues lack pupils and irises and, uh, thus appear to have no eyes. In fact, most Greek and Roman statues were painted in colorful hues, but the paint wore off over time and left behind white stone. In the second century A.D.—uh, that was during the Roman Empire—Roman sculptors began carving eyes, irises, and pupils. They also started making very realistic depictions of living people in their portrait sculptures so that even wrinkles and blemishes such as moles are apparent.

Over time, the Romans also became less influenced by the Greeks with respect to the sizes of their statues. In the early Roman Empire, Roman sculptors started making colossal statues of their own gods. The Romans worshipped their emperors as gods, so they created massive statues of them as well. Roman emperors were often posed on horseback or standing tall while dressed in regal clothing and with an arm stretched out as if they were waving to their adoring subjects. If you look at page seventy-three in your books, you'll see a picture of a statue of Emperor Augustus in that classic pose . . . That statue is a mere two meters high. There was once, however, a statue of Emperor Nero in Rome that was thirty meters high. Sadly, it's been lost. Now, uh, I think that's enough background information. Let me show you some Greek and Roman statues so that you can see what I'm talking about.

Answer Explanations

12 Gist-Content Question

Ⓑ The professor mainly talks about how the Greeks influenced Roman art.

13 Connecting Content Question

Ⓒ The professor says, "The Greeks strove to make their statues perfect representations of the human body, an aspect greatly admired by the Romans. The Greek style varied from the Etruscan style, which had influenced the Romans in earlier times. The Etruscans, in case you are curious, were less concerned about representing the human body accurately."

14 Understanding Organization Question

Ⓓ The professor remarks, "The carvings and sculptures on the Arch of Constantine and Trajan's Column mostly depict people. These people were typically Roman warriors, conquered enemies, and Roman emperors."

15 Detail Question

Fact: ①, ②, ④ Not a Fact: ③
The professor states, "When the supply of original Greek statues was exhausted, the Romans founded two schools to train sculptors to make copies. One school was in Rome while the other was in Athens. There was even heavy demand for miniature replicas of Greek statues, which Romans used as decorations for their homes" About the Romans, she says, "They also started making very realistic depictions of living people in their portrait sculptures so that even wrinkles and blemishes such as moles are apparent." However, the professor also points out, "The Greeks made statues of people and animals but also heavily used statues of mythological figures and gods for their buildings. The Romans, on the other hand, preferred more realism. The carvings and sculptures on the Arch of Constantine and Trajan's Column mostly depict people."

16 Detail Question

②, ③ The professor mentions, "Roman emperors were often posed on horseback or standing tall while dressed in regal clothing and with an arm stretched out as if they were waving to their adoring subjects."

17 Understanding Function Question

Ⓐ The professor implies that, due to the value of metal, many Roman statues made of metal were recycled in later times.

PART 2

Conversation [1-5]

| Script |

Listen to part of a conversation between a student and an event organizer.

W Student: Mr. Cartwright, have all of the bands that will be performing at this year's spring fling been determined yet? I'd like to print the flyers and post them around campus, but I need to make sure that the information on them is correct.

M Event Organizer: We're still negotiating with a couple of the bands, Brenda.

W: Which ones?

M: The Red Riders and the Larry Walker Band.

W: Oh, so that means you've concluded talks with the Bogeys, right? They're going to be the headliner, aren't they?

M: That's correct. The Bogeys are one of the most popular bands in the country, and we managed to secure them for a low price. They gave us a discount of around half of what they normally charge to play at college events.

W: Wow, how did you manage that?

M: You don't know that two of the members attended college here? Lee Duncan and Charles Little both graduated from this school about five years ago.

W: Ah, I wasn't aware of that. I don't really listen to rock music, so the only thing I know about the Bogeys is that everyone was saying they're supposed to be the main event.

M: You should check out their music. It's not too bad.

W: I will.

M: Anyway, we made offers to the managers of both the Red Riders and the Larry Walker Band, and both said they would give us a response no later than five this evening. If they agree, we'll fax them a copy of the contract to sign at once. As soon as we get that, you can print the flyers.

W: That's great.

M: Uh, wait. You'd better give me a copy of each flyer you've made to let me confirm that the information on them is accurate. We have a limited budget, and I'd hate to waste money by having to reprint flyers at the printer's office.

W: Good thinking. I don't have any physical copies on me right now, so I'll email you the three flyers I was planning on printing. I'll do that right after my next class concludes.

M: Sounds good. By the way, have you obtained permission from the student activities office to put the flyers up on campus?

W: I already spoke with Ms. Worthy in that office. She told me she needs to see the flyers first before she can approve them. She said it normally takes a day or two to get approval, but she understands how important this event is to the student body, so she told me she'd check the flyers over and approve them within an hour of them being submitted. After she does that, we can start posting flyers.

M: That's exactly what I needed to hear. Okay, is there anything else you'd like to discuss? I've got to meet with a few people right now to make sure this event goes well, so I don't have much more time to chat.

W: I've got a couple of questions regarding tickets to some of the minor events, but they can wait until later.

M: Perfect. Why don't you come back here around 5:30, and we can discuss a few minor matters?

W: I can do that. All right, I need to get going. My next class is halfway across campus.

M: See you later.

Answer Explanations

1 Gist-Content Question

Ⓐ Most of the conversation involves the speakers discussing preparations for the school's spring fling.

2 Making Inferences Question

Ⓓ When talking about the Bogeys, the student remarks, "I don't really listen to rock music, so the only thing I know about the Bogeys is that everyone was saying they're supposed to be the main event."

3 Detail Question

Ⓓ The man tells the student, "You'd better give me a copy of each flyer you've made to let me confirm that the information on them is accurate."

4 Understanding Function Question

Ⓑ The man asks, "By the way, have you obtained permission from the student activities office to put the flyers up on campus?"

5 Detail Question

Ⓑ The man instructs the student, "Why don't you come back here around 5:30, and we can discuss a few minor matters?"

Lecture [6–11]

| Script |

Listen to part of a lecture in a child studies class.

W Professor: One key component in the development of the brain is visual stimulation. This is true both when we are born and when we grow up, but it's especially true in our early years. A baby's brain is one of the body's most immature organs when a child is born. The brain must grow, and the best way to help it develop is through visual stimulation.

A baby's vision can be stimulated in a multitude of ways. For instance, parents frequently adorn baby cribs with objects that their children can easily see and try to grasp. One example of these decorations is a mobile that can be hung above a crib. The mobile may have colorful objects that move, which prompt babies to passively observe the objects and to follow them with their eyes. Soon, the babies will attempt to grasp the objects. This is a sensory-motor response. The sensory part is the visual stimulation of the brain by seeing objects. The motor part is the babies' attempts to touch the objects. The sensory aspect is passive while the motor one is active. When babies repeat these exercises, their brains begin to grow.

A second way to increase babies' visual stimulation is to take children to different environments. Parents should take their babies out of their cribs and allow them to move around the house, uh, under close supervision, of course. Taking babies outside into the world in strollers also helps so long as it is done initially in a safe, quiet area such as a park. The more visual stimulation babies have, the more new and interesting things they see. Parents should also start associating the things that their babies see with the words that represent the objects, which is the first step toward speaking. Babies will additionally form the cognitive ability to understand that objects don't disappear simply because they cannot be seen at the moment.

Visual stimulation at an early age is vital because vision is the primary sense which babies rely upon when they are first born. Therefore, sensory-motor experiences must be repeated constantly. As babies age, their brains begin to grow in size. In fact, the brain typically doubles in size during the first year of life. Keep in mind that the reverse is also true. Studies done on babies living in poor circumstances, um, such as those who live in poverty or those who have vision problems, show a twenty- to thirty-percent decrease in brain growth in the first year. This lack of brain growth at an early age contributes to a decrease in their cognitive abilities as they become older.

Another issue involves parents placing too much stress on their babies. Some parents are a bit overactive and try to induce their babies to do too much too soon. By overstimulating their children, they are causing a negative effect on brain growth. Studies have showed that too much stress on babies impairs their neurological growth. One way to avoid stress is to have no negative visual stimulation. For example, trying to frighten a baby with a scary monster toy or attempting to surprise a baby will only result in harm, not good. Parents should allow their babies to learn and grow at their own pace and with as little stress as possible.

M Student: Pardon the interruption, but I'm curious about the brain growth of babies that you mentioned. How can we measure it? Is that even possible?

W: Thanks to modern-day equipment such as MRIs and various diagnostic tools, we are capable of studying the brain growth of babies. But much of our learning comes from studies performed on animal brains. I recently read one interesting study done on tadpole brains. Scientists were able to stimulate a natural protein in the tadpoles' brains that's called the green fluorescent protein. This protein moves through every part of the brain and therefore gave them a visual way to track brain growth in tadpoles. The scientists conducted experiments during which they put tadpoles in complete darkness for many hours and then exposed them to light. They saw a dramatic increase in brain activity when the tadpoles were in well-lit areas. The tadpoles' brain neurons grew larger, and new branches, some of which became permanent, formed. Further research showed that four different proteins were activated by this visual stimulation, which allowed the neurons to grow. How and why this happened is still being studied.

The mechanics in human brain growth are similar. Neurons grow and branch out, forming complex networks within the brain. For babies, neuron growth was the most pronounced with visual stimulation. By increasing visual stimulation, parents can improve their babies' overall brain growth and cognitive abilities. As I mentioned earlier, repetition is one of the best ways to do this. Getting babies to repeat tasks can stimulate the sensory-motor responses that are necessary for brain growth and cognitive ability growth.

Answer Explanations

6 Gist-Content Question

Ⓒ During her lecture, the professor focuses mainly on the ways that visual stimulation can help stimulate brain growth in babies.

7 Detail Question

②, ③ The professor points out, "The mobile may have colorful objects that move, which prompt babies to passively observe the objects and to follow them with their eyes. Soon, the babies will attempt to grasp the objects. This is a sensory-motor response. The sensory part is the visual stimulation of the brain by seeing objects. The motor part is the babies' attempts to touch the objects. The sensory aspect is passive while the motor one is active. When babies repeat these exercises, their brains begin to grow."

8 Understanding Attitude Question

Ⓐ The professor tells the class, "Taking babies outside into the world in strollers also helps so long as it is done initially in a safe, quiet area such as a park. The more visual stimulation babies have, the more new and interesting things they see."

9 Connecting Content Question

Ⓒ The professor says, "As babies age, their brains begin to grow in size. In fact, the brain typically doubles in size during the first year of life. Keep in mind that the reverse is also true. Studies done on babies living in poor circumstances, um, such as those who live in poverty or those who have vision problems, show a twenty- to thirty-percent decrease in brain growth in the first year. This lack of brain growth at an early age contributes to a decrease in their cognitive abilities as they become older." The likely outcome of a baby growing up in poverty during the first year of the child's life is that the child will not be able to think as well as a baby living in better conditions.

10 Detail Question

Ⓓ The professor comments, "Studies have showed that too much stress on babies impairs their neurological growth. One way to avoid stress is to have no negative visual stimulation."

11 Understanding Function Question

Ⓑ In stating, "The scientists conducted experiments during which they put tadpoles in complete darkness for many hours and then exposed them to light. They saw a dramatic increase in brain activity when the tadpoles were in well-lit areas. The tadpoles' brain neurons grew larger, and new branches, some of which became permanent, formed," the professor shows the students how exposure to light and darkness affected the tadpole brains.

| Vocabulary Review

p. 76

Answers

A

1 negotiates	2 suffice	3 activates
4 removal	5 superstitious	

B

1 b	2 a	3 a	4 b	5 a
6 b	7 b	8 a	9 b	10 a

Practice with Short Passages

p. 80

A

| Answers | 1 Ⓒ | 2 Ⓐ |

| Script |

Listen to part of a conversation between a student and a student activities office employee.

W Student: Good afternoon, Mr. Martinson. How are you doing today?

M Student Activities Office Employee: Hi, Katie. I'm all right. Is there something I can do for you?

W: Yes, there is. You remember I told you that I make various handicrafts in my free time, right?

M: Sure. You've mentioned that to me before a couple of times. I don't think I've ever seen anything you've made, but I know it's your hobby. Why do you ask?

W: I showed some items I made to my art professor, and she told me that the quality was pretty good and that I ought to sell them.

M: Hey, that's a great idea. You could probably set up a webpage and sell them online. You could get buyers from all over the world.

W: Uh, slow down, Mr. Martinson . . . That's a bit too ambitious for me at this time. Instead, I'm considering selling the items here on campus. There are always people selling things on the sidewalks here. In fact, uh, I've even bought some items from them. Do they have to get permission to sell things on campus, or can they set up a booth without asking anyone?

M: They most definitely must get permission from us. If they don't, we call the campus police and have them escorted off the university grounds.

W: Wow, that's pretty harsh.

M: It appears severe, but it isn't. After all, we're responsible for everything which gets sold on campus, so we have to make sure every vendor complies with the various state and federal laws.

W: I see. It sounds like it might be a bit, uh, difficult for me to get permission. Should I not even bother trying?

M: Not at all. The process is relatively simple. I do it for vendors all the time. Basically, you need to let me know precisely what types of items you're going to be selling. Pictures, uh, or even a few samples, would be nice. And then you have to fill out a form. Lastly, you have to pay a fee of $25 a day to set up a booth on campus.

W: That's not too bad. Do you think I could fill the form out right now? I can visit my dorm, pick up some samples, and return here with them in a few hours.

M: Sure. I've got a copy of the form right here on my desk.

Answer Explanations

1 Ⓒ The student and the man speak as though they know each other well. In addition, the man states, "Sure. You've mentioned that to me before a couple of times. I don't think I've ever seen anything you've made, but I know it's your hobby." So it can be inferred that the two of them are well acquainted.

2 Ⓐ At the end of the conversation, the student says, "Do you think I could fill the form out right now?"

B

| Answers | 1 Ⓒ | 2 Ⓐ |

| Script |

Listen to part of a conversation between a student and a professor.

M Student: Pardon me, Professor McClellan, but would it be all right if I borrowed a few moments of your time?

W Professor: This won't take too long, will it, Chris? I've got to attend a staff luncheon ten minutes from now.

M: This should only require two or three minutes, ma'am. I have a question about a couple of classes I'm considering taking next semester.

W: If that's the case, then I've got time to speak with you.

M: Great. Thanks so much.

W: All right, tell me: Which classes are you debating signing up for?

M: Well, I've got my entire schedule settled except for one class. I've narrowed it down to the following. Um, I'm either going to take German 1, uh, that's a basic German language class, or I'm going to take English 43, which is an introduction to Shakespeare class.

W: Hmm . . . Remind me again what your major is, please.

M: I'm double-majoring in Chemistry and Economics.

W: So neither class has anything to do with your major, right?

M: Yes, ma'am. I suppose I might travel to Germany one day, so that's a reason I'm contemplating learning German. But I don't need to study German for my foreign language requirement since I'm fluent in Italian. And I've always been interested in English literature, but I don't consider myself particularly well read.

W: So the Shakespeare class would be an opportunity for you to read some plays and to become better acquainted with his work, right?

M: That's correct. ∩2 Oh, uh, just so you know, I'm not concerned in the least bit about what my grade in either class will be. I figure I can get at least a B in each class. Since there's no way I'm going to graduate with honors next year, taking a class that will give me an easy A isn't a major concern of mine. **I didn't take my classes seriously my freshman year, and now I'm paying for that.**

W: I understand. In that case, if I were you, I'd register for the language class. You can always read Shakespeare's works in your free time, but it would be much better to learn a foreign language in a classroom setting.

M: What you said makes a lot of sense. Thanks. Now I know exactly how my schedule is going to look.

Answer Explanations

1 ⓒ The professor advises the student, "I understand. In that case, if I were you, I'd register for the language class. You can always read Shakespeare's works in your free time, but it would be much better to learn a foreign language in a classroom setting." So she implies that people ought to study foreign languages with an instructor.

2 ⒶWhen the student says, "I didn't take my classes seriously my freshman year, and now I'm paying for that," he implies that he got his lowest grades at school that year.

C

| Answers | 1 Ⓐ | 2 Ⓑ |

| Script |

Listen to part of a lecture in an ecology class.

M Professor: Fish is one of the main food sources for bears, and they have a particular love of salmon. In places where brown, black, and grizzly bears live, such as Alaska, Western Canada, and Kamchatka in Russia, there are countless rivers, streams, and brooks where salmon can be found. There are almost always trees growing alongside those sources of water, too. What might surprise you is that these three living things, uh, salmon, bears, and trees, have a very special relationship that helps each survive. Why don't we find out how . . . ?

Every year, salmon swim upriver to reach their traditional breeding and spawning grounds. Let's take a look at a video of them doing that . . . The salmon are swimming upstream here. Notice the tree-lined stream and the shady places where they're breeding and spawning . . . ? Well, um, that shade is a necessity, not a luxury. If salmon lay their eggs in unshaded spots, the sunlight will make the

water temperature higher, and the eggs will have less of a chance of surviving. The reason is that in warmer water, the oxygen level is reduced, thereby negatively affecting the eggs. Now, do you see how the bed of this stream has plenty of gravel? Gravel is important because it supports the eggs in moving water. And that's how trees play a significant role. Without trees, there would be more erosion, which would leave rivers, streams, and brooks filled with silt, so there would be few—if any—places for salmon eggs to be laid without running the risk of being washed downstream and most likely failing to hatch.

Oh, but what about bears . . . ? Before salmon can even reach their breeding spots, they have to run a gauntlet of bears trying to catch them. And once they arrive at their destinations, there are even more bears waiting. As we can see in the video now . . . the bears like to grab the salmon, bite it once or twice, and then drag it onto land and eat it. But they don't eat the entire fish. They only eat the best parts, so they leave both flesh and bone behind. This, in turn, attracts other predators and insects, which consume the leftovers, but some of the remainder goes into the soil, which provides nutrients. And when the bears and other animals defecate, their nitrogen-rich feces get into the soil, which helps the trees grow.

So let's recap . . . Salmon need shade and gravel to lay their eggs. Trees provide shade and prevent erosion. Bears need salmon for food, and trees need nitrogen and other nutrients to grow, which they get from the salmon that bears kill. Thus all three help one another in key ways.

W Student: ∩2 But surely there aren't enough bears to make that much of a difference.

M: **In point of fact, you'd be surprised.** A conservative estimate of just one species—the black bear—in the Canadian province of British Columbia is about 80,000. The average black bear eats 700 salmon per spawning season, and that provides the bear with about seventy percent of its yearly protein supply. Each bear contributes around twelve kilograms of nitrogen from dead salmon per hectare of forest in salmon breeding grounds. So, um, if we do the math, we'll discover that these 80,000 bears are putting nearly one million kilograms of nitrogen nutrients into the soil alongside rivers, streams, and brooks each year. One study has shown that more than half of the nitrogen that trees absorb in these regions comes from dead salmon.

Answer Explanations

1 Ⓐ The professor remarks, "Each bear contributes around twelve kilograms of nitrogen from dead salmon per hectare of forest in salmon breeding grounds. So, um, if we do the math, we'll discover that these 80,000 bears are putting nearly one million kilograms of nitrogen nutrients into the soil alongside rivers, streams, and brooks each year. One study has shown that more than half of the nitrogen that trees absorb in these regions

comes from dead salmon." Thus it can be inferred that there would be fewer trees in some places without salmon.

2 (B) When the professor responds to the student's comment by saying, "In point of fact, you'd be surprised," he is indicating that the student's opinion on the matter they are discussing is wrong.

D

Answers   1 (B)   2 (A)

| Script |

Listen to part of a lecture in a geology class.

W Professor: When we think of diamonds, images of beautiful, clear gemstones come to mind. But diamonds come in a variety of colors due to various impurities in them. They can be pink, yellow, red, and green, and there are even orange diamonds, too. Rarest of all is the black diamond, of which there are two kinds. Some are like regular diamonds yet have impurities making them black in color. These diamonds are rare but can be found in places where diamonds are normally unearthed, especially near areas that are or once were volcanically active. The second type of black diamond is called carbonado. Some Portuguese explorers in Brazil gave them this name in the mid-eighteenth century because of their similarity to black coal. At present, there are only two known sources of carbonado: the Central African Republic and Brazil.

I'd like to discuss the properties of carbonado with you for a bit. To begin with, carbonado doesn't always look like a diamond. It looks more like a rock, even when it's polished. It's not always pure black either but is instead more grayish-green in color. Carbonado isn't used as a gemstone much but is mainly useful to various industries. Remember that diamonds are the hardest known substances and score a ten on the Mohs scale of hardness. Carbonado is actually harder than regular diamonds due to its unique structure, which is a very dense crystal lattice of carbon, graphite, and diamond. So, uh, essentially, three substances combined to form a single one in the guise of carbonado.

How it was created is a matter of some debate in geological circles. You see, uh, it's not found in the typical places where diamonds are located. That, of course, is nearby seams of kimberlite in areas of volcanic activity. Most diamonds are produced deep within the Earth in a process requiring millions of years, but they aren't particularly old when compared to the Earth as a whole. After being formed, diamonds are then brought to the surface through volcanic activity. Carbonado is different though. You see, um, it's been dated at almost three billion—yes, billion with a B—years old. It's not found near volcanically active sites but is instead found near the surface and sometimes in sedimentary deposits near the

outflows of rivers. As I just mentioned, it's found only in Brazil and parts of Africa. So . . . does anyone know what those two places were like three billion years ago?

M Student: Weren't they, uh, joined together as part of the supercontinent that used to be on the planet?

W: Bingo. You got it in one. This has led to two theories on carbonado's origin. First, some believe that a large meteorite crashed and hit the Earth where Africa and Brazil were joined. This massive impact caused a tremendous amount of heat and pressure to fuse the minerals that made carbonado. As for the second theory, some hypothesize that carbonado was created in space and arrived on the Earth on a meteorite. No, really. Don't scoff at the idea. It would go a long way toward explaining why we can't find this unique rock anywhere else on the planet. You should stop and consider that for a moment before you dismiss the theory. Okay, I've got some real carbonado up here, so why don't we take a close look at it?

Answer Explanations

1 (B) The professor comments, "Most diamonds are produced deep within the Earth in a process requiring millions of years, but they aren't particularly old when compared to the Earth as a whole. After being formed, diamonds are then brought to the surface through volcanic activity. Carbonado is different though. You see, um, it's been dated at almost three billion—yes, billion with a B—years old." In saying that, she implies that carbonado is much older than other types of diamonds on the Earth.

2 (A) At the end of the lecture, the professor tells the class, "Okay, I've got some real carbonado up here, so why don't we take a close look at it?"

Practice with Long Passages   p. 84

A

Answers

1 (C)   2 Fact: [2], [3]   Not a Fact: [1], [4]
3 (A)   4 (B)

| Script |

Listen to part of a conversation between a student and a housing office employee.

W1 Housing Office Employee: Hello. Is there something I can assist you with this morning?

W2 Student: I sure hope so. I'm here because I'd like to change dormitory rooms. Do you know if it's too late to do that?

W1: We're only one week into the fall semester, so it's still possible for you to move to another dormitory room.

W2: Great.

W1: However, you should understand that roughly 98% of all the dormitory rooms on campus are occupied, so don't expect to get your first choice.

W2: I understand that. I simply need to escape from the current situation I'm in.

W1: Why is that? Is there a problem with your room or your roommate?

W2: Both, actually.

W1: Why don't you tell me what the problem with each of them is in that case?

W2: Sure, I can do that. The issue with my room is quite simple. I'm a freshman here, so I didn't get to choose the dorm I'm currently living in. The school assigned me to live in Kenwood Hall, which is an absolutely awful dorm for a couple of reasons. To begin with, it's located on the easternmost part of campus, but I'm enrolled in the school of business, so most of my classes are on the far western side of the campus. It takes me more than twenty minutes to walk across campus to get to my classes.

W1: What's the other problem?

W2: Kenwood Hall is a huge party dorm. I mean, I think I'm the only person in the entire dorm that even tries to study. It's always loud, and I can't concentrate on my studies or get any sleep at night.

W1: Yeah, we've received similar complaints about that dormitory from other students. So, uh, what about your roommate?

W2: Ah, Rachel . . . I think she came here to have fun and not to study. I haven't seen her open a single book ever since classes began. She's constantly playing loud music, and she goes to bed very late at night. She and I have nothing in common, and I have to get out of my present situation before she ruins my semester.

W1: Yes, uh, it sounds like you're in a pretty bad situation. So should I guess that you'd like a dormitory which is closer to your business classes?

W2: Yes, that would be perfect. I was thinking of a place such as Patterson Hall or Martin Tower. Do there happen to be any rooms available in either of them?

W1: Yes, I believe there are a couple of vacant rooms in each. How about taking a look and seeing what your options are?

W2: Excellent. Let's see what you have available.

Answer Explanations

1   Ⓒ The student cannot stand the dormitory that she is currently staying in.

2   Fact: ②, ③ Not a Fact: ①, ④
About her dormitory, the student comments, "To begin with, it's located on the easternmost part of campus,

but I'm enrolled in the school of business, so most of my classes are on the far western side of the campus. It takes me more than twenty minutes to walk across campus to get to my classes." She also notes, "Kenwood Hall is a huge party dorm. I mean, I think I'm the only person in the entire dorm that even tries to study. It's always loud, and I can't concentrate on my studies or get any sleep at night." However, she did not choose to live in it as she says, "I'm a freshman here, so I didn't get to choose the dorm I'm currently living in." And it is not true that it has many students eager to study living in it since she says, "I think I'm the only person in the entire dorm that even tries to study."

3   Ⓐ The student complains about her roommate when she states, "Ah, Rachel . . . I think she came here to have fun and not to study. I haven't seen her open a single book ever since classes began. She's constantly playing loud music, and she goes to bed very late at night. She and I have nothing in common, and I have to get out of my present situation before she ruins my semester."

4   Ⓑ At the end of the conversation, the employee says, "Yes, I believe there are a couple of vacant rooms in each. How about taking a look and seeing what your options are?" Then, the student agrees with her suggestion.

Dictation

1   I'm here because I'd like to change dormitory rooms.

2   I simply need to escape from the current situation I'm in.

3   Yeah, we've received similar complaints about that dormitory from other students.

B

Answers

1 Ⓑ   2 Archaic Period: ① Classical Period: ③, ④
Hellenic Period: ②   3 Ⓐ, Ⓓ   4 Ⓒ

| Script |

Listen to part of a lecture in an archaeology class.

M Professor: During the time of ancient Greece and Rome, coins dominated the economies of the Mediterranean world. Since Greece is the older of the two, I'd like to examine its coinage first. The history of Greek coins can be divided into three periods: the Archaic Period, the Classical Period, and the Hellenic Period. The first period lasted from approximately 700 B.C. to 479 B.C., which was when the Classical Period began. The Classical Period didn't end until the Macedonian conquests of Alexander the Great in 336 B.C., which heralded the Hellenic Period. It lasted until the Roman expansion.

The Greeks first minted coins around 700 B.C. These early coins were made of electrum, which is an alloy of silver and gold. The coins had some markings indicating both who had made them and what their values were.

Later, the Greeks developed coin punches, which could make more elaborate designs with images on both sides. Following that, they created superior etched coin molds, which made the best designed coins. Around 560 B.C., the Greeks began minting gold and silver coins for the first time. These coins had different denominations and were widely used. The gold coin was called the *slater* and the silver coin the *siglos*. Soon, nearly every Greek city-state began making similar coins but with different images, uh, depending on where the coins were minted.

During the Classical Period, the coins of Athens predominated. The main Athenian silver coin was called the *tetradrachm*. A lesser coin was called the *drachmae*. Four of them made a *tetradrachm*. Over the next century and a half, Athenian coins spread far and wide, and, when the Macedonians conquered Greece, they adopted the Athenian coins and used them during the Hellenic Period. During Alexander the Great's conquests, the *tetradrachm* had an image of Hercules on one side and Zeus on the other. As Alexander's armies Hellenized the Near East, their coins accompanied them.

W Student: What happened to the Greek coins after Alexander died?

M: Hmm . . . Alexander died in 323 B.C., and his empire was divided amongst his generals. For the most part, those generals established their own kingdoms and minted their own coins. We still consider them to be a part of the Hellenic Period since they were Greek coins, but the Romans began dominating the region soon afterward.

As for the Romans . . . Roman coinage started around the fourth century B.C. Their first coins were made of bronze, were rough in shape, and were called the *aes rude*. By the third century B.C., the rounder *aes grave* had become the standard coin. It was a heavy bronze coin that would become reduced in size over time. These bronze coins had marks showing their value as well as carved images. Different cities in Italy issued their own bronze coins. It was around the time of the Punic Wars, in 241 B.C., that the Romans first minted silver coins. The main silver coin was the *denarius*, and it remained the standard Roman coin until the third century A.D. Another silver coin, called the *sestertius*, was issued from time to time during the Roman Republic but, uh, was never as widely used as the *denarius*. The Romans also minted a gold coin, called the *aureus*, during the Republic years. It was worth twenty-five *denarii*.

Roman minting technology closely followed the Greek style as there was a strong connection between the two regions. Initially, the Romans minted images of animals and their gods on their coins. When Julius Caesar came to power in 45 B.C., he issued coins with his own image on them. He was the first person to do so, but his actions became a tradition followed by Roman emperors for centuries to come. The reverse sides of the coins were often used to show off images of the great achievements

of either the Roman Empire or the emperor himself. As Rome expanded, its coins gradually spread all across the empire.

Now, I've got a small collection of Greek and Roman coins I'd like to show to you. Everyone come up here to the front and gather around, but be sure not to touch any of the coins as they're quite old.

p. 88

Answers

PART 1

Conversation [1–5]

| Script |

Listen to part of a conversation between a student and a professor.

M Student: Thank you very much for agreeing to be my thesis advisor for the coming year, Professor Haynes.

W Professor: It's my pleasure, Jason. You've taken several classes with me ever since you arrived here, and you've not only excelled in them but have also proven to be an impressive scholar. I'm looking forward to assisting you with your research during your senior year.

M: Thanks for saying that, ma'am.

W: So . . . have you given any thought regarding what you want to do your senior thesis on?

M: I'm thinking of doing it on some of the ancient cultures that once lived in West Africa.

W: Hmm . . . That would be an interesting topic. May I ask why you're choosing it?

M: Sure. Last summer, my parents and I traveled to Africa. We sailed up the Niger River for a couple of weeks and visited Timbuktu and some other sites of ancient African empires. I was, uh, I was totally fascinated by what I saw and learned there. When I returned home, I tried to find a few books on ancient African cultures and empires, but, well, there wasn't all that much available.

W: There's not a lot of scholarship available in English, but there is much more in French. You don't happen to speak French, do you?

M: I've studied it for four semesters, and I spent six weeks in France during the summer after my freshman year. So, uh, while I wouldn't say I'm fluent in the language, I do have a decent understanding of it.

W: All right. Well, you're going to be doing the bulk of your research in French, so I suggest that you take an intensive

course in the French language this summer. Are you planning to remain on campus again this summer?

M: Yes, I'll be working in the library like always. I guess I could take a night class in French if one is being offered here.

W: Good. Find out about that. If you can't take a class here, you can study at the Paris Institute downtown. The prices there are fairly inexpensive, and the teachers are highly dedicated and effective.

M: Thanks for the tip.

W: You'll also need to start doing research this summer. I can put together a list of books you ought to read. Most of them will be general books about West Africa and some of the kingdoms and empires which thrived in that area. You should read them and then find something specific to focus on for your thesis topic.

M: Okay. Since the library is quiet in summer, I should be able to read a great deal while I'm working.

W: Good. Furthermore, I encourage you to speak with Professor Mankins in the History Department.

M: Who is he?

W: He's new. He was hired this semester. His expertise is African history, so he might be able to give you some assistance.

M: Okay. I'll set up a meeting with him.

W: I know him well, so let me contact him first. I'll tell him about you and ask if he'd be willing to give you some advice.

M: Thanks.

W: It's no problem. I'll email him after lunch, and, once he responds to me, I'll call you. Now, uh, let me think about which books you need to read. I'll come up with a list of authors and titles and email them to you no later than six this evening.

M: Thanks so much, Professor Haynes. I really appreciate everything.

Answer Explanations

1 Gist-Content Question

Ⓑ The speakers are mostly talking about how the student needs to prepare for a project that he will do in the future.

2 Making Inferences Question

Ⓐ The professor implies that the student needs to improve his skills in the French language when she says, "Well, you're going to be doing the bulk of your research in French, so I suggest that you take an intensive course in the French language this summer."

3 Understanding Attitude Question

Ⓒ The professor remarks, "If you can't take a class here, you can study at the Paris Institute downtown. The prices there are fairly inexpensive, and the teachers are highly dedicated and effective."

4 Understanding Function Question

Ⓐ The professor talks about Professor Mankins to let the student know that he might be able to provide the student with assistance on his thesis.

5 Detail Question

①, ② The professor tells the student, "I'll email him after lunch, and, once he responds to me, I'll call you. Now, uh, let me think about which books you need to read. I'll come up with a list of authors and titles and email them to you no later than six this evening."

Lecture #1 [6–11]

| Script |

Listen to part of a lecture in an education class.

W Professor: Learning is something we all start doing from the time we're young children. I'd even go as far as to state that it's a process that never ends throughout our entire lives. How we learn depends upon numerous factors; however, for the most part, there are seven basic methods. They are, um, visual, aural, verbal, physical, logical, social, and solitary. Everyone learns in one or more of these ways, yet some students may prefer one to another, and some may be strong in certain styles but not in others. Let's look at each of them in turn.

Visual learning refers to the use of all forms of images to learn. Students who prefer the visual style of learning tend to use images to absorb information. These individuals have a good understanding of colors and shapes and have good spatial awareness. They like to read and usually have well-developed handwriting, yet they also struggle in some ways. For instance, if you tell them how to do something but don't give them a visual demonstration, they may not understand how to do it. They can also remember faces, uh, but not names, they're easily distracted, and they must look at people directly when speaking to others. When you're teaching children who prefer the visual style, you should be sure to use flashcards, colored blocks, and written directions, and you also need to speak to these students face to face.

Aural learning . . . um, that's A-U-R-A-L rather than O-R-A-L, by the way . . . is related to listening. Individuals who prefer this style are more talkative and social and often do better in music and performing arts such as acting. As for the drawbacks, some students struggle with written directions, have trouble staying quiet for long periods, and remember names but not faces. When teaching these types of learners, you'd be better off using verbal instructions and having your students read them aloud, and you could also utilize music to help your students learn.

Verbal learners learn best by using the written word. They like reading and writing, prefer to read instructions and

write reports, and absorb information by reading books. They struggle when given oral instructions, don't fully understand body language, and may have difficulty in social situations. To help these kinds of learners, you need to let them take lots of notes while studying. You also ought to write instructions on the board in class, give your students writing assignments, and not place much emphasis on oral reports. You should additionally have resources in your classrooms such as dictionaries and thesauruses.

🎧11 What about physical learners . . . ? Well, they like moving about while they learn. They . . . um, yes? Question?

M Student: **Our textbook calls physical learning, um, the kinesthetic learning style, so, um, which of these two terms would you like for us to use?**

W: Ah, both of them are correct, so you all can use whichever term you prefer. Okay . . . ? Good . . . Let's see . . . Physical learners like touching and using things as well as exploring the environments they're in while learning. They don't want to sit still, listen, read, or write. They also often don't like getting instructions but instead prefer to jump in, try to do something themselves, and figure out how to do it on their own. They excel at sports and performing arts, may struggle to control themselves, and tend to lash out physically when they're upset. To help these learners, we, as teachers, must let them do things on their own before providing instructions. We also ought to have plenty of hands-on learning tools in our classrooms, do plenty of physical activities, plan outdoor lessons, and have these students play games or do projects.

The logical style of learning relates to mathematics. These learners can easily see patterns and make connections between things that seem unconnected. These students like solving problems in a systematic way, step by step, and using a schedule. Such students are good at explaining things with examples and statistics and can easily see the mistakes other people make. One of their weaknesses is that they have a need to point out these mistakes, which may upset others. These learners excel at math and the sciences. The best way to teach them is to help them explore by doing logic games, difficult math problems, and science experiments and by encouraging the learning of strategy games such as chess.

Learners may possess elements of one or two or perhaps all five types of learning. For example, I myself am more of a verbal and logical learner but am quite weak in the visual and physical areas of learning. Oh, yes, there are two other learning areas that most people fit into. Some people are social learners while others are solitary ones. Social learners prefer the company of others, and solitary learners like being left alone. At schools, many teachers emphasize group work so that students can build their social skills. In my experience, visual, aural, and physical students tend to prefer group work because they enjoy socializing. Verbal and logical learners, on the other hand, prefer working by themselves.

6 Gist-Content Question

Ⓑ The lecture is about the various styles of learning that students have.

7 Detail Question

Fact: ②, ③   Not a Fact: ①, ④

About visual learners, the professor remarks, "They can also remember faces, uh, but not names, they're easily distracted, and they must look at people directly when speaking to others. When you're teaching children who prefer the visual style, you should be sure to use flashcards, colored blocks, and written directions, and you also need to speak to these students face to face." However, they are not talkative or social, and they do not like taking large amounts of notes in their classes.

8 Detail Question

Ⓑ About physical learners, the professor declares, "Physical learners like touching and using things as well as exploring the environments they're in while learning. They don't want to sit still, listen, read, or write. They also often don't like getting instructions but instead prefer to jump in, try to do something themselves, and figure out how to do it on their own."

9 Understanding Function Question

Ⓓ The professor says, "Learners may possess elements of one or two or perhaps all five types of learning. For example, I myself am more of a verbal and logical learner but am quite weak in the visual and physical areas of learning."

10 Making Inferences Question

Ⓑ Throughout the lecture, the professor talks to the students as if they will be teachers in the future. She makes comments such as, "When you're teaching children who prefer the visual style, you should be sure to use flashcards, colored blocks, and written directions, and you also need to speak to these students face to face," and, "When teaching these types of learners, you'd be better off using verbal instructions and having your students read them aloud, and you could also utilize music to help your students learn."

11 Making Inferences Question

Ⓐ When the student asks the question about physical learning and kinesthetic learning, it can be inferred that he does not know which of the two terms is correct.

Lecture #2 [12–17]

| Script |

Listen to part of a lecture in an architecture class.

M Professor: One of the goals in building design is to make each building extremely efficient. There are two main purposes in doing this: to reduce costs during the construction process as well as during the lifetime of the building and to reduce the energy needs of the building while maintaining an ecologically sound environment. These two goals go hand in hand, for by making a building energy efficient, future costs will be lowered while less harm will be caused to the environment. 🎧16 **Let me emphasize that planning is the key to efficient building design.** The architect and the building owner must see eye to eye on all matters during the design phase. Communication must be open between the two sides to avoid any misunderstandings, so all targets and objectives have to be clearly stated during every phase of design. When it comes time to build a structure, the same is true for the relationship between the architect and the construction team.

The first thing that must be considered in any new building project is the building site. How much harm the new building will cause to the local environment is a key point. Care must be taken to avoid damage to the soil and nearby water resources. There must be a good local source of electricity and water for the building, and it should be located near transportation hubs so that the people who eventually use the building can get to and from it with ease. As for parking, underground parking garages are the preferred mode these days as large outdoor parking lots disrupt the greenery around the building. An eye to future landscaping must be taken into consideration when planning the building. Greenery, which includes lawns and trees, is more pleasing and can additionally act as a, um, as a cooling agent since concrete parking lots absorb large amounts of heat, which contribute to the urban heat island problem we studied the other day.

The position of the building is another factor since it should be situated to receive the maximum amount of sunlight, thereby lowering energy costs. A building with large windows facing the sun for most of the day lets in more light and heat and reduces the need for artificial light and heat sources. Moreover, sunlight is important if the building depends on solar energy for power. Proper sealing and ventilation are vital, too, because you want to keep heat in, but you don't want too much moisture to build up inside a building due to poor ventilation. Such moisture can result in mold damage, so efficient ventilation systems are crucial. Buildings should use good air filters to reduce the amount of pollution entering them as well.

Yet another consideration is the wind. A building should be designed so that it doesn't cause irregular wind patterns to flow around it. Buildings placed too close to other ones can cause a canyon effect, uh, where winds howl through the spaces at great speeds and bother pedestrians. I'm sure anyone who has been in a large city has experienced practically being knocked down by a sudden gust of wind coming from around a building. The building must be strong enough to withstand the most extreme wind speeds a region experiences. Furthermore, you must be sure to consider rain and snow when designing a building. Rooftops need be able to handle the accumulation of snow lest they collapse after heavy snowstorms, and they should also have places for rain to run off. Nowadays, one trend is to have rain capture systems that can collect rainwater to use in waste removal systems in buildings.

Another factor in building design efficiency is to utilize low-impact materials, which are ones that have a minor effect on the environment while being produced and additionally cause little harm to it in the future if they ever become waste materials. So, um, I'm talking about nontoxic materials, and I'm talking about using recycled materials to make buildings. 🎧17 Plastic, wood, and metal can all be recycled and used in new buildings, and this is good for the environment.

W Student: Are you sure about that? **I was under the impression that recycled materials aren't as strong as new materials.**

M: That may be true for some materials, but it isn't always the case. Recycled materials that meet building codes can be safely used to make buildings. But keep this in mind: As architects, we should never forgo safety when designing buildings just to save a few dollars or to say that we're protecting the environment. So, um, it's good to use recycled materials, but always make sure that they're strong enough for the building you're working on.

All right, now that I've told you several ways to make a building more efficient, I think it's time for us to look at a few examples in depth. The first we're going to examine is a remarkable building in Sydney, Australia, called One Central Park. It has some amazing hanging gardens that are an innovative utilization of greenery and which make it an environmentally conscious building. Take a look up here as I show you a few pictures and point out some interesting aspects of its design.

Answer Explanations

12 Gist-Content Question

Ⓐ The professor spends most of the lecture telling the students how to make buildings more efficient.

13 Understanding Organization Question

Ⓐ The professor comments, "Greenery, which includes lawns and trees, is more pleasing and can additionally act as a, um, as a cooling agent since concrete parking lots absorb large amounts of heat, which contribute to the urban heat island problem we studied the other day."

14 Detail Question

Ⓒ About low-impact materials, the professor points out, "Another factor in building design efficiency is to utilize low-impact materials, which are ones that have a

minor effect on the environment while being produced and additionally cause little harm to it in the future if they ever become waste materials. So, um, I'm talking about nontoxic materials, and I'm talking about using recycled materials to make buildings."

15 Understanding Attitude Question

Ⓑ About One Central Park, the professor states, "The first we're going to examine is a remarkable building in Sydney, Australia, called One Central Park. It has some amazing hanging gardens that are an innovative utilization of greenery and which make it an environmentally conscious building."

16 Understanding Attitude Question

Ⓒ When the professor says, "Let me emphasize that planning is the key to efficient building design," he means that it is important to plan buildings properly in order for them to be efficient.

17 Understanding Function Question

Ⓓ When the student makes her comment, she implies that she does not want to use recycled materials in the construction of buildings since she believes they are not as strong as new materials.

PART 2

Conversation [1–5]

| Script |

Listen to part of a conversation between a student and an Archaeology Department employee.

W Student: Mr. Fleming, I would like to have a word with you about my work schedule here in the Archaeology Department this semester if you have a spare moment.

M Archaeology Department Employee: I'm really sorry, Amy, but I already told you that there simply aren't any more hours to give you this semester. We've got three other workers, and they need to be assigned a few hours as well.

W: It's not that, sir. I understand I can't get any more hours. But I wonder if it would be possible for me to change one of my shifts. I'm referring to the shift I'm scheduled to work on Friday from one to four in the afternoon.

M: Huh? Didn't you specifically request that shift last week?

W: Um . . . Yes.

M: But now you want me to change it? I'm a bit confused. What's going on?

W: It has to do with my schedule, sir. You see, I was enrolled in a creative writing course that was supposed to meet on Tuesdays and Thursdays. Unfortunately, not enough people signed up for the class, so it was canceled this morning.

M: Okay. But what does that have to do with your Friday schedule?

W: The professor assigned to teach the course has a

second creative writing class on Wednesday and Friday afternoons. I really want to study with Professor Marino, but the class time is right in the middle of my scheduled work shift.

M: Aren't there other creative writing classes you could take? What's so special about Professor Marino?

W: I'm a big fan of his. He has published several novels in the fantasy genre, and that's what I want to write in. The other professors who teach creative writing aren't nearly as accomplished as he is. I just feel that I, uh, I wouldn't learn as much in one of their classes.

M: All right. I suppose that makes sense.

W: Wonderful. So I can change shifts with someone else?

M: Woah, slow down. I didn't say that. I can definitely give the shift to someone else, so you'll be free to sign up for the class. Chad just told me this morning that he'd love to work a few more hours, and he mentioned Friday as being the perfect day for him.

W: Do you think I could switch shifts with Chad?

M: You can ask him, and if your schedules match and he's willing to trade shifts with you, then I don't have a problem with that. But I doubt he'll agree.

W: Why do you say that?

M: He wants more hours. He's determined to earn more money this semester, so I don't think he'll be okay with trading shifts, but he'll definitely want to take an extra shift if he can.

W: Then what can I do? I really need to work at least twelve hours this semester. My books this semester cost more than normal, and I need the money from working to pay for them.

M: You could try talking to Gretel or Peter to see if they're willing to switch shifts. Or you could find a second job on campus. I know for a fact that the secretary in the Anthropology Department upstairs is looking for two student employees. I'd be more than willing to put in a good word for you with her.

Answer Explanations

1 **Gist-Content Question**

ⓒ The student tells the man that she wants to take a class at a time when she is scheduled to work in the office, so she has a conflict between her work and school schedules.

2 **Understanding Attitude Question**

ⓓ About Professor Marino, the student remarks, "He has published several novels in the fantasy genre, and that's what I want to write in. The other professors who teach creative writing aren't nearly as accomplished as he is. I just feel that I, uh, I wouldn't learn as much in one of their classes."

3 **Making Inferences Question**

ⓑ When the man tells the student that Chad will probably take her shift but not trade hours with her, the student replies, "I really need to work at least twelve hours this semester. My books this semester cost more than normal, and I need the money from working to pay for them." It can therefore be inferred that she does not want to lose any of her work hours.

4 **Making Inferences Question**

ⓒ The man states, "You could try talking to Gretel or Peter to see if they're willing to switch shifts." He therefore implies that Gretel and Peter are employed in the Archaeology Department.

5 **Detail Question**

ⓓ The man tells the student, "I know for a fact that the secretary in the Anthropology Department upstairs is looking for two student employees. I'd be more than willing to put in a good word for you with her." So he is willing to recommend the student for a job in another office.

Lecture [6–11]

| **Script** |

Listen to part of a lecture in an urban development class.

M Professor: In the ancient world, as humanity began moving on from living in small villages to establishing towns and cities, at first, there was minimal effort made at urban planning. As cities developed, they grew in a haphazard fashion with crooked streets, houses built here and there, and few central locations for markets or for people to meet. While there were some minor attempts to create better urban landscapes, there were few notable examples until the fifth century B.C. in Greece. Historians give much of the credit to one man, Hippodamus of Miletus, who is considered the father of modern urban planning.

Hippodamus was born in Miletus in 498 B.C. and died in 408 B.C., so he lived quite a long time. Besides urban planning, he is noted for his work in philosophy. Much of what we know about him comes from Aristotle. The idea that Hippodamus was the father of urban planning mainly comes from Aristotle's work *Politics*. At that time, politics included all aspects of life in a city, which was called a *polis* in Greek, so urban planning and Hippodamus's ideas on it fit nicely into Aristotle's work.

Unfortunately, little is known about Hippodamus's life or personality except for a quote from Aristotle describing him as being a vain man who behaved in an eccentric manner, such as by dressing oddly at times. Some scholars believe that when Aristotle wrote that, he was both criticizing and making fun of Hippodamus. Whatever the case, it's from Aristotle that we have a few descriptions of Hippodamus's life. When and how Hippodamus received any training in urban planning is unknown. What is known, though, is that he had a hand in planning the rebuilding of the city of Miletus, his hometown. Miletus was a port city on the coast of what is western Turkey today. During the fifth century B.C., it was Greek territory as several small Greek city-states had sprung up in that region. However, the Persian Empire became powerful and conquered much of the area, including Miletus. During the many years of warfare between Greece and Persia, Miletus suffered a great amount of damage.

When it came time to rebuild the city, Hippodamus had a role in laying out the new plan for Miletus. Today, we would refer to what he created as a grid system. The system he designed had streets meeting at right angles, which were neat and tidy in comparison to the layouts of other cities. They formed regular square city blocks with groups of two-story houses in these blocks and straight, wide streets on all sides of the blocks. His plans also called for open areas that evolved into marketplaces. The famous Greek agora, or marketplace, most likely developed around that time. The ideas of Hippodamus created a more functional city that was appealing to the eye and would be a place people would want to live.

Hippodamus additionally helped rebuild another city, Piraeus, which was the port city of Athens, a major Greek city-state of the time. He designed a grid system with central markets around the large harbor. The main agora was later named for him as a sign of honor for his work. There's additional evidence that Hippodamus planned some Greek colonies in Italy as well as the city of Rhodes.

W Student: Did others copy his work? I ask because the layout you described sounds similar to Roman urban areas and military camps, and you also mentioned that he did work in Italy.

M: The Romans acquired a lot of knowledge from Greece, and city planning was no exception. This is especially true since many small Greek colonies were founded in Italy. Alexander the Great himself borrowed the ideas of Hippodamus when designing the city of Alexandria at the mouth of the Nile River in Egypt in 331 B.C. Later, the Romans did the same thing with regard to city planning. In fact, people all throughout history have utilized the grid pattern. So, yes, Hippodamus clearly had a tremendous influence on urban planning.

He was also a philosopher of how city life should be structured. He believed the ideal city would be inhabited by 10,000 free male citizens plus another 40,000 women, children, and slaves. That made a total of 50,000 residents. Hippodamus further believed that the free men could be divided into three groups: soldiers, artisans, and husbandmen. The term husbandman refers to a common worker in case you don't know. He also divided the land into three parts. One part was sacred, another was private, and the last was public. Aristotle disagreed with Hippodamus's ideas on city structures, and that's one reason Aristotle wrote so much about him. Aristotle's

biggest issue with the beliefs of Hippodamus was that only the soldiers in cities would be armed. He felt that would place too much power in the hands of one group. Aristotle also believed that the leadership of a city should be in the hands of a large middle class.

Answer Explanations

6 Gist-Content Question

ⓒ During his lecture, the professor focuses mainly on discussing the contributions of Hippodamus to urban planning.

7 Detail Question

ⓑ The professor remarks, "When it came time to rebuild the city, Hippodamus had a role in laying out the new plan for Miletus. Today, we would refer to what he created as a grid system."

8 Making Inferences Question

ⓐ In stating, "His plans also called for open areas that evolved into marketplaces. The famous Greek agora, or marketplace, most likely developed around that time," the professor implies that Hippodamus played a major role in the creation of the agora.

9 Understanding Organization Question

ⓓ Regarding Alexander the Great, the professor notes, "Alexander the Great himself borrowed the ideas of Hippodamus when designing the city of Alexandria at the mouth of the Nile River in Egypt in 331 B.C."

10 Detail Question

1, 3 About Hippodamus's ideal city, the professor mentions, "Hippodamus further believed that the free men could be divided into three groups: soldiers, artisans, and husbandmen. The term husbandman refers to a common worker in case you don't know. He also divided the land into three parts. One part was sacred, another was private, and the last was public."

11 Understanding Organization Question

ⓒ When discussing Hippodamus's philosophy of city life, the professor first describes Hippodamus's thoughts, and then he compares some of them with those of Aristotle.

Vocabulary Review　　　　　　　　　　p. 98

Answers

A

1　hub	2　elaborate	3　forgo
4　verbal	5　standard	

B

1　b	2　a	3　b	4　b	5　a
6　b	7　b	8　a	9　a	10　b

Practice with Short Passages
p. 102

A

| Answers | 1 Ⓑ | 2 Ⓓ |

| Script |

Listen to part of a conversation between a student and a professor.

M Student: Hi, Professor Wilkinson. Um, do you think I could, uh, I could come in for a minute? I have something that I, uh, I'd like to talk about.

W Professor: Of course, you can. Please have a seat over there.

M: Thanks so much.

W: My pleasure. Now, um, what's on your mind?

M: I'm a student in your History 42 class. It's kind of big, so you probably don't know who I am. My name is Peter Hampton.

W: Nice to meet you, Peter. I've noticed you in class since you always make a point of sitting in the front row, but, uh, because I don't call roll and we haven't had any tests or assignments yet, you're right . . . I haven't learned your name yet, so thanks for letting me know.

M: Um, my pleasure, ma'am. Anyway, um, I'm here because I was kind of confused about your lecture in class today.

W: Which part of it didn't you understand?

M: 🎧2 It was the part when you spoke about the Fourth Crusade. I guess, uh, I guess what happened between the Venetians and the Byzantines was a bit too confusing for me. I wonder if you could explain to me exactly what happened.

W: **Well, unfortunately, I've got to head to my next class in about two minutes.**

M: Oh, then I suppose I'd better get going in that case.

W: Hold on a second, Peter. While I don't have enough time to rehash my lecture for you, let me give you some reading material. If you look at it, you should be able to understand exactly what happened in the Fourth Crusade. And by that, uh, I mean that you'll understand what happened in the fifty or so years before the crusade began, what happened during the Fourth Crusade itself, and what the results of the crusade were.

M: Awesome. Thanks. So, uh, what books should I read?

W: Here's a list . . . You want to read this book by Norwich here . . . I can't recall what chapter the information is in, so you'll have to use the index. And this book, um . . . here by Runciman is outstanding. If you read both, you'll

have a complete understanding of that period in history.

M: Thanks so much, Professor Wilkinson. You've been a tremendous help.

W: You're welcome, Peter. I'll see you in class on Thursday.

Answer Explanations

1 Ⓑ The professor tells the student, "While I don't have enough time to rehash my lecture for you, let me give you some reading material. If you look at it, you should be able to understand exactly what happened in the Fourth Crusade. And by that, uh, I mean that you'll understand what happened in the fifty or so years before the crusade began, what happened during the Fourth Crusade itself, and what the results of the crusade were."

2 Ⓓ When the professor tells the student that she has to go to her class in a couple of minutes, it can be inferred that she does not have time to comply with the request that the student makes.

B

| Answers | 1 Ⓐ | 2 Ⓒ |

| Script |

Listen to part of a conversation between a student and a student employment center employee.

W Student: So, um, what do you think of the résumé I've written?

M Student Employment Center Employee: Hmm . . . It's fairly well done overall. However, there are a number of places where you could make improvements that would help you tremendously in trying to secure an interview.

W: Yeah? What do you think I should change about it?

M: 🎧2 To begin with, your résumé should be a single sheet of paper rather than the two pages you've got here.

W: Just a single page? B-b-b-but . . . I've got so many accomplishments that I need two pages to let companies know about them.

M: **That's what you might think, but the people who will be reading your résumé won't see it that way.** They'll most likely simply toss your two-page résumé in the trashcan without even reading it.

W: Why would they do that?

M: First, you haven't even graduated yet, so there is absolutely no way you have two pages of worthwhile accomplishments to list. Second, the ability to be concise is highly desired by the people doing the hiring. Tailor your résumé so that it points out the accomplishments, skills, and experiences that are relevant to the job for which you're applying. That will result in a much more focused document.

W: Um . . . If I did that, I might have to write three or four different versions of my résumé.

M: So? You want a job, don't you?

W: Ah, yes, I see your point. In that case, what else do you believe I should do?

M: I've got a paper prepared which explains how to write a good résumé. The things you need to improve upon are all covered in the list, so how about studying it on your own time? Right now, I'd like to focus on the interview process with you.

W: That's fine.

M: Now, have you ever had a job interview before?

W: Yes, I have. It was for a job at a fast-food restaurant I applied to work at around, uh, six years ago when I was in high school. Would you like me to tell you how it went?

M: Yes, I would. Even though you might not realize it, that experience will be extremely helpful to you in the interviews you do in the coming months.

Answer Explanations

1 Ⓐ The man says to the student, "I've got a paper prepared which explains how to write a good résumé. The things you need to improve upon are all covered in the list, so how about studying it on your own time?"

2 Ⓒ The student protests what the man says, and then he responds by commenting, "That's what you might think, but the people who will be reading your résumé won't see it that way." In stating that, he is expressing his disagreement with the student's opinion.

C

| Answers | 1 Ⓓ | 2 Ⓑ |

| Script |

Listen to part of a lecture in a physics class.

M1 Professor: Electricity is a natural phenomenon that we've harnessed to use in countless ways, one of which is to produce light. In its natural state, it's capable of producing light as we can see when lightning flashes in the sky. The question I'd like to answer right now is the following: How can we make a controlled form of light from electricity? The method of doing this was well known in the nineteenth century, but that theory couldn't produce a working device until Thomas Edison developed the first practical incandescent light bulb in 1879.

The basics of a light bulb are quite simple. Basically, uh, electricity passes through a filament, that is, a thin wire, inside an enclosed glass bulb. Edison used carbon filament wires, but the wires in today's light bulbs are made of tungsten, which is more resistant to heat. In addition,

tungsten wires produce brighter light and last longer. As electricity flows through the filament, it meets resistance, which it fights, resulting in the filament turning white hot. The filament, however, does not burn up completely. Instead, both heat and light are produced. The filament is enclosed in a glass bulb that either lacks air or contains an inert gas such as argon, so it doesn't catch on fire or cause the oxidation of the tungsten filament. The light bulb will continue to produce light until the filament burns out, which eventually happens to every light bulb.

Now, uh, that's a relatively simple explanation of what happens. The physics behind it, however, is a bit more complex. Light is a type of energy that atoms release. It comes in the form of particles called photons. Each light photon comes from an excited electron. When electricity meets resistance in the tungsten filament, the atoms in the tungsten absorb more energy. The electrons in each tungsten atom become more energized and then return to a weaker state of energy while the excess energy is cast off the electron in the form of light photons.

M2 Student: Pardon the interruption, but how do the electrons get more energy?

M1: I was about to explain that. The principle behind this energy increase is called Joule heating. That's spelled J-O-U-L-E with a capital J. It's named after English scientist James Joule, who discovered it in 1841. The principle states that when the moving particles in an electric current interact with the atom in the substance that the current is moving through, it will result in resistance. As the electrons in the electric current collide with the atoms in the substance, the electrons give up some of their energy. This energy is absorbed by the electrons in the atoms of the substance the current is passing through. 🎧2 It just so happens that carbon can absorb a lot . . . Wait a minute. I'm sorry. **I didn't mean to say carbon; I meant to say tungsten.** So, uh, tungsten can absorb a lot of this energy without burning up. As the atoms grow excited, they move into higher orbits around the nucleus of the atom. But this happens briefly. Then, the electrons return to their normal positions, and the excess energy gets released as light photons.

Interestingly, only around six percent of the electricity passing through the filament produces light. The rest produces heat, which is mostly wasted since light bulbs can't warm anything more than a couple of feet away from them. The tungsten wire in a typical light bulb is heated to more than 2,000 degrees Celsius whenever you turn it on. Impressive, isn't it?

Answer Explanations

1 Ⓓ The professor focuses on how tungsten filament is better than carbon filament in saying, "Edison used carbon filament wires, but the wires in today's light bulbs are made of tungsten, which is more resistant to heat. In addition, tungsten wires produce brighter light and last

longer."

2 Ⓑ When the professor makes that statement, he is correcting a speaking mistake that he made by saying "carbon" when he should have said "tungsten."

D

| Script |

Listen to part of a lecture in an art history class.

M Professor: The next painting we need to examine is this one . . . Does anyone know who painted this . . . ? Nobody wants to guess . . . ? Okay. It's *Girl with a Pearl Earring*, and it was painted by Dutch master Johannes Vermeer. He painted this oil on canvas around 1665. This work is an example of a tronie . . . that's T-R-O-N-I-E . . . which was commonly done by Dutch artists in the seventeenth century. A tronie is typically a head or a head and upper body painting that's stylized or exaggerated so as to make it appear grotesque or comical. A tronie isn't exactly a portrait as it's not intended to show a recognizable person; hence one of the mysteries of this painting is, uh, who exactly the girl with the pearl earring is.

But before we attempt to answer that question, let's examine the work in more detail, shall we . . . ? First, I'll tell you a bit about its background. At present, the work is a deep, dark black color, but Vermeer intended it to have a translucent green glaze. As you can see up here on the screen, that has faded away. A detailed analysis of the painting indicated that the glaze went on top of the darker background, uh, where it was perhaps intended to provide a sharp contrast with the girl's pale skin tones. Vermeer likely used the dark background since it enabled him to show the girl in a sharper three-dimensional form. It worked, didn't it? Notice how the girl practically appears to be here in the room with us and looks as if she's about to say something.

Let's examine the girl . . . She's obviously Caucasian . . . Her clothing suggests a Middle Eastern influence. The most obvious aspect is the turban wrapped so snugly around her head that we can't see a hint of her hair color. The blue band with the yellow knot on top here . . . and the long, trailing yellow piece over her back here . . . give her the appearance of blond hair though. ∩1 Turbans weren't common headgear in the Netherlands during Vermeer's time, so most art historians speculate he got the idea from Michael Sweerts' painting *A Boy in a Turban Holding a Nosegay*. Here it is side by side with Vermeer's work . . . **The paintings by Vermeer and Sweerts are so similar in composition that some people mistakenly believe the same artist painted them.**

The other main object in *Girl with the Pearl Earring* is the pearl itself. It's ovoid in shape, not round . . . giving it a weighty appearance. Such a large pearl would have been expensive, uh, both then and now, so perhaps she didn't actually wear a pearl earring while posing. Or perhaps it was a smaller pearl or an earring made of something else. Knowing Vermeer's skill, it's possible he merely painted the pearl by using his imagination.

The big mystery, of course, is who the model is. ∩2 A recent book and movie suggest that she was a serving girl named Griet, who lived with the Vermeer family, yet there's no historical evidence to support this claim. Yes, Judy?

W Student: I read somewhere that it's Vermeer's daughter Maria.

M: That's a distinct possibility, but, um, again, there's no evidence. **Maria would have been around twelve when this painting was done, and most critics, uh, as well as I, agree that the girl in the painting is a bit older than that.** A third candidate is Magdalena, the daughter of Vermeer's patron Pieter van Ruijven. Still, there's no firm evidence, so it's likely that we'll never know for sure who she really is.

Answer Explanations

1 Ⓒ In making that statement, the professor implies that Vermeer and Sweerts used similar painting styles since "The paintings by Vermeer and Sweerts are so similar in composition that some people mistakenly believe the same artist painted them."

2 Ⓐ The professor casts doubt upon the student's suggestion when he makes his comment regarding who the girl in the painting really is.

Practice with Long Passages p. 106

A

| Script |

Listen to part of a conversation between a student and a professor.

W1 Professor: I took a look at the class schedule you want for next semester, Catherine, and everything looks fine to me.

W2 Student: I'm glad you approve of the classes I'm taking. But I'm curious: Do you think it's going to be too hard for me to take three classes in my major?

W1: Well . . . it's fairly unusual, but it can be done, so I wouldn't worry very much about it. However, there's one thing you definitely ought to be aware of.

W2: What's that?

W1: You realize, don't you, that you're not going to be able to graduate in four years?

W2: I'm not?

W1: Catherine, you're going to be starting the first semester of your junior year in the fall, and you have so far taken a grand total of one . . . just one . . . class in your major.

W2: Well, uh, the reason is that I switched majors this semester. I had originally been in the Physics Department, but I didn't enjoy studying that subject, so I decided to make the move to Art History this semester. So, uh, that's why I've only taken one class.

W1: Right. I understand exactly what happened since we've covered this topic before. However, have you taken a look at the requirements for Art History majors? Do you know how many classes and what types of classes you need to get a major in it?

W2: Er . . . I looked at the requirements a few weeks ago, but I can only, uh, vaguely remember them. Anyway, they can't be that hard, can they? I'm sure I can handle them.

W1: I too believe you can, uh, handle them, as you just said, but you can't do everything in four semesters. It's simply an impossible task.

W2: Why is that?

W1: You need to take a total of twelve Art History classes to begin with. So that means you would have to take three classes during three of the next four semesters and two in the other one. However, you also need to take some required classes in math, a foreign language, economics, and science. And, uh, in case you don't know—which I'm pretty sure is the case here—you need to take a couple of history and literature classes as an Art History major.

W2: Um . . . I wasn't aware of that.

W1: Yes, that's what I assumed. So you're basically going to have to spend another year here to be able to graduate as an Art History major.

W2: Isn't there anything I can do to graduate in four years?

W1: 🎧4 Hmm . . . If you're willing to stay here and take summer school classes during both sessions for the next two years, then, yes, you could possibly avoid staying here for a fifth year. But you'd have to plan your schedule very carefully.

W2: **Would you mind showing me what classes I'd need to take during the summer terms and in my junior and senior years?**

Answer Explanations

1 Ⓒ The professor tells the student, "You can't do everything in four semesters. It's simply an impossible task."

2 Ⓓ The student tells the professor, "Well, uh, the reason is that I switched majors this semester. I had originally been in the Physics Department, but I didn't enjoy studying that subject, so I decided to make the move to Art History this semester."

3 Ⓓ While telling the student about the courses that she will need to take, the professor also mentions, "And, uh, in case you don't know—which I'm pretty sure is the case here—you need to take a couple of history and literature classes as an Art History major." When she makes that comment, it can be inferred that she believes the student has not done enough thinking about her future and how she is going to graduate.

4 Ⓑ When the student asks the professor that question after the professor states, "If you're willing to stay here and take summer school classes during both sessions for the next two years, then, yes, you could possibly avoid staying here for a fifth year. But you'd have to plan your schedule very carefully," the student implies that she does not want to stay at school for her fifth year but would instead prefer to graduate in only four years.

Dictation

1 However, there's one thing you definitely <u>ought to be aware of</u>.

2 <u>The reason is that</u> I switched majors this semester.

3 So <u>that means</u> you <u>would have to</u> take three classes during three of the next four semesters.

B

Answers

1 Ⓑ   2 Ⓐ   3 Forming Biofilms: ☒2, ☒4
Consuming Unusual Food Sources: ☒3   Going Dormant: ☒1
4 Ⓒ

| Script |

Listen to part of a lecture in a biology class.

W Professor: 🎧4 Bacteria are single-celled organisms found everywhere on the Earth. And when I say everywhere, I mean it. I'm not exaggerating in the least bit. Bacteria are unlike any other organism in that they're the one form of life which can survive virtually anywhere. **They are found in all environments, from freezing cold places in Antarctica to the intense heat of the Sahara Desert to areas beneath the surface in the deepest, darkest parts of the oceans.** This ability to survive has enabled them to thrive for millions of years and also to play a profound role regarding life on the planet.

There are three main ways that bacteria manage to survive in extreme environments. They are, um, by forming biofilms, by availing themselves of unusual food sources, and by going dormant. Let me tell you about each in turn.

Forming biofilms is the most common method bacteria employ. Biofilms are massive colonies of bacteria that join together when they endure some kind of stress. These colonies can be found almost anywhere. For instance, there are many kinds of bacteria in our bodies. Some are in the digestive system, which is extremely acidic. But by forming biofilms, bacteria avoid being killed. When formed into complex biofilms, bacteria can create new pathways that allow them to consume food and to remove waste matter in more effective ways. That allows them to endure whatever stress they are under. Naturally, many bacteria die, but others survive. That's actually good for humans since our bodies require some bacteria to digest food.

M Student: But what about *E. coli* and other similar bad bacteria?

W: Well, sure, *E. coli* can sicken people so much that they die, but there are scientists working on ways to destroy the ability of some bacteria to form biofilms. With luck, their efforts will meet with success in the near future.

What about the second way bacteria survive . . . ? Again, they find food sources in unusual locations. It was long believed that all life forms received their food needs from the sun and photosynthesis. Plants use photosynthesis to make food, and many animals consume plants. Others, of course, consume animals. But deep underneath the ocean's surface, there's no sunlight, so it was once believed that no life could survive there. Then, in the 1970s, deep-sea explorers discovered hydrothermal vents, which are areas where hot water gushes up from the ocean floor. Around those vents, uh, they found numerous life forms. Later examinations determined that many of those creatures were feeding on sugars that were produced by bacteria. The bacteria were utilizing a chemical form of photosynthesis by extracting sulfur from the hot water, processing it, and making sugar that enabled both them and the other life there to survive.

The third way bacteria endure extreme environments is by going dormant for extended periods of time. Bacteria can survive with the bare minimum of the necessities of life only to grow in tremendous numbers when the opportunity arises. Do you remember when the oil platform exploded in the Gulf of Mexico a few years ago? Well, a great amount of oil was spilled into the ocean. It turns out that there was a tremendous increase in bacteria blooms all around the oil platform. The bacteria had been lying dormant on rocks on the seabed, but, due to the sudden influx of oil, the bacteria became active. Researchers discovered that the bacteria survived by processing methane from oil to make food. They also learned that the bacteria has a gene permitting it to live in low-oxygen, low-food environments for very long times.

M: Does that mean that some bacteria could survive on other planets?

W: That's an interesting question. So far, we haven't found any signs of bacteria anywhere other than the Earth, but, uh, that doesn't mean they aren't there. I suppose it's possible—maybe even probable—that bacteria exist elsewhere, but we probably won't know for sure until we send astronauts to other celestial bodies.

Answer Explanations

1 Ⓑ The professor mostly focuses on the manner in which bacteria manage to survive in extreme environments.

2 Ⓐ When the student asks a question about *E. coli*, the professor talks about it by stating, "Well, sure, *E. coli* can sicken people so much that they die, but there are scientists working on ways to destroy the ability of some bacteria to form biofilms. With luck, their efforts will meet with success in the near future."

3 Forming Biofilms: ②, ④
Consuming Unusual Food Sources: ③
Going Dormant: ①
About forming biofilms, the professor states, "Biofilms are massive colonies of bacteria that join together when they endure some kind of stress," and, "When formed into complex biofilms, bacteria can create new pathways that allow them to consume food and to remove waste matter." As for the consuming of unusual food sources, the professor talks about hydrothermal vents and points out, "Later examinations determined that many of those creatures were feeding on sugars that were produced by bacteria. The bacteria were utilizing a chemical form of photosynthesis by extracting sulfur from the hot water, processing it, and making sugar that enabled both them and the other life there to survive." As for going dormant, the professor says, "The third way bacteria endure extreme environments is by going dormant for extended periods of time. Bacteria can survive with the bare minimum of the necessities of life only to grow in tremendous numbers when the opportunity arises. Do you remember when the oil platform exploded in the Gulf of Mexico a few years ago? Well, a great amount of oil was spilled into the ocean. It turns out that there was a tremendous increase in bacteria blooms all around the oil platform. The bacteria had been lying dormant on rocks on the seabed, but, due to the sudden influx of oil, the bacteria became active."

4 Ⓒ When talking about the very harsh places where they live, the professor implies that bacteria can adapt to any of the environments in which they live.

Dictation

1 I'm not exaggerating in the least bit.

2 But what about *E. coli* and other similar bad bacteria?

3 It turns out that there was a tremendous increase in bacteria blooms all around the oil platform.

p. 110

Answers

PART 1

1 Ⓑ	2 Ⓒ	3 Ⓐ	4 Ⓐ	5 Ⓒ
6 Ⓑ	7 Ⓐ	8 ②, ④	9 Ⓐ	10 Ⓒ
11 Ⓓ	12 Ⓐ	13 ②, ③	14 Ⓐ	15 Ⓐ
16 Ⓒ	17 Ⓑ			

PART 2

1 Ⓐ	2 Ⓒ	3 Ⓒ	4 Ⓓ	5 Ⓓ
6 Ⓐ	7 Ⓓ	8 Ⓑ		

9 Pre-Automobile City: ②, ④
　 Post-Automobile City: ①, ③　10 Ⓒ　11 Ⓒ

PART 1

Conversation [1–5]

| Script |

Listen to part of a conversation between a student and an admissions office employee.

M Student: Hello, Ms. Johnson. I'm Matt Potter, and I'm here to interview for the campus tour guide position.

W Admissions Office Employee: It's a pleasure to meet you, Matt. Please have a seat, and then we can get this interview started.

M: Thank you.

W: I looked at the information you submitted on your application, and you appear to be an outstanding student. You've gotten straight A's every semester, which is quite impressive since you're in the Chemical Engineering Department.

M: Well, I study as hard as I can, and I've happened to do well on my tests.

W: Ah, I see you're modest as well. That's good. So, uh, it appears that your academic qualifications are excellent, but let's be honest . . . You're going to be giving tours, which isn't very, shall we say, academically rigorous. You need other skills to be a good tour guide.

M: Such as?

W: First, you need to love the school. Every guide we have giving tours to prospective students and their parents absolutely loves being here. It's so apparent to the people taking the tours that they often comment on it. We in the admissions office are only interested in hiring students who want to be here. So how do you feel about this school?

M: This was my first choice. In fact, I successfully applied for early admission, so I immediately accepted a place here and withdrew my applications at other universities. I, well . . . I can't imagine myself anywhere else.

W: That's good to know. Out of curiosity, how familiar are you with the campus?

M: What do you mean?

W: Do you know the names of all the academic buildings, dormitories, and other places on campus?

M: Ah, I understand. Hmm . . . I'd say I know the names of around half the buildings on campus. Since I'm an engineer, I spend most of my time in Paxton Hall, but I've taken classes in at least six other buildings on campus. I also visit my friends in their dorms, and I go to the campus center, library, and gym a lot.

W: That sounds good.

M: Is it bad if I'm not familiar with every building here?

W: Not really. We have a booklet we give to our tour guides that has the names of the buildings on campus along with short descriptions of them. Therefore, uh, you can study the booklet and learn what to tell the visitors.

M: Okay.

W: Well, that's just about it. Oh, wait a minute . . . I need to know when you'd be available to give tours. A standard tour lasts thirty-five to forty minutes.

M: Ah, sure. I anticipated this question, so I made a copy of my schedule. Here it is . . . The time blocks that are circled are the ones when I would prefer to work. I'd love to do around ten hours of tours a week.

W: That should be doable. Now, uh, I can't give you the job right away because I have to discuss this with my superior in a few minutes, but between you and me, you're the best of all the applicants I've interviewed. So I'm going to highly recommend hiring you.

M: Thank you for saying that, ma'am.

W: I should be able to let you know by the end of the day. I'll send you a text message around, uh, probably around five or so.

M: Perfect. Thanks a lot, Ms. Johnson. I really hope I get the job.

Answer Explanations

1 Gist-Purpose Question

Ⓑ At the beginning of the conversation, the student says, "Hello, Ms. Johnson. I'm Matt Potter, and I'm here to interview for the campus tour guide position."

2 Detail Question

Ⓒ The woman comments, "We in the admissions office are only interested in hiring students who want to be here."

3 Understanding Function Question

Ⓐ The woman remarks, "We have a booklet we give to our tour guides that has the names of the buildings on campus along with short descriptions of them. Therefore, uh, you can study the booklet and learn what to tell the visitors."

4 Understanding Attitude Question

Ⓐ The woman indicates that she is impressed with the student when she remarks, "Now, uh, I can't give you the job right away because I have to discuss this with my superior in a few minutes, but between you and me, you're the best of all the applicants I've interviewed. So I'm going to highly recommend hiring you."

5 Making Inferences Question

Ⓒ The woman will likely speak with her boss next as she says, "Now, uh, I can't give you the job right away because I have to discuss this with my superior in a few minutes."

Lecture #1 [6–11]

| Script |

Listen to part of a lecture in a geology class.

W1 Professor: Beneath the Earth's surface, there are riches to be found in the form of precious minerals. The most valuable include metals such as gold, silver, and platinum as well as gems like diamonds, sapphires, and rubies. There are also more common, but quite useful, minerals, including iron and copper, which we use to make many of the items we require in our daily lives. What I'd like to talk about now is how geologists know where to dig for these minerals. Finding mineral deposits is a vital aspect of mining, which makes geologists crucial to mining companies. To detect mineral deposits, geologists rely upon a wide range of methods and tools, including, um, let's see . . . traditional prospecting, historical knowledge of where minerals are found, satellite imagery, airborne magnetic surveys, and detailed analyses of mineral samples.

The oldest way to find minerals is to prospect for them. Prospecting refers to the actual physical work of walking over the land and looking for signs of mineral deposits. Very often, mineral deposits leave clues near the surface that professional geologists and miners recognize, which means that a large mineral deposit is close by. Gold, for example, is often found in streambeds, where old-fashioned panning can find samples that indicate the potential for large deposits of gold in the area. Outcroppings of exposed minerals may also mean that there are larger deposits underground. Modern tools are useful to prospectors as well. For example, some employ handheld magnetic detectors to find iron ore deposits.

Geologists study historical records and rely upon the wealth of knowledge that has been gathered over the years to locate minerals as well. As an example, copper is found in areas that saw volcanic activity in the past. The reason is that volcanic activity creates large areas where the water underground is very hot. It then flows through the bedrock and causes changes in the rocks that it comes into contact with. That's the way copper ore is created.

Volcanic activity is also known for producing seams of kimberlite, which is a kind of rock. If you find kimberlite, you're also likely to discover diamonds, so that's why prospectors know to look near volcanoes for diamonds.

In this modern age, geologists have myriad high-tech tools to assist them in finding minerals. For instance, satellite imagery and magnetic mapping are used by geologists. Satellite images can help geologists gain a better understanding of the land that they want to survey. Satellites can take pictures which interpret different wavelengths on the electromagnetic scale, including infrared wavelengths. These images allow geologists to see the land in a way that the human eye simply is not capable of doing. The images also show the land in a larger scope than is possible when looking at it from ground level. Satellite images in infrared wavelengths can additionally allow geologists to determine soil and rock compositions. From these pictures, geologists can identify different types of rocks and then determine whether or not valuable minerals are likely to be found nearby. Magnetic aerial surveys can be used in a similar manner. Here's what happens. Magnetic detectors are placed on helicopters, which then fly in a grid pattern back and forth over a region in order to cover all the land in a targeted area. Once that is accomplished, computers then use the data to create a magnetic composite picture of the region. This can be beneficial when attempting to locate deposits of magnetic minerals such as iron.

W2 Student: What happens once geologists collect all the data?

W1: Well, when I was working as a geologist, I would analyze the data to determine which places most likely had whatever mineral I was looking for, and then I'd head out into the field to find out what exactly was in the land. I'd do things such as take samples from streambeds and rock outcroppings, and I also frequently dug deep under the ground.

W2: How did you do that?

W1: My team and I would use drills to extract sample cores of rocks from several hundred feet underground. As soon as we thought we had located a deposit, we would analyze the samples we had found. 🎧11 We needed to figure out if it was worth the mining company's time and money to extract the minerals. If the deposit was estimated to be large enough and easy enough to extract from the ground, then mining began. **However, we usually came up empty.** We would only find signs of small deposits or no signs of minerals at all, so we packed our bags and moved to another region to start the entire process anew.

Let me stress one thing to you . . . No matter how much technology geologists use, there's no guarantee that they'll find a large, profitable mineral deposit once mining begins. There are many times when geologists think they've found a huge deposit, but, as soon as the digging starts, very little is extracted. This can cost mining companies millions of dollars in survey fees, land claim fees, and other assorted costs, including the actual mining. Fortunately, that never happened to one of my teams. But let me tell you about something interesting that happened to me once . . .

Answer Explanations

6 Gist-Content Question

Ⓑ During her lecture, the professor talks about which methods geologists use when they are looking for valuable minerals.

7 Connecting Content Question

Ⓐ About gold, the professor notes, "Gold, for example, is often found in streambeds." About copper, she states, "As an example, copper is found in areas that saw volcanic activity in the past."

8 Detail Question

②, ④ The professor lectures, "In this modern age, geologists have myriad high-tech tools to assist them in finding minerals. For instance, satellite imagery and magnetic mapping are used by geologists. Satellite images can help geologists gain a better understanding of the land that they want to survey. Satellites can take pictures which interpret different wavelengths on the electromagnetic scale, including infrared wavelengths. These images allow geologists to see the land in a way that the human eye simply is not capable of doing. The images also show the land in a larger scope than is possible when looking at it from ground level. Satellite images in infrared wavelengths can additionally allow geologists to determine soil and rock compositions." Then, she adds, "Magnetic aerial surveys can be used in a similar manner. Here's what happens. Magnetic detectors are placed on helicopters, which then fly in a grid pattern back and forth over a region in order to cover all the land in a targeted area. Once that is accomplished, computers then use the data to create a magnetic composite picture of the region. This can be beneficial when attempting to locate deposits of magnetic minerals such as iron."

9 Understanding Function Question

Ⓐ The professor talks to the students about how she used to look for minerals when she discusses the time when she was a geologist.

10 Making Inferences Question

Ⓒ At the end of the lecture, the professor tells the students, "But let me tell you about something interesting that happened to me once," so she will probably continue her lecture.

11 Understanding Attitude Question

Ⓓ When the professor says, "However, we usually came up empty," she means that she and her team usually found nothing of value, so their searches were unsuccessful.

Lecture #2 [12–17]

| Script |

Listen to part of a lecture in a marine biology class.

M Professor: If you've ever spent any time on the ocean or even around boats and wharves in ports, you almost certainly noticed that fish have a tendency to swarm around any object that's floating in the water. Close to shore, fish like swimming near wharves and boats that are docked as well as any mooring devices and buoys. Out at sea, they'll congregate around driftwood, masses of seaweed, and even lone coconuts floating in the water. Fishermen have observed this characteristic ever since people first took to the water. They have also long used this habit as a way to catch fish as they lure fish to various manmade floating devices. The term that marine biologists use to describe this trait is fish aggregation. The manmade devices are called fish aggregating devices, or FADs, for short.

Why fish gather around these objects isn't known for certain, but it's likely there are a few reasons. One is that out in the ocean, floating objects are about the only things that fish see which is different. FADs therefore provide some kind of stimulus to their brains when they see the object. The fish therefore swim over to check it out and then remain around it for long periods of time. Another theory is that small fish may be seeking protection by staying near these floating objects. This is especially true in the case of natural objects such as seaweed and floating trees that get swept out to sea. Small fish can hide within these objects and avoid being preyed upon by larger predators. But, interestingly enough, larger fish also swim around these objects, mostly because they are seeking smaller fish to eat. This, in turn, attracts fishermen, who go to places where they have the opportunity to catch both big and small fish.

Many fishermen make their own FADs and then place them in the water to attract fish to places convenient to them. So that there's no confusion regarding what they look like, let me describe them for you. Manmade FADs come in all kinds of shapes and sizes and are made of materials that can float, uh, usually some sort of plastic or wood. They tend to be round in shape and can be attached to the seafloor with long ropes, cables, or chains that are connected to heavy concrete blocks. The bottom half of a FAD is underwater while its top half is above water. On top of a FAD is a high pole with a flag so that fishing vessels can find them while other ships can avoid them. Other FADs are placed entirely underwater, um, beneath the depth of a large ship's keel. Their locations are known only to those who place them. In some instances, fishermen place FADs on top of artificial reefs, which also attract large numbers of fish.

Typically, a FAD, uh, either a natural or manmade one, takes a couple of weeks to a month to attract enough fish to make it profitable for fishermen to cast their nets. Small fish arrive first in search of shelter or simply because they're curious. Big fish such as tuna arrive later. The small fish swim right next to the FADs while the big fish swim in circles a hundred meters away or so. Then, they swim in from time to time to feed on the smaller fish. Some fishermen are only after bigger fish while others want all of them. After the fishermen cast their nets and haul in the fish, they have to wait another few weeks before they can go fishing again since new fish need to be attracted to replace the ones they just caught.

W Student: 🎧17 Hold on a second. It sounds like these fishermen are engaging in overfishing. Is it legal to place FADs in the ocean? If it is, it shouldn't be.

M: **Well, it's a bit of a gray area as far as the law is concerned, so people in some nations are seeking to pass laws regarding FADs.** And, um, those nations that do have laws already have trouble enforcing them since the fishermen can either move their FADs or place them deep underwater. Another concern regarding FADs is that some fisherman may stake a claim to a specific area after placing a FAD in it. This upsets other fishermen and can result in conflict. Furthermore, FADs are a nuisance to maritime navigation since other boats can get entangled in the mooring lines or even strike the FADs, which can damage their hulls. Finally, the long lines anchoring FADs frequently ensnare dolphins, turtles, sharks, and other animals, and those marine creatures end up dying.

And, uh, yes, overfishing is a major concern. One of the biggest problems with FADs is that many of the fish attracted to them are juveniles which haven't reached adulthood yet, so they haven't mated and produced the next generation of fish. By catching such large numbers of young fish, fishermen are endangering the futures of various species. So, yes, they're quite controversial. However, fishermen see FADs as a way to protect their livelihoods and resent governments and environmentalists from intruding on their lives. But there are some FADs that are less harmful than others. Let me tell you about one right now.

Answer Explanations

12 Gist-Content Question

Ⓐ The professor mostly talks about how fish aggregating devices can be used to attract and catch fish.

13 Detail Question

② , ③ The professor lectures, "Why fish gather around these objects isn't known for certain, but it's likely there are a few reasons. One is that out in the ocean, floating objects are about the only things that fish see which is different. FADs therefore provide some kind of stimulus to their brains when they see the object. The fish therefore swim over to check it out and then remain around it for

long periods of time. Another theory is that small fish may be seeking protection by staying near these floating objects. This is especially true in the case of natural objects such as seaweed and floating trees that get swept out to sea. Small fish can hide within these objects and avoid being preyed upon by larger predators."

14 Gist-Purpose Question

Ⓐ The professor remarks, "So that there's no confusion regarding what they look like, let me describe them for you."

15 Making Inferences Question

Ⓐ The professor comments, "After the fishermen cast their nets and haul in the fish, they have to wait another few weeks before they can go fishing again since new fish need to be attracted to replace the ones they just caught." So it can be inferred that fish aggregating devices can be used multiple times to catch fish.

16 Understanding Organization Question

Ⓒ In talking about overfishing, the professor declares, "And, uh, yes, overfishing is a major concern."

17 Understanding Function Question

Ⓑ When the professor states, "Well, it's a bit of a gray area as far as the law is concerned, so people in some nations are seeking to pass laws regarding FAD," it can be inferred that the laws about fish aggregating devices vary from country to country.

PART 2

Conversation [1–5]

| Script |

Listen to part of a conversation between a student and a professor.

M Professor: Mary, what a pleasant coincidence. I was hoping to see you today. Are you going to class right now? Do you have a moment to step into my office? There's something I'd like to discuss.

W Student: Oh, hello, Professor Jackson. Uh, sure, I guess I have a few moments. I'm supposed to meet one of my friends for lunch at the student center, but she's always late, so it's all right if I talk to you now.

M: Great. Uh, why don't you come into my office so that we can talk in private?

W: Sure. Um . . . this isn't anything bad, is it? I mean, um, we've only been in class for a couple of weeks, and I haven't even turned in any assignments yet.

M: No, Mary. There's nothing bad at all, so please don't feel alarmed.

W: That's a relief. Thanks.

M: Do you remember that at the end of Monday's lecture, I mentioned we would be forming study groups starting next week?

W: Oh, yes, I recall you saying that. I was planning to sign up for one because I want to be sure I understand the material that you go over in class.

M: Er . . . Well, um, the reason I'm bringing this up is that I'd like you to be a leader of an individual study group.

W: Excuse me?

M: I don't have any graduate students to be TAs, so I have to rely upon upperclassmen like you to provide assistance. You're definitely one of the top students in the class, so you'd be ideal for helping out others. So what do you say?

W: I guess I'd say this is totally unexpected. I mean, uh, we just started the class, so how do you know I'm one of the best students? Uh, don't get me wrong. I'm incredibly flattered that you think so highly of me, but I'm not sure what makes you feel that way.

M: 🎧5 Mary, this is the third class of mine you've taken so far. **You got high grades in the other two, and several professors in the Biology Department think well of you, too.** When I consulted with some of my colleagues on who to ask to lead the study groups, your name was the only one to receive unanimous support.

W: Wow . . . I had no idea.

M: That's another thing we like about you, Mary. You're not conceited and don't think highly of yourself, unlike some other students. I'm positive you'd do a great job of teaching. And didn't you tell me once that you were considering finding a job in the teaching profession?

W: Yes, sir, and I still feel that way.

M: Then this is exactly the kind of experience you need. You'll essentially be the teacher of a small group of students, so you'll get to find out if you enjoy it or not.

W: Hmm . . . When you put it that way, I guess I can do it.

M: Wonderful. Thanks for agreeing. I'm sure you'll do a terrific job. Take a look at this, please . . . It's the scheduled meeting times for the four study groups we'll be having. You're the first person I've asked, so you get first choice.

W: Tuesday evening is perfect for me. I'll take that one.

M: Okay. Now, about your compensation . . .

Answer Explanations

1 Gist-Purpose Question

Ⓐ The professor calls the student in to his office to speak with him in order to offer her a job, so he wants to discuss some work that he would like for her to do.

2 Making Inferences Question

Ⓒ The professor tells the student, "I don't have any graduate students to be TAs, so I have to rely upon upperclassmen like you to provide assistance." Since the professor mentions that the student is an upperclassman, he is implying that she is either a junior or a senior.

3 Understanding Attitude Question

Ⓒ The professor notes, "That's another thing we like about you, Mary. You're not conceited and don't think highly of yourself, unlike some other students."

4 Making Inferences Question

Ⓓ At the end of the conversation, the professor states, "Now, about your compensation . . ." So he will probably tell the student how much money she will earn next.

5 Understanding Function Question

Ⓓ When the professor says, "Several professors in the Biology Department think well of you, too," he is implying that the student has previously taken several Biology classes.

Lecture [6–11]

| Script |

Listen to part of a lecture in an architecture class.

W Professor: Urban design has been ongoing for thousands of years, so it may come as a surprise to learn that during that entire time, um, for the most part, the structures of cities have been based on four common design shapes. By design shapes, I am referring to how city blocks are designed. Imagine looking down on several cities from above as if you were in a helicopter or plane . . . You'd be able to distinguish four main designs: medium-sized rectangular blocks, small blocks in various shapes, larger blocks in various shapes, and small square blocks.

I'd like for you all to open your textbooks to page 101. On that page—as well as the next three or four pages— you'll see examples of these four designs. The pictures should enable you to visualize what I'm talking about. Oh, and in case you're curious, the information I'm going to give you comes from a study of 131 cities around the world. The study's authors examined the layout of each city from a mathematical point of view. Take a look at the four pictures on page 101 . . . You'll see that Buenos Aires, Argentina, has a layout of medium-sized rectangular blocks . . . Athens, Greece, is comprised of small blocks in various shapes . . . New Orleans, United States, has a layout of larger blocks in various shapes . . . And, finally, Mogadishu, Somalia, has a pattern of small, square blocks.

M Student: 🎧11 I find it hard to believe that every one of the cities they examined fit perfectly into a mere four designs. That doesn't, um, that simply doesn't seem possible.

W: Please don't misunderstand, Todd. **They don't fit—as you said—perfectly into the four design types, but they all conform in some way to the four basic designs I mentioned while also possessing unique aspects of their own.** And even within some cities, there are differences between districts. Take, for example, New York City and its five boroughs of Manhattan, Brooklyn, Staten Island, Queens, and the Bronx. You can see their layouts on the next page, um, by the way . . . Manhattan has a regular structure of small blocks while the blocks in the other four boroughs aren't so regular or small. Staten Island, for example, has twice as many medium-sized blocks as it does small blocks, and its blocks are more rectangular than square.

Overall, the greatest differences can be seen in cities founded before the invention of the automobile and those established after its creation. Pre-automobile cities encompass the vast majority of cities in Europe and Asia and a few in the Americas, Africa, and Oceania. These cities often developed in haphazard manners without any of our modern concerns for automobile traffic. There are exceptions though. Most of them are cities that had some initial structured planning, um, like many European cities that grew up where Roman cities had once been. Yet even these cities developed somewhat randomly as their populations grew, and many were subsequently redesigned in modern times to take the automobile into account. This has resulted in some cities having sections with winding streets and misshapen blocks alongside sections with streets laid out in a grid pattern and more square and rectangular blocks.

In contrast, post-automobile cities developed with more structure, with more regulated street design, and with more grid-like patterns that considered automobile traffic. You can see both types in the United States. Cities on the east coast that were established early on, such as Boston, have random patterns to their block arrangements with a wide variety of shapes and sizes. I believe the picture of downtown Boston is on page 103 . . . And even a city such as Washington, D.C., which was planned, has more of an irregular grid pattern mostly because its designers designed long, wide boulevards that cut diagonally across the city and met at intersections, thereby giving the city many irregularly shaped blocks. Cities farther west that grew during the age of automobiles, such as Los Angeles, have more grid-like patterns and blocks shaped and sized in more regular ways. They also have wider streets and many freeways to take into account the growing traffic problems modern cities face. In modern times, many pre-automobile cities in the U.S. have gone through massive redesigns to make it easier for drivers.

Another consideration of urban design that can lead to less-than-ideal grid patterns and regular blocks is the terrain. Rivers, mountains, and coastlines can disrupt the flow of regular block layouts in urban areas. Paris, for example, has the Seine River flowing straight through it while the Thames Rivers cuts through the heart of London. New York is built on several islands, so designing and building its streets required taking its coastlines and rivers into consideration. So, um, it's obvious that these four basic designs aren't perfect examples of all cities. Nevertheless, most of them do share certain characteristics that make them similar to one another.

Answer Explanations

6 Gist-Content Question

Ⓐ Most of the professor's lecture is about how individual sections of cities such as blocks are shaped.

7 Understanding Function Question

Ⓓ The professor instructs the students, "I'd like for you all to open your textbooks to page 101. On that page—as well as the next three or four pages—you'll see examples of these four designs. The pictures in your textbooks should enable you to visualize what I'm talking about."

8 Connecting Content Question

Ⓑ About the two places, the professor says, "Manhattan has a regular structure of small blocks while the blocks in the other four boroughs aren't so regular or small. Staten Island, for example, has twice as many medium-sized blocks as it does small blocks, and its blocks are more rectangular than square." So she compares the sizes of their blocks in her lecture.

9 Connecting Content Question

Pre-Automobile City: ②, ④ Post-Automobile City: ①, ③ Regarding pre-automobile cities, the professor states, "Pre-automobile cities encompass the vast majority of cities in Europe and Asia and a few in the Americas, Africa, and Oceania. These cities often developed in haphazard manners without any of our modern concerns for automobile traffic." As for post-automobile cities, the professor notes, "They also have wider streets and many freeways to take into account the growing traffic problems modern cities face."

10 Detail Question

Ⓒ The professor points out, "Another consideration of urban design that can lead to less-than-ideal grid patterns and regular blocks is the terrain. Rivers, mountains, and coastlines can disrupt the flow of regular block layouts in urban areas."

11 Detail Question

Ⓒ The professor is clarifying a statement she made in response to the student's comment.

| Vocabulary Review   p. 120

Answers

A
1	principles	2	determine		
3	subsequently	4	rehash	5	nuisances

B
1 a	2 b	3 b	4 b	5 a
6 a	7 b	8 a	9 b	10 a

Chapter 06 | Understanding Attitude

Practice with Short Passages

p. 124

A

| Answers | 1 Ⓑ | 2 Ⓓ |

| Script |

Listen to part of a conversation between a student and a housing office employee.

M Student: Good morning. Um . . . Is this the place where I should come if I lost the key to my dorm room?

W Housing Office Employee: Well, that depends. Can you tell me where you might have lost it?

M: Actually, I know exactly where I lost it.

W: Yes?

M: I feel sort of silly about what happened. You see, uh, I was having dinner at the dining hall last night. I put my dorm room key on the tray while I was eating, and, um . . . I simply forgot it was there when I finished my meal, so I left it on the tray. It must have gotten lost in the uh, the dishwashing process.

W: Did you talk to anyone at the dining hall to see if somebody washing the dishes found it? I mean, um, they find lost items there all the time. There's a good chance your key was found by someone.

M: Yes, ma'am. I went there this morning and asked somebody, but nobody had turned anything in.

W: This morning? Why didn't you go last night right after you realized your key was gone?

M: Um . . . To be honest, I didn't know that I had thrown it away for a few hours. You see, um, after I finished dinner, I didn't go back to my dorm room. Instead, I headed straight to the library, where I stayed until around eleven at night. It was only when I was heading back to my room that I suddenly noticed I didn't have my key. And, uh, by that time, the dining hall had closed for the night.

W: Ah, I see. Well, it's unfortunate, but these things sometimes happen.

M: So . . . I'll be able to get a new key, right?

W: 🎧2 Yes, of course. All you have to do is fill out this form right here . . . I'll need to see your student ID as well. Oh, and a replacement key costs $20. You have to pay for it right now.

M: **Wow, that's more than I had expected, but, uh, you take cash, right? I think I've got enough on me.**

W: Yes, that's an acceptable form of payment.

Answer Explanations

1 Ⓑ When explaining how he lost his key, the student says, "I feel sort of silly about what happened." So it can be inferred that he is embarrassed about what happened.

2 Ⓓ When the student states, "That's more than I had expected," he means that he believes the price of a replacement key is very expensive.

B

| Answers | 1 Ⓐ | 2 Ⓐ |

| Script |

Listen to part of a conversation between a student and a professor.

W Student: Professor Richardson, I can't wait to visit the museum of natural history. I've never been there before, so it should be a great experience.

M Professor: You've never gone there? 🎧2 Aren't you a senior, Vicky?

W: Actually, I'm only a junior, but you're right in implying I should have checked out the museum earlier. I guess I've just been too busy with my schoolwork to get to the city very much.

M: **Well, you're going to be in for a real treat this Wednesday.**

W: Are we going to take a tour of the museum to see all of the exhibits?

M: No, we're not doing that because the museum has exhibits on a wide variety of things. For instance, the dinosaur exhibit may be fascinating, and I highly recommend it, but it has nothing to do with ancient Rome, so we're going to bypass that part of the museum. If you want to see exhibits like fossils and, uh, modern art, you'll have to go to the museum on your own time.

W: So, uh, in that case, what exactly are we going to do?

M: For starters, we're going to look at the items from ancient Rome that the museum has on permanent display. It will take us about an hour to do that since I'm going to be lecturing about the relics at the same time. After that, we're going to visit some of the backrooms in the museum.

W: Yeah? What's there?

M: You may not be aware of this, but the museum has one of the largest collections of relics from ancient Rome in the entire country. However, due to space limitations, it only exhibits a tiny percentage of those artifacts at one time. The rest are kept in storage rooms in the museum's basement, but we're going to get to see those items.

W: Wow. How did you pull something like that off?

M: The curator is rather considerate of the needs of local scholars, so he permits instructors at some schools to bring their classes to the museum every year.

W: It's nice of him to contribute to the advancement of knowledge like that.

M: You're right. Since every item can't be displayed, it's great to get the opportunity to see everything else. You're going to be astounded by some of the items we get to see.

Answer Explanations

1 Ⓐ About the curator, the student says, "It's nice of him to contribute to the advancement of knowledge like that."

2 Ⓐ When the professor tells the student, "You're going to be in for a real treat," it can be inferred that he expects the student to be impressed by what she sees at the museum.

C

Answers 1 Ⓑ   2 Ⓒ

| Script |

Listen to part of a lecture in an anthropology class.

W Professor: Prior to the onset of civilization several thousand years ago, most of humanity was grouped together in hunter-gatherer bands. For anthropologists, studying the lives of prehistoric people is problematic for several reasons. For starters, they left no written records, so we have no firsthand accounts of them. Secondly, we tend to ascribe our modern values and way of life on the people in the past that we study, but we simply must avoid doing this to understand how they lived. Finally, we can't assume that all hunter-gatherers were identical; thus they can't be studied as if they were one large group with the same structure and habits everywhere around the world. ∩2 Instead, these groups lived differently depending upon their environments, which included, hmm, let me think . . . the local geography, the available food supplies, and the climate. For instance, a hunter-gatherer clan in Africa had an extremely different lifestyle than one living in the Arctic. **Anthropologists who make any of these mistakes are doing their profession a disservice and will arrive at incorrect conclusions.**

Nevertheless, we can make some generalizations about early hunter-gatherer bands. They were small groups comprising a few dozen people at the most. It's believed they were primarily family groups covering several generations, yet there may have been a few different families in one clan. Within the band, each member had certain tasks, which were often divided based on sex and age, to perform. For the most part, women who were of child-bearing age or who had given birth already were responsible for taking care of the children. These women

included both mothers and grandmothers, and they likely reared the children as a group activity.

As for the men, their primary tasks were to protect the clan and to hunt for meat. Almost all hunter-gatherer groups ate meat. Besides the flesh of mammals, they consumed fish, birds, reptiles, and even insects. Those in the Arctic regions pretty much only ate meat while those in warmer climates had access to and, uh, therefore ate various fruits, vegetables, and grains. The men hunted in groups and used spears as well as bows and arrows to kill prey. Men, women, and children all took part in preparing the meat for cooking, curing the hides, and using other animal parts, such as bones, to make useful tools.

All members of the clan, um, except for the youngest children, foraged for edible plant matter. Sometimes the group had to wander far to find sufficient amounts of sustenance, but that wasn't always the case. In certain regions, there was enough food that a clan could survive in one place for several generations. Each member ate while foraging but would take food back to those protecting the children or out hunting for meat. The group members also shared duties when it came to doing tasks such as gathering firewood, building shelters, and carrying loads to new campsites.

M Student: What about the leaders? Did they also engage in this work?

W: You may be surprised to hear this, but we believe these hunter-gatherer groups had no leaders. Instead, they all had equal roles in the group.

M: How can you be sure of that if there aren't any written records, uh, like you pointed out a moment ago? I don't see how it's possible to know any of this.

W: Well, uh, we don't know this for sure, but that's what most modern-day anthropologists feel happened in the past. We aren't positive though, so we just go by what we think most likely happened.

Answer Explanations

1 Ⓑ The student remarks, "How can you be sure of that if there aren't any written records, uh, like you pointed out a moment ago? I don't see how it's possible to know any of this." In saying that, he expresses his skepticism toward what the professor is saying. His tone of voice also indicates that he doubts what the professor is saying is true.

2 Ⓒ When the professor says, "Anthropologists who make any of these mistakes are doing their profession a disservice and will arrive at incorrect conclusions," it can be inferred that she believes some anthropologists do poor work.

D

Answers 1 Ⓓ   2 Ⓐ

Listen to part of a lecture in an environmental science class.

M Professor: Okay, would everyone please quiet down because we need to get started with today's lecture . . . ? All right, let's begin . . . Sound travels four times faster in water than it does in air. The actual rate is 1,230 meters per second for sound in water compared to 340 meters per second for sound in air. This faster rate is due to the way molecules are packed more tightly in water than in air, thereby permitting a swifter transfer of sound. Some sounds are capable of traveling through water for miles. Sounds are additionally louder in water than in air because of water's greater density, which leaves less room for them to dissipate. Interestingly, on account of the way that sound moves in air, a person a short distance away may not hear it, yet sounds made in water will almost always be heard by the people or creatures around it.

And this fact is causing problems. There's an environmental issue called sound pollution in water. Sound pollution is mainly made by humans. Think about it . . . All of our oceangoing ships, motorboats, jet skis, oil-drilling platforms, navy ships with sonar, and other manmade machines are filling the oceans with sound. This isn't new either as it has been a problem since the 1970s. Scientists at that time estimated that the sounds in the ocean had increased ten decibels since the 1950s, mostly due to the global increase in shipping and the use of recreational boats. In the past forty years, this problem has worsened.

W Student: How is sound pollution affecting marine life forms? It can't be good for them, can it?

M: 🎧2 Most certainly not. Still, uh, it's hard to say exactly how big of a problem it is since we can't ask dolphins, whales, and other marine life what they think of all the noise. **It's also a matter of dispute between those making the pollution and environmentalists since, unlike oil and gas drilling and pollution in the oceans, we don't know for sure how dangerous or harmful sound pollution is.** We can make some good estimates of what trouble it's causing though. For instance, mammals such as dolphins and whales use sound in their daily lives. How . . . ? Well, they use sounds to communicate with one another, to find food and mates, and to navigate. But the increased levels of noise in the oceans are making it harder for them. Or, uh, at least we think it's becoming harder.

Here's an example of what may be happening . . . Whales use a frequency to communicate with one another which is in the same sound range that most ocean noise pollution is at. At times, whales hear the sounds of ships' engines, get confused, and then slam into the sides of huge oceangoing vessels. The number of whale collisions with ships is increasing, and the unfortunate result is that many whales are dying. Another problem is that the noise which recreational boaters closer inshore make sometimes drives whales and dolphins out of the same locations, which are where they frequently feed or mate.

Yet another problem has to do with navigation. It's widely believed that naval ships using sonar can interfere with whales' ability to navigate. Sonar utilizes high-energy pulses that are some of the loudest sounds in the ocean. Whales are thought to beach themselves to try to escape from these pulses. In other instances, they lose the ability to navigate, so they mistakenly swim into shallow water, get trapped, and then die. So, uh, as you can see, sound pollution in the water is a huge issue, and something really needs to be done about it.

Answer Explanations

1　Ⓓ The professor indicates that he believes sound pollution is causing harm to marine creatures when he says, "Still, uh, it's hard to say exactly how big of a problem it is since we can't ask dolphins, whales, and other marine life what they think of all the noise. It's also a matter of dispute between those making the pollution and environmentalists since, unlike oil and gas drilling and pollution in the oceans, we don't know for sure how dangerous or harmful sound pollution is. We can make some good estimates of what trouble it's causing though. For instance, mammals such as dolphins and whales use sound in their daily lives. How . . . ? Well, they use sounds to communicate with one another, to find food and mates, and to navigate. But the increased levels of noise in the oceans are making it harder for them. Or, uh, at least we think it's becoming harder."

2　Ⓐ When the professor remarks, "It's also a matter of dispute between those making the pollution and environmentalists since, unlike oil and gas drilling and pollution in the oceans, we don't know for sure how dangerous or harmful sound pollution is," he means that nobody is certain how much harm sound pollution in the oceans actually causes.

Practice with Long Passages　　p. 128

A

Answers	1　Ⓐ	2　Ⓒ	3　Ⓑ	4　Ⓒ

| Script |

Listen to part of a conversation between a student and a student services office employee.

M1 Student: Good afternoon. I'm looking for Ms. Linda Anderson. Would you happen to know where she is? I've got an appointment to see her at three thirty today.

M2 Student Services Office Employee: I'm sorry, but Ms. Anderson is currently out of the office. She fell ill and had to leave for the day.

M1: Oh . . . That's unfortunate. I hope she gets better soon. Um . . . Do you happen to know when she's going to be back? I understand that she's sick, but I have something of importance that I need to discuss with her.

M2: Would your name happen to be Eric Kennedy?

M1: Yes, that's me.

M2: Ah, that's great. Linda sent me an e-mail about you around thirty minutes ago. She told me I should expect you to drop by to make a request. So, uh, is there something I can assist you with?

M1: Yes, that would be wonderful. I'm pleased Ms. Anderson was thoughtful enough to write about me to you even though she's unhealthy.

M2: That's the kind of person she is.

M1: She seems like she's pretty dedicated to her job.
🎧4 Anyway, uh, I'm the president of the club Movie Matters, and I'm here to reserve a room.

M2: Shall I assume that you're going to screen a movie in this room, or is this merely going to be a meeting of some sort?

M1: **Does it make a difference?**

M2: Yes, it makes a big difference. Er . . . You're new to this, aren't you?

M1: Um . . . Is it that obvious?

M2: A bit, but don't worry about it. There's a first time for everything. Let me explain why I asked you the question. You see, uh, if you're just going to have a regular meeting, I can assign you any number of empty rooms on campus. However, if you're going to show a movie, you need for the room to have a projector—or a computer if you're showing a DVD—as well as a screen. We've only got a few rooms on campus like that, and they tend to be in high demand. So you might not get the room you're looking for at the time you desire if that's what you're going to be doing.

M1: Ah, I get it. Well, we plan to show a movie, so I guess we're going to need one of those special rooms you mentioned. I hope there's something available. We're going to screen the film this coming Sunday night.

M2: All right. What time are you hoping to do that? Oh, and how long will the movie last?

M1: We'd like to have the room from, um . . . eight to eleven at night would be ideal. How does that sound?

M2: Hold on a second and let me put everything in the computer . . . Huh, you're in luck. It looks like you'll get your choice of two rooms. Why don't I describe each room to you, and then you can tell me which one you prefer?

Answer Explanations

1 Ⓐ At the beginning of the conversation, the student tells the employee, "I'm looking for Ms. Linda Anderson. Would you happen to know where she is? I've got an appointment to see her at three thirty today."

2 Ⓒ About Ms. Anderson, the student remarks, "I'm pleased Ms. Anderson was thoughtful enough to write about me to you even though she's unhealthy," and he also states, "She seems like she's pretty dedicated to her job."

3 Ⓑ At the end of the conversation, the employee tells the student, "Huh, you're in luck. It looks like you'll get your choice of two rooms. Why don't I describe each room to you, and then you can tell me which one you prefer?" So the student will probably select a room to reserve next.

4 Ⓒ When the student asks the employee, "Does it make a difference?" with regard to the type of room he is going to reserve, it can be inferred that the student has never reserved a room for the movie club.

Dictation

1 She seems like she's pretty dedicated to her job.

2 Let me explain why I asked you the question.

3 Why don't I describe each room to you, and then you can tell me which one you prefer?

B

Answers

1 Ⓐ	2 Toothed Whale: 1, 2, 4 Baleen Whale: 3		
3 Ⓑ	4 Ⓓ		

Script

Listen to part of a lecture in a marine biology class.

W Professor: Aside from being the largest creatures on the planet and mammals that live in the ocean, whales are unique in other ways. One of them concerns the sounds they're capable of making. Whales use sounds both for communication and navigation purposes. Have you ever wondered why they use sound . . . ? It's simple. In the water, sound is more useful and effective than both sight and smell. The reason concerns the manner in which water molecules slow down and scatter light and odors yet permit sound to travel at greater speeds than it does in the air.

The way whales produce sound depends upon the species. There are two main types of whales. First are toothed whales such as sperm whales, dolphins, and porpoises. Uh, the last two are considered whales in case you don't know. The second type are baleen whales such as the blue whale. Baleen whales don't have teeth but instead have thick batches of bristle-like barriers in their mouths used to filter out marine life forms from water passing over them.

Okay, so how do whales make sounds . . . ? Toothed whales make clicking sounds with what marine biologists call phonic lips. They aren't real lips, of course, but are sort of like, um, hmm . . . they're sort of like the sinuses we have in our nasal area. The phonic lips are connected to an organ in the whale's forehead. This soft organ is called the melon. It acts in a manner similar to a sonar dome on the underside of a ship. The melon emits clicking sounds through the water in an arc in front of the toothed whale.

As for baleen whales, they produce sound in a simpler manner. They have a larynx which is in the shape of a large sac and can inflate and deflate by the whale contracting muscles in its chest and throat. The larynx sac presses against what's called a vocal fold, uh, a thick U-shaped mass of tissue. When air passes in and out of the larynx sac, it vibrates against the vocal fold and produces sounds. The sounds then leave the whale's body through the slit-like openings on the sides of its head called ventral throat pleats. The pleats are what help the baleen whale expand its mouth when it sucks in lots of water to filter it to find food.

M Student: 🎧4 Which produces louder sounds, toothed whales or baleen whales?

W: **Well, loudness is a subjective way to measure sounds, so it's not particularly good to call one whale's sounds louder than another's.** What we can do, however, is compare their frequency range. That's one thing we know about both types of whales. Baleen whales produce sounds in a lower frequency range than toothed whales. The sounds baleen whales make get only as high as thirty kilohertz whereas the sounds toothed whales make can get as high as 150 kilohertz.

Next, let's explore how whales use their sounds. Toothed whales mainly use them for echolocation, which is a way to navigate underwater. The whales send out bursts of clicks on short wavelengths. These sounds hit objects in the water and bounce back to the whales, just like, uh, just like sonar. That enables them to know what's in the water surrounding them. Toothed whales additionally produce more unique sounds, called whistles by researchers. These whistles are like a toothed whale's signature, and it's believed they use these whistles in pods of other whales to identify one another. Baleen whales, on the other hand, aren't believed to use sounds for echolocation. Instead, researchers speculate that they use sounds mainly to find mates or to communicate with their pod members to get them to change directions or to warn them of danger. But, uh, that's merely a hypothesis. We don't know for sure.

I think now is a good time to play some whale sounds for you so that you can appreciate their beauty. Listen closely to the sounds these whales make . . .

1 Ⓐ During the lecture, the professor compares and contrasts toothed whales and baleen whales.

2 Toothed Whale: ①, ②, ④ Baleen Whale: ③
About the toothed whale, the professor states, "Next, let's explore how whales use their sounds. Toothed whales mainly use them for echolocation, which is a way to navigate underwater," and, "Baleen whales produce sounds in a lower frequency range than toothed whales. The sounds baleen whales make get only as high as thirty kilohertz whereas the sounds toothed whales make can get as high as 150 kilohertz." She also adds, "Toothed whales additionally produce more unique sounds, called whistles by researchers. These whistles are like a toothed whale's signature, and it's believed they use these whistles in pods of other whales to identify one another." Regarding the baleen whale, the professor mentions, "As for baleen whales, they produce sound in a simpler manner. They have a larynx which is in the shape of a large sac and can inflate and deflate by the whale contracting muscles in its chest and throat. The larynx sac presses against what's called a vocal fold, uh, a thick U-shaped mass of tissue. When air passes in and out of the larynx sac, it vibrates against the vocal fold and produces sounds."

3 Ⓑ At the end of the lecture, the professor tells the class, "I think now is a good time to play some whale sounds for you so that you can appreciate their beauty. Listen closely to the sounds these whales make . . ."

4 Ⓓ When the professor makes her response to the student, it can be inferred that she does not like the way that he phrased his question when she remarks, "It's not particularly good to call one whale's sounds louder than another's."

Dictation

1 The way whales produce sound <u>depends upon</u> the species.

2 <u>As for</u> baleen whales, they produce sound in a <u>simpler manner.</u>

3 I think now is a <u>good time to play</u> some whale sounds for you <u>so that you can</u> appreciate their beauty.

Answers

PART 1

1 Ⓑ   2 ①,④   3 Ⓑ   4 Ⓒ   5 Ⓒ

6 Ⓐ   7 ①,③   8 Ⓑ   9 Ⓒ

10 Gene Theory: ②   Reactive Oxygen Theory: ①,③,④

11 Ⓑ   12 Ⓒ   13 Ⓐ   14 Ⓐ-Ⓒ-Ⓓ-Ⓑ

15 ②,③   16 Ⓐ   17 Ⓓ

PART 2

1 Ⓒ   2 Ⓓ   3 Ⓐ   4 Ⓓ   5 Ⓑ

6 Ⓐ   7 Ⓒ   8 Ⓐ   9 Ⓑ   10 Ⓑ

11 Ⓐ

PART 1

Conversation [1–5]

| Script |

Listen to part of a conversation between a student and a professor.

M Professor: Good morning, Rachel. Thank you for agreeing to come here to see me today.

W Student: No problem, Professor Lewis.

M: Um . . . I think I'd better be blunt and just come out and say what's on my mind . . . Rachel, the quality of your work has declined a great deal in the past two months. Are you having trouble understanding the material we're going over in class?

W: No, sir. I comprehend everything you're teaching in all of the lessons.

M: Are you sure about that? I mean, we have homework in every class, but you haven't submitted a homework assignment in, um . . . let me check my files . . . Ah, here it is. It's been six weeks since you've turned in your homework.

W: Yes, I know that.

M: Are you aware that homework counts for twenty percent of your class grade? If you continue this trend of not turning in any homework, the highest grade you'll be able to get in my class will be a C⁺, and that's assuming you get a perfect score on the final exam. I strongly urge you to start doing your homework.

W: Yes, sir. I understand. I'm truly sorry about not doing my homework.

M: Is there something going on that you'd like to discuss with me?

W: Well, to be honest, I haven't really been able to focus on schoolwork this entire semester.

M: Are you sick? Or, uh, do you have a family or financial issue?

W: It's a personal issue involving my parents, but, um, if you don't mind, I'd rather not discuss it. However, I guess I should inform you that I probably won't be here at school next semester, so I guess that's why I've been a bit, er, lax regarding my homework.

M: Ah, okay . . . Well, I won't pry into your personal business, but do you mind if I give you a bit of advice?

W: No, sir. That's fine.

M: First, you should speak with your academic advisor. Out of curiosity, who is your advisor?

W: Professor Kenmore in the Biology Department.

M: Ah, she's a great teacher. I sometimes have lunch with her. Why don't you speak with her about your issues? Now, uh, you don't have to be specific, but she can help you make it through the semester without failing all of your classes.

W: What difference does it make if I'm not planning to come back?

M: Things may change. Perhaps something will happen, and you'll make it back here next semester. Or, uh, maybe you'll return here in a year or two after taking some time off. If that happens, you don't really want to have three or four F's on your transcript, do you?

W: Oh . . . Now that you put it that way, I see your point.

M: That's good. So why don't you talk to her, and then she can start the process of getting you extensions on all your assignments? That will enable you to get caught up with your classes, and you won't be penalized for being late with them. 🎧5 You know, I'm fairly certain Professor Kenmore is in her office right now, so I can call her and see if she has time to speak with you today. How does that sound?

W: **It seems like the right thing to do.**

Answer Explanations

1 Gist-Purpose Question

Ⓑ The professor asks the student, "I think I'd better be blunt and just come out and say what's on my mind . . . Rachel, the quality of your work has declined a great deal in the past two months. Are you having trouble understanding the material we're going over in class?"

2 Detail Question

①, ④ The professor advises the student, "I strongly urge you to start doing your homework." He also adds about the student's advisor, "Why don't you speak with her about your issues? Now, uh, you don't have to be specific, but she can help you make it through the semester without failing all of your classes."

3 Making Inference Question

Ⓑ Regarding Professor Kenmore, the professor comments, "Ah, she's a great teacher. I sometimes have lunch with her." So it can be inferred that Professor Lewis is on good terms with her.

4 Understanding Attitude Question

Ⓒ During the entire conversation, the professor shows that he is very concerned about the well-being of the student.

5 Understanding Attitude Question

Ⓒ When the student responds to the professor's comment by saying, "It seems like the right thing to do," she means that she supports what the professor suggests doing.

Lecture #1 [6-11]

| Script |

Listen to part of a lecture in a physiology class.

M Professor: At some point in all people's lives, their bodies begin aging. Several things happen when people begin the aging process. As examples, um, obviously, their bodies start deteriorating, and the classic signs of aging appear. Those include, um, baldness, the graying of hair, the diminishing of sight and hearing, frailty in the bones and muscles, wrinkles on the skin, and numerous health issues commonly associated with aging, such as dementia, heart disease, and many forms of cancer. Why we age has been studied extensively, especially during the past century, yet the exact mechanism behind aging remains a mystery. We do, however, have some reasonable suppositions about what causes it.

Researchers believe that factors related to genes play a big role in the aging process, and they further believe that the introduction of reactive oxygen species—more commonly known as free radicals—into the body are of vital importance. Both of these factors lead to cell death, which results in the deterioration of the body. Okay, uh, this is going to require a bit of explaining, but I'll try to make it as uncomplicated as possible. To begin, understand that the human body is comprised of trillions of cells, each of which acts differently. For instance, some cells die quickly and get replaced while other cells can survive for decades but don't get replaced when they die. Cells die for a variety of reasons, but, um, for the most part, they're preprogrammed to die early and then to be replaced, or they may suffer some kind of damage, which shortens their lives.

Genes are connected with cell damage, death, and patterns of aging in some groups of people. They are also different in each person, and we pass our genes on to the next generation. Therefore, over time, we can see some patterns of aging and age-related health problems in individual groups, um, such as ethnic groups and families. In some groups, cancer and heart disease are common, in others, dementia happens with great frequency, and in others, early-onset baldness, vision problems, and other signs of aging occur. These are all the results of genes which the members of particular groups have in common.

Some genes have been discovered to cause various types of cancer. The BRCA1 and BRCA2 gene mutations, as an example, cause breast cancer. For almost everyone, gene damage prevents the replication of cells or, um, at least slows down the regenerative process when cells die. Therefore, nearly everyone's body slowly starts deteriorating as gene damage in cells accumulates over time. Why and how genes are damaged are still points of discussion among experts though. Oh, uh, you should also be aware that good genes can increase a person's life span. The gene called FOXO3A is common in people who live to be more than 100 years old. Exactly how this helps them live longer isn't known but is, unsurprisingly, being studied intensively. It's a mystery that many people, myself included, hope is unraveled in the near future.

W Student: Pardon the interruption, Professor Duquesne, but what about diet and exercise? Don't factors such as these play a role in longevity?

M: That's true, especially with regard to diet. Studies done on the diets of people who live long lives show some patterns, such as a greater consumption of fish, vegetables, and fruit than red meat and starchy grains. And, um, interestingly enough, diet and longevity are tied to the reactive oxygen theory of aging. You may have heard this term by a different name since it's frequently called the free radical theory. This theory posits that atoms with missing electrons seek new electrons to achieve balance. Electrons normally orbit the nucleus of an atom in pairs, but sometimes an electron goes missing. Those atoms with missing electrons are known as free radicals. The lone electron seeks an electron from another molecule in order to create a pair again. It does this by pulling an electron off a nearby molecule. This, in turn, creates a new free radical, which then seeks a new electron from another molecule. As you can surmise, this results in a never-ending chain reaction as new free radicals seek electrons. Interestingly enough, this causes damage to the cell which the molecules are part of. The cell may die or, in worse cases, mutate and become cancerous. The free radical chain theory has also been linked to some effects of aging, including the increase of wrinkled skin and the buildup of plaque in arteries, which can lead to heart disease.

There's an entire food industry that has arisen in recent decades on account of this theory. The notion is that we can undo the damage caused by free radicals by ingesting foods like vegetables and fruits that have antioxidant properties. Antioxidants are molecules that can lose an electron yet not become free radicals. Hence they can replace the lost electrons on free radicals without causing the chain reaction leading to cell death, faster aging, and potentially fatal diseases.

6 Gist-Content Question

Ⓐ The lecture is mostly about some of the possible causes of aging in humans.

7 Detail Question

1, 3 The professor lectures, "Genes are connected with cell damage, death, and patterns of aging in some groups of people. They are also different in each person, and we pass our genes on to the next generation. Therefore, over time, we can see some patterns of aging and age-related health problems in individual groups, um, such as ethnic groups and families. In some groups, cancer and heart disease are common, in others, dementia happens with great frequency, and in others, early onset baldness, vision problems, and other signs of aging occur."

8 Connecting Content Question

Ⓑ The professor states, "Some genes have been discovered to cause various types of cancer. The BRCA1 and BRCA2 gene mutations, as an example, cause breast cancer." So a person with the BRCA1 gene will likely get a type of cancer.

9 Understanding Organization Question

Ⓒ The professor expresses her hope that the research on the FOXO3A gene will be successful in commenting, "The gene called FOXO3A is common in people who live to be more than 100 years old. Exactly how this helps them live longer isn't known but is, unsurprisingly, being studied intensively. It's a mystery that many people, myself included, hope is unraveled in the near future."

10 Connecting Content Question

Gene Theory: 2 Reactive Oxygen Theory: 1, 3, 4
About the gene theory, the professor notes, "Genes are connected with cell damage, death, and patterns of aging in some groups of people. They are also different in each person, and we pass our genes on to the next generation. Therefore, over time, we can see some patterns of aging and age-related health problems in individual groups, um, such as ethnic groups and families. Regarding the reactive oxygen theory, the professor remarks, "You may have heard this term by a different name since it's frequently called the free radical theory." The professor also states, "This theory posits that atoms with missing electrons seek new electrons to achieve balance. Electrons normally orbit the nucleus of an atom in pairs, but sometimes an electron goes missing. Those atoms with missing electrons are known as free radicals. The lone electron seeks an electron from another molecule in order to create a pair again. It does this by pulling an electron off a nearby molecule. This, in turn, creates a new free radical, which then seeks a new electron from another molecule. As you can surmise, this results in a never-ending chain reaction as new free radicals seek electrons." The professor then adds, "The free radical chain theory has also been linked to some effects of aging, including the increase of wrinkled skin and the buildup of plaque in arteries, which can lead to heart disease."

11 Understanding Organization Question

Ⓑ The professor focuses on the relationship of the food industry with the reactive oxygen theory in saying, "There's an entire food industry that has arisen in recent decades on account of this theory. The notion is that we can undo the damage caused by free radicals by ingesting foods like vegetables and fruits that have antioxidant properties. Antioxidants are molecules that can lose an electron yet not become free radicals. Hence they can replace the lost electrons on free radicals without causing the chain reaction leading to cell death, faster aging, and potentially fatal diseases."

Lecture #2 [12–17]

| Script |

Listen to part of a lecture in a performing arts class.

W Professor: Before we delve into modern theater, I think it would be best if we were to discuss the roots of theater first. Just so you know, I'm only going to focus on theater in the Western world. Both the Eastern world and Africa have rich and extensive histories of their own when it comes to theater; nevertheless, they had very little influence on Western theater until modern times. And, uh, to be clear, when I say Western theater, I'm referring to that which developed and evolved over time in Europe and the Americas.

The starting point for the history of Western theater is Greece. Theater in the ancient world is believed to have begun as an offshoot of festivals. You see, in many ancient societies, there were festivals for various occasions. Most were related to specific gods, and music and dancing were typically integral to them. Costumes and masks were additionally worn during some religious festivals, and the festivals included rituals which were performed by priests while the audience looked on as spectators. So, as you can see, those were the two sides to any theatrical performance: the performers and the spectators.

In Greece, one such festival was held in honor of Dionysus, the god of fertility and wine. By the sixth century B.C., the festival for Dionysus had taken on a structured form as singers and dancers related stories from Greek mythology. These individuals became the first chorus in theatrical history. One priest of Dionysus, a man named Thespis, started the tradition of interacting with the chorus by speaking to them in plain language, uh, that is, by engaging them in dialogue. In effect, he became the first actor on a stage, so today we call our actors thespians in honor of Thespis. The Greek tradition of theater was thusly born with its two main elements:

the actor on stage and the chorus. Thespis and others like him started staging theatrical competitions during the festival of Dionysus, and from them arose the first of the Greek theatrical styles, which was tragedy. Here's an interesting tidbit of information for you . . . In 534 B.C., Thespis was given an award for his performance at one of these competitions, so I guess you can say he was the first best actor award winner in history.

At that time, Greek plays consisted only of one actor and the chorus. By the early fifth century B.C., another of the great Greek actors and playwrights, named Aeschylus, expanded the concept of the stage performance by adding a second actor. A later innovation by the playwright Sophocles added a third actor, thereby allowing for even more diversity in stage performances. In the fifth century B.C., Euripides emerged as a noted playwright of Greek tragedies. Of all the great Greek writers, more of his works—nineteen in all—have survived to this day while we only have a handful of the works of others. It was around that time that comedy began to be a part of the competitions at festivals. The first great comedic playwright was Aristophanes. The Greeks also designed the common theater structure, the amphitheater, with its rising tiers of benches or seats with the stage in front of the spectators, a style still utilized in modern-day theaters around the world.

Greek culture spread far and wide throughout the Mediterranean region, and elements of their theater followed them. One place they colonized was Italy, and that had a profound influence on the future history of theater in the Western world. The Romans went on to conquer all of Italy and Greece itself, but that happened after they had already been influenced by many aspects of Greek culture, including theater. There were, of course, many differences. Um, let's see . . . The Romans preferred comedies to tragedies, and they also allowed women to appear on stage, um, something the Greeks did not permit to happen.

🎧17 As I hope you all know, the Romans conquered much of the land that comprises modern-day Europe. As a result, aspects of Roman theater accompanied them elsewhere. **However, after the fall of Rome in the fifth century, the Christian church came to dominate Europe, and it frowned upon theatrical performances.**

M Student: Wait a minute. In Professor Rudolph's medieval English literature class, we learned about some of the miracle plays that were performed during Easter service. Don't those count as theatrical performances? I'm pretty sure they do.

W: Ah, yes, Paul, that was an exception. Just in case you don't know, class, Paul is referring to how churches in the Middle Ages would stage plays about the events involved in the death and resurrection of Jesus Christ. While these miracle plays, as they were called, were quite popular, of more importance were the traveling performance

troupes that could be found throughout Europe. They were crucial because they preserved the traditions of theater from Greece and Rome, uh, albeit in a different form. They performed a wide variety of acts, including singing, storytelling, music, and juggling. It wasn't until the Renaissance, when there was a revival of Greek and Roman theater in Italy and other places, that there was a true return to the roots of traditional theater. Let me talk for a bit about that now . . .

Answer Explanations

12 Gist-Content Question

Ⓒ The professor focuses on the origin of the theater as well as its early years in her lecture.

13 Understanding Organization Question

Ⓐ The professor talks about the contributions to the development of theater there were made by Thespis when she covers him.

14 Connecting Content Question

Ⓐ–Ⓒ–Ⓓ–Ⓑ Regarding the development of the theater, the professor first states, "The starting point for the history of Western theater is Greece. Theater in the ancient world is believed to have begun as an offshoot of festivals." Then, she mentions, "By the sixth century B.C., the festival for Dionysus had taken on a structured form as singers and dancers related stories from Greek mythology. These individuals became the first chorus in theatrical history." Next, she says, "By the early fifth century B.C., another of the great Greek actors and playwrights, named Aeschylus, expanded the concept of the stage performance by adding a second actor." Last, she notes, "It was around that time that comedy began to be a part of the competitions at festivals. The first great comedic playwright was Aristophanes."

15 Detail Question

②, ③ The professor remarks, "The Romans preferred comedies to tragedies, and they also allowed women to appear on stage, um, something the Greeks did not permit to happen."

16 Understanding Attitude Question

Ⓐ The professor tells the class, "While these miracle plays, as they were called, were quite popular, of more importance were the traveling performance troupes that could be found throughout Europe."

17 Understanding Attitude Question

Ⓓ When the professor says, "However, after the fall of Rome in the fifth century, the Christian church came to dominate Europe, and it frowned upon theatrical performances," she means that the Christian church did not like theatrical performances.

PART 2

| Script |

Listen to part of a conversation between a student and a librarian.

M Student: Good evening. I'm supposed to write a report for a class, but I'm not sure how to find any of the books I need.

W Librarian: Okay. If you could give me a bit of information about what you're planning to write on, I can lend you a hand. What's your topic?

M: Uh, basically, my professor told the class we should research mathematical knowledge from ancient times and then choose a couple of mathematicians and write about their accomplishments.

W: Okay. Do you have any particular mathematicians in mind?

M: I'm completely lost. I don't think I can even name a single mathematician from the past.

W: All right. Then it looks like you'll be starting from scratch. The first book I can recommend to you is A *Comprehensive History of Mathematics and Mathematicians*. It contains information on virtually every single mathematician of note from cultures around the world. 🎧5 If you look through this book, you'll be able to determine which individuals you can write about.

M: *A Comprehensive History of Mathematics and Mathematicians* sounds like it's precisely the book that I need. Do you know where on the shelves it is so that I can check it out?

W: **Actually, it's a reference book.**

M: Oh, I see. How big is it?

W: It's more than 1,000 pages long. I suggest looking through the book here since you can't borrow it and then making copies of some of the pages you find to be of particular interest.

M: Are there any other books on math and mathematicians that you think would be useful and which I actually can check out?

W: Sure. There are plenty. But first, why don't you tell me if you have a particular region or time period in mind? That way, we can narrow down our search for the appropriate books.

M: Okay. I guess I'd be the most interested in some mathematicians who lived during the time of ancient Greece. I'm currently taking a class in the ancient Greek language, and that's kind of cool, so it might be nice to learn about some mathematicians who lived then.

W: That's a good choice. We have plenty of books on them. Let me think . . . *Ancient Greek Mathematicians* by David Cornwall is one. So are *Math in Ancient Times* and *A Guide to Greek Mathematicians*.

M: You really seem to know all of these books.

W: Well, I am the science and math librarian here, so it's my job to know which books we have and which ones students might be interested in. You know, most of the books on Greek mathematicians are located in the same place in the stacks, so why don't you follow me upstairs to them, and I can show you where they are?

M: Wonderful. Oh, uh, what should I do if any of these books are already checked out?

W: You have a couple of options. You can buy them from an online bookstore. That could get a bit expensive though, uh, even if you purchase e-books. Or you can request them through interlibrary loan. That won't cost you a thing.

M: How long will it take to get books through interlibrary loan?

W: It depends. You can get popular books in three or four days. If you want something more esoteric, it could take longer.

Answer Explanations

1 Gist-Content Question

Ⓒ After the student explains the project he is working on, he mentions, "I'm completely lost." So he does not know how to start his research project.

2 Understanding Attitude Question

Ⓓ After the librarian names some books that might be helpful, the student comments, "You really seem to know all of these books."

3 Gist-Purpose Question

Ⓐ About interlibrary loan, the librarian states, "Or you can request them through interlibrary loan. That won't cost you a thing."

4 Making Inferences Question

Ⓓ The librarian tells the student, "You know, most of the books on Greek mathematicians are located in the same place in the stacks, so why don't you follow me upstairs to them, and I can show you where they are?" So she will probably show the student where some books are located.

5 Understanding Function Question

Ⓑ When the librarian says, "Actually, it's a reference book," when talking about a certain book, she is implying that the student cannot borrow the book.

| Script |

Listen to part of a lecture in an environmental science class.

M Professor: The word plastic comes from the Greek language and means to be malleable and easily shaped, which is precisely what plastics are: substances that can be shaped into many different forms. As a result, we can find plastics virtually everywhere nowadays. They're mainly used to make containers and for packaging, but we can also find plastics in countless industries, where they're utilized to make, uh, let's see . . . clothing, parts of cars and airplanes, furniture, toys, games, and, uh . . . Well, you get the idea.

Let me tell you about the science behind plastics. They're a type of polymer, which is a substance that's made of long chains of cells. In nature, we can find polymers in plants. Cellulose, for example, is a polymer that makes up the walls of plant cells. The long polymer chains in plastics can easily slide past one another, which allows them to assume many shapes. One can imagine plastics being made of cell chains that are like long, cold pasta noodles that slide together easily. The first polymers that could be used to make things were found in nature. For instance, rubber is formed when resin secreted by rubber trees is collected and processed. When treated in a process called vulcanization, it becomes hardened but still retains the ability to change its shape without breaking. Rubber therefore has similar properties as plastics.

The first modern plastics also came from nature. In 1862, at an exhibit in London, England, British scientist Alexander Parkes presented a material he called Parkesine. He made the substance from cellulose that he had bathed in nitric acid. He then added pigments to give it color. When heated, Parkesine could be shaped into various forms. Unfortunately, while Parkes was a good scientist, he was not good at conducting business, and his product was quickly copied by an American company. It made some changes to Parkesine, and in 1870, the company released a new product called celluloid, which was later used to make film for cameras.

Other people in different countries attempted to make plastics, but most failed to provide any durable and malleable substances. Then, in 1907, came the first modern plastic, called Bakelite. It was created by American Leo Baekeland. His key breakthrough was to avoid using plant cellulose and instead to make his plastic from petrochemicals. So I guess we can call Bakelite the first synthetic polymer since he didn't use a substance from nature. Baekeland used phenol, which is an acid that he acquired from coal tar. Bakelite was useful in electronic products because it was heat resistant. It became a commercial success, and this opened the floodgates to new ways to make plastics. By the 1940s, there were polystyrene, polyester, nylon, and PVC, which is commonly used in pipes for plumbing. Today, there are even more types of plastics, most of which are derived from petrochemicals.

During World War Two in the 1940s, the plastics industry found ways to make many useful products for the military. By the 1950s, plastics were everywhere. They were mainly used to make clothing, packing materials, and commercial household products. And because plastics were much cheaper than glass, we began seeing the widespread use of plastics in water, juice, and soda bottles while glass usage declined. And that's when we started getting in trouble.

W Student: Getting in trouble? What do you mean by that?

M: Well, we made plastics so useful and strong and virtually indestructible that they started becoming a problem. Most people use plastic products such as water bottles once and then throw them away. But plastics can last for thousands of years without breaking down to their base components. Today, plastic pollution is everywhere. Landfills are full of plastic products, and there are massive patches of plastic garbage floating in the oceans.

W: But we recycle plastics, too. Don't you think that recycling will help solve the problem?

M: Recycling helps but isn't perfect. Recycling plastics is a difficult process, and the cost benefit is very low. Additionally, newly recycled plastics have structural weaknesses, so more plastic must be added to them. One estimate I saw is that only about ten to twenty percent of all plastics are recycled, so there's plenty of room for improvement.

The solution to our plastic problem may be found elsewhere. Scientists are working on making substances that can easily dissolve plastics. In one big breakthrough, Japanese researchers discovered a bacterium that can eat away at plastics. Then, scientists at a university in Britain found a way to make the bacterium the Japanese found into an enzyme which can dissolve plastics twenty percent faster. One drawback is that the enzyme only works on a form of plastic called PET. That's good news since most plastic bottles are made from PET, but with luck, ongoing research will find a way to make the enzyme viable for large-scale usage.

Answer Explanations

6 **Gist-Content Question**

Ⓐ During his lecture, the professor focuses mainly on the development of plastics over time.

7 **Understanding Organization Question**

Ⓒ The professor makes a comparison in stating, "The long polymer chains in plastics can easily slide past one another, which allows them to assume many shapes. One can imagine plastics being made of cell chains that are like long, cold pasta noodles that slide together easily."

8 **Understanding Attitude Question**

Ⓐ About Alexander Parkes, the professor remarks, "Unfortunately, while Parkes was a good scientist, he was not good at conducting business, and his product was quickly copied by an American company."

9 **Detail Question**

Ⓑ The professor tells the class, "His key breakthrough

was to avoid using plant cellulose and instead to make his plastic from petrochemicals. So I guess we can call Bakelite the first synthetic polymer since he didn't use a substance from nature."

10 Connecting Content Question

Ⓑ The professor states, "And because plastics were much cheaper than glass, we began seeing the widespread use of plastics in water, juice, and soda bottles while glass usage declined." Then, he adds, "Well, we made plastics so useful and strong and virtually indestructible that they started becoming a problem. Most people use plastic products such as water bottles once and then throw them away. But plastics can last for thousands of years without breaking down to their base components."

11 **Detail Question**

Ⓐ The professor comments, "In one big breakthrough, Japanese researchers discovered a bacterium that can eat away at plastics. Then, scientists at a university in Britain found a way to make the bacterium the Japanese found into an enzyme which can dissolve plastics twenty percent faster."

| Vocabulary Review

p. 142

Answers

A
1 astounded   2 esoteric   3 emit
4 surmise   5 malleable

B
1 b   2 a   3 b   4 b   5 a
6 b   7 a   8 b   9 a   10 b

Practice with Short Passages
p. 146

A

| Answers | 1 ⓒ | 2 Ⓐ |

| Script |

Listen to part of a lecture in an art class.

W1 Professor: When the camera was invented in the mid-nineteenth century, an entirely new way of visualizing the world came about. Photographs captured the realism of people, the land, and the objects people used. Over time, painters began aping the manner in which the camera worked by adding more elements of realism to their work. And photography itself began to take on an artistic aspect. This resulted in a debate, um, one that is still ongoing, regarding whether or not photography is an actual art. Sally? You have something to add?

W2 Student: Well, of course it's art. Who could possibly think differently?

W1: To be honest, lots of people would. But, um, let's hold off on the argument that it's not art for a moment and consider photography as if it were art. The main argument for it being art is rather simple. A photograph, like a painting, is a visual representation of the world around us. Much like a painter does, a photographer uses tools. A painter utilizes canvas, an easel, and paint whereas a photographer utilizes a camera and film. By adjusting their tools, both can create different visual effects, thereby enhancing the way their work is seen. Hence a photograph is art on an equal standing as a painting or drawing. A second argument is that what is art is in the eye of the beholder, so each person can decide whether a photograph is art or not.

What about the arguments against it . . . ? Well, the primary one is that a camera is a machine, and a camera simply can't create art. You see, there's a, um, a kind of disconnect between the person operating the camera and the subject matter. Yes, the photographer may set the lighting or set the camera's operating functions, but, in the end, it's the film itself or the digital magic that produces the actual photograph. A true artist, the argument goes, has a brush or pencil in hand and employs his skill with it to create art. It's not just traditional artists who think this way. At the beginning of the debate, photographers themselves wanted to be separate from artists. At a meeting of the Photographic Society of London in 1853, it was argued that photographs were too literal in their interpretations of the world and therefore couldn't elevate a person's imagination to a point where they could be considered art.

And for the most part, at its inception, photography was primarily utilitarian as it was used to take portraits, to capture scenes in nature, and to record historical events. It wasn't until the twentieth century that it started moving toward a more artistic bent. In the 1960s and 1970s, photography galleries grew in popularity, but even then, photography was considered a niche form of art that hadn't been accepted by the mainstream public. In some ways, I understand this attitude. Your mother's old snapshots of your fifth birthday party surely can't be considered art. Nevertheless, there's a wide body of excellent work, such as that by Ansel Adams, which makes you stop, stare, and appreciate the finer qualities of photography.

M Student: Aren't we perilously close to the debate regarding what the definition of art is?

W1: That's correct. What is art . . . ? Are movies and comic books art . . . ? How about writing . . . ? Some may say yes while others may say that only paintings and sculptures are art. As for me, I say that if something grabs your attention and moves you at a deeper level, then it must be art no matter what the medium.

Answer Explanations

1 ⓒ About Ansel Adams, the professor remarks, "Nevertheless, there's a wide body of excellent work, such as that by Ansel Adams, which makes you stop, stare, and appreciate the finer qualities of photography."

2 Ⓐ During the lecture, the professor first explains why photography can be considered art, and then she discusses some reasons why it should not be considered art.

B

| Answers | 1 Ⓑ | 2 Ⓑ |

| Script |

Listen to part of a lecture in an environmental science class.

M Professor: Okay, now that we've gone over the syllabus, it's time to begin this semester's class on climatology. I think the best thing for me to do would be to define what it is that we climatologists do. Climatology is the study of weather patterns over a long period of time. Through this study, climatologists hope to gain insight into the normal climate of a region. By understanding it, we can then understand when changes occur and therefore provide warnings to people about any coming changes. For example, knowing if an early frost is going to happen can help farmers avoid crop damage, or, uh, if it's likely that an unseasonable snowstorm is going to hit an area, we can let people know so that they'll have time to prepare for it.

It's also used for other purposes. Let's see . . . If you've ever traveled anywhere, one of the first things you likely did before leaving was check out the local climate. It's usually expressed in two ways: the temperature and the amount of precipitation. The charts used in most guidebooks and on websites are based on information gathered by global weather services over decades. These charts show monthly temperature highs and lows as well as the average precipitation per month. So you can find out when to avoid certain places and when to visit others based on the local climate.

W Student: How do climatologists collect all this data?

M: Climate patterns are mainly understood through the examination of historical records and present-day observations. Let's use the United States as an example. Its National Weather Service has hundreds of weather stations around the country. It has been collecting data ever since it was founded in 1870. There are also thousands of volunteer weather observers who submit whatever data they collect. Each day, these people observe the weather conditions and take records on things such as the high, low, and average temperatures, the humidity, the dew point, the atmospheric pressure, wind speed, precipitation amounts and types, and the condition of the sky, uh, such as the amount and type of cloud cover. This data gets collected and is then used by the National Weather Service to create weather maps, um, like the ones you see on TV and in the newspaper, and to make weather forecasts. It's also used to create an accurate picture of the normal climate in a region.

Three more ways we collect data are by making observations on the oceans, by collecting data in the upper atmosphere, and by using radar and satellites. On the oceans, ships collect data on weather conditions and transmit it to weather centers around the world. These reports let us construct weather maps of oceanic conditions, which are useful to fishermen and sailors since they can be used to forecast approaching storms. In the upper atmosphere, data on the temperature, humidity, and air pressure is collected, primarily by sending aloft instruments attached to weather balloons. When a balloon reaches a certain height, it bursts, and a parachute helps the instrument package float back down to the ground. Radar is used to find bands of rain and snow and, uh, even more importantly, to determine where tornadoes might develop. And satellite images can help us see where large storms are developing, especially hurricanes on the oceans.

C

| Script |

Listen to part of a lecture in an anthropology class.

M1 Professor: New Guinea is a large island in the southwestern part of the Pacific Ocean and is located north of Australia. It's one of the biggest islands in the world, and it's also one of the most primitive. Except for its coastline, it's extremely mountainous and is covered in dense jungle growth. These factors made New Guinea rather hard for European explorers to examine since they couldn't explore the deep interior until aircraft were invented, allowing people to fly over the island in the early twentieth century. What they saw then astonished them, for deep in the island's interior was a vast population of natives living in societies that hadn't had any contact with the outside world for thousands of years. Even today, many of the island's natives live in extremely primitive conditions compared to the rest of the world.

Due to the rugged terrain, the natives are not only isolated from the outside world but are also kept apart from one another. This has led to hundreds of languages developing over time, so the people in one valley frequently cannot communicate with the people in the next valley. It's estimated that there are more than 700 tribes in New Guinea, and those are just the ones we know about. There may be even more in the island's thick jungles.

For the most part, the natives of New Guinea are farmers living in small tribal groups. They plant crops such as yams and taro in valleys and on hillsides and also hunt and fish. They gather bananas and other fruits, and they make a starchy food called sago from palm trees. Some raise pigs, but that's not too common, and there's a relative lack of domesticated animals. Most people live in huts made from wood, but some tribes, such as the Korowai, build huts in trees very high above the jungle floor. Along rivers and swamps, tribes erect their huts on stilts to avoid flooding. Tribes are usually male-dominated societies, and they have some aspects of religion. The economy is typically subsistence based, but some tribes make handicrafts which they trade with other tribes or with outsiders.

M2 Student: Is there a difference between the highland people and the coastal people?

M1: There is a huge difference because the coastal people are more in touch with the modern world. In big coastal towns such as Port Moresby, there are cars, TVs, phones, electricity, and other trappings of modern life. Many people along the coast and along some rivers in the interior have been in contact with Western missionaries, so some of them speak Western languages. They tend to be more accepting of outsiders. But, um, that's not always the case in the interior.

M2: I've heard that lots of those isolated tribes are cannibals. That can't possibly be true, can it?

M1: Well . . . it was quite common in the past. In case you're curious, cannibalism was practiced due to the lack of protein in many natives' diets. You see, the interior has few large animals that can be hunted for meat. So people ate, well, they ate other people. That also caused warfare between tribes since murdering someone to eat that person would set off years of warfare between rival tribes. Nowadays, many tribes state that they have abandoned cannibalism, but some anthropologists are doubtful of their claims. As for what's happening deep in the jungles, who knows?

Answer Explanations

1 Ⓐ The professor comments, "Most people live in huts made from wood, but some tribes, such as the Korowai, build huts in trees very high above the jungle floor."

2 Ⓑ The student asks a question about cannibalism, so that is the reason the professor discusses it.

D

Answers   1 Ⓐ   2 Ⓓ

| Script |

Listen to part of a lecture in a zoology class.

W Professor: The life cycles of insects vary from species to species, but almost all insects start their lives as eggs. The eggs hatch, and then, in various stages, the insects grow to become adults, whereupon they can then mate and reproduce. To get to the adult stage, insects go through a process called metamorphosis, which basically means that their bodies change. How they change depends on the insect. Entomologists divide insects into three basic types based upon their process of metamorphosis. Insects exhibiting very little change are ametabolous, those which undergo gradual or partial changes are hemimetabolous, and those insects which completely change are holometabolous. Oh, yeah, if you want to know how to spell those words, please take a look at the second page of the handout I gave you at the start of class.

Ametabolous insects exhibit virtually no changes from the egg to the adult stage. Basically, these insects look like miniature versions of adults once they hatch. Over time,

they eat, molt, uh, which means they shed their skin, and get bigger, but there are no major distinctive changes in their body structures as they become adults. Examples of these insects are the silverfish, firebrat, and springtail. By the way, the silverfish is not a fish but a small, wingless insect that's silvery in color and sort of moves around like a fish by wriggling its body, so that's how it acquired its name. As a general rule, ametabolous insects are small, lack wings, and have simple body structures.

The second type, um, hemimetabolous insects, go through three distinct stages in their lives: egg, nymph, and adult. The insects enter the nymph stage as soon as they hatch. The nymphs look similar to the adult versions yet are not identical. They eat, grow, molt, and finally become adults. The most common change for these types of insects is that the adult versions have wings, which emerge when the nymphs molt and grow bigger. Nymphs share nearly all the same characteristics as adults of their species, live in the same habitats, and eat the same foods, but they have no wings and cannot reproduce. Examples of hemimetabolous insects are grasshoppers, termites, and cockroaches.

M Student: Pardon me for the interruption, but isn't this type of metamorphosis sometimes called incomplete metamorphosis? I remember reading that somewhere.

W: Yes, that's correct. Some entomologists use that term, but I think it's misleading. The word incomplete suggests that metamorphosis has been arrested in midstride, which isn't the case at all. So I'd rather that we avoid the term in this class. All right . . . ? Thanks.

The third type of metamorphosis is likely the most familiar to all of you since butterflies and many other insects go through it. It's holometabolous, which typically has four stages: egg, larva, pupa, and adult. Let's see what happens . . . First, larvae hatch from their eggs and then begin eating a great deal, whereupon they grow bigger. At some point in their lives, they form cocoons around their bodies and enter the pupa stage. During it, the larvae undergo a great transformation. Think about butterflies as an example. In their pupa stage, they develop wings and grow much larger. Then, when they become adults, they burst from their cocoons and appear much different than they were in their pupa stage. Moths, ants, bees, flies, and beetles are all types of holometabolous insects.

Answer Explanations

1 Ⓐ While discusses holometabolous metamorphosis, the professor states, "Think about butterflies as an example. In their pupa stage, they develop wings and grow much larger. Then, when they become adults, they burst from their cocoons and appear much different than they were in their pupa stage."

2 Ⓓ During her lecture, the professor goes into detail about each of the three different kinds of metamorphosis.

Practice with Long Passages

A

Answers   1 Ⓑ   2 Ⓑ, Ⓒ   3 Ⓐ   4 Ⓒ

| Script |

Listen to part of a lecture in a zoology class.

M Professor: The term megafauna refers to the group of animals which are larger than humans are. This term refers not just to animals alive today but to those that lived in the past but are presently extinct, too. In modern times, there are numerous examples of megafauna . . . Let's see, um, the elephant, the rhino, the whale, the big cats, the bear, the moose, and many others. There are also countless examples of megafauna that lived thousands of years ago but went extinct. Among them are the saber-toothed tiger, the giant sloth, the giant beaver, the mammoth, and, um, in more recent times, the auroch and moa, a bird that once dwelled in New Zealand. We're not positive why all of these species vanished, especially for ones that died out in the distant past. We do, however, have many theories, two of which have more adherents than the others. They are climate change and human hunting.

I want to discuss the climate change theory with you for a bit. Climate change has occurred all around the world at various times in the past. Some changes were quite dramatic when they happened during ice ages. One theory states that lots of megafauna evolved during ice ages, when they thrived, um, but when the ice ages ended, the conditions that had allowed them to exist were suddenly gone. For example, the mammoths, which dwelled on the tundra in the Northern Hemisphere, had little competition for food when the glaciers were advancing. When the glaciers started receding though, the southern lands became filled with life, and large herds of deer, elk, and reindeer began consuming a great amount of the vegetation, which likely affected the mammoth's food supply, therefore causing it to starve. Climate change also caused once-fertile lands in North Africa and Australia to turn arid and to transform into deserts, and that certainly caused the extinction of some species of megafauna. These changing conditions may have also altered the nature of the plants and animals which the megafauna relied on for sustenance, so, um, perhaps their food supplies gradually disappeared, and they couldn't adapt quickly enough to avoid dying out.

The second theory, uh, that human hunters caused the extinction of many megafauna, has numerous supporters. One reason is that there's ample physical evidence for this. Massive pits with huge collections of megafauna bones have been found around the world. The bones have spear nicks and human teeth marks. It's additionally clear from the patterns of human migration why these huge beasts fell prey to small humans. Megafauna that had lived in isolation for tens of thousands of years were suddenly confronted with skilled hunters. This most certainly happened in the Americas, Australia, New Zealand, and northern Siberia. Facing humans, the megafauna didn't know what these unfamiliar creatures were and failed to flee since their instincts didn't indicate that humans were dangerous, so they were easily hunted.

And, um, if you think about it, it was the ice ages that caused sea levels to drop, thereby forming land bridges allowing humans to cross into the Americas and other lands, at which point they began hunting the megafauna. Thus climate change and human hunting jointly factored into the demise of some megafauna.

W Student: Which would you say had a greater effect?

M: It depends on the animal mostly. Let's take the moa as an example. It was a four-meter-high bird that weighed more than 200 kilograms. Having no wings, it was flightless. Polynesian seafarers, the ancestors of today's Maori people, landed in New Zealand around the year 1300 and started hunting the bird. By 1450, the moa was gone. Maori oral histories tell of great hunts during which hundreds of moa were easily killed and then subsequently cooked and eaten at feasts. Basically, the moa had no fear of humans, and that cost them their lives. So I'd say that the moa went extinct due to human hunting. But what about a megafauna that probably went extinct on account of climate change? Here's an example of one . . .

Answer Explanations

1 Ⓑ The professor focuses on the reasons that megafauna went extinct in the past.

2 Ⓑ, Ⓒ The professor comments, "For example, the mammoths, which dwelled on the tundra in the Northern Hemisphere, had little competition for food when the glaciers were advancing. When the glaciers started receding though, the southern lands became filled with life, and large herds of deer, elk, and reindeer began consuming a great amount of the vegetation, which likely affected the mammoth's food supply, therefore causing it to starve. Climate change also caused once-fertile lands in North Africa and Australia to turn arid and to transform into deserts, and that certainly caused the extinction of some species of megafauna."

3 Ⓐ In talking about human hunters and the fact that they made some megafauna go extinct, the professor implies that they were able successfully to hunt animals much larger than they were.

4 Ⓒ About the moa, the professor states, "So I'd say that the moa went extinct due to human hunting."

B

| Script |

Listen to part of a lecture in an archaeology class.

W Professor: Prior to the Roman invasion of Britain in the year 43 A.D., most of England was peopled by a group we call the Celtic Britons. They arrived in England from mainland Europe in the middle of the British Iron Age, which happened sometime around 500 B.C. Following the Roman invasion and later Anglo-Saxon invasions, the Celtic Britons were mostly assimilated. Nonetheless, we still know about them, mostly from the roughly 100 archaeological sites scattered around the country as well as the artifacts that have been excavated at them.

Celtic Briton settlements were characterized by the development of hill forts surrounded by cultivated farmland. These were forts constructed mainly of earth and wood that were placed on high hills and surrounded by ramparts and ditches. Many artifacts found at these hill forts are related to daily living and warfare, but there have also been some works of an artistic nature unearthed. Some of the items found include, hmm . . . let's see . . . carved stone statues, tankards for drinking, mirrors, spoons, buckets, cauldrons, armlets, torcs, horse bits, pins, bolts, shields, armor, swords, and daggers.

Most of these artifacts are made of stone, bronze, iron, or gold. The Celtic Britons' workmanship shows signs of influence from mainland Europe, and there's ample evidence of cultural diffusion in their artifacts. The Britons are known to have copied the common European Iron Age style known as La Tène culture. It, um, it dates from around 450 B.C. In case you're wondering, this culture is named after La Tène, a village in Switzerland that yielded a veritable treasure trove of artifacts in the mid-nineteenth century. This culture was once widespread throughout both Europe and parts of England and is commonly thought to have evolved from the Hallstatt culture that preceded it.

Take a look at this item up on the screen . . . It's a mirror found near Desborough in Northampton, called, appropriately enough, the Desborough Mirror, and dates back to the first century B.C. Note the intricate spiral patterns on the back . . . that are characteristic of the La Tène style. Putting such intricate designs on a simple device such as a mirror must have required both a considerable amount of time and great skill. It also gives us some insight into the higher levels of culture of the Celtic people, whom the Romans later tried to depict as uncivilized barbarians. Here's another example for you . . . It's a large bronze shield known as the Battersea Shield. It was discovered in London in the Thames River mud and has been dated back to 350 B.C. Again, um, note the La Tène influence as there are spiral patterns on the three sections. A shield such as this was likely owned by a powerful chieftain or elite warrior who might have died in the river. Or, um, perhaps it was cast into the river as an offering to their gods. Without written proof, we can't be positive.

M Student: Since they made shields with bronze, did they use bronze to make their swords as well? Or did they make them with another metal?

W: By the time of the La Tène culture, most of the people living in Europe and England had switched to iron weapons. Most of the artifacts found at the La Tène site were weapons, including a large haul of Iron Age swords. There were two main types of swords used. They were the long sword and the short sword. 🎧4 In the northern parts of Europe, the long sword was the dominant weapon of choice while the short sword prevailed in southern areas.

M: Why is that?

W: **The reason has been debated endlessly.** A widely accepted theory is that the more loosely organized Celtic people preferred open warfare, which favored individual combat using long swords. The Romans and Greeks to the south favored fighting in units such as the phalanx and legion, where the short sword was more practical in tightly packed fighting units. Okay, um, since we're talking about swords, let me show you a few images of swords that have been excavated in England.

Answer Explanations

1 Ⓒ The professor points out, "Celtic Briton settlements were characterized by the development of hill forts surrounded by cultivated farmland. These were forts constructed mainly of earth and wood that were placed on high hills and surrounded by ramparts and ditches. Many artifacts found at these hill forts are related to daily living and warfare, but there have also been some works of an artistic nature unearthed."

2 Ⓐ The professor says, "It's a mirror found near Desborough in Northampton, called, appropriately enough, the Desborough Mirror, and dates back to the first century B.C. Note the intricate spiral patterns on the back . . . that are characteristic of the La Tène style." Then, the professor adds, "It's a large bronze shield known as the Battersea Shield. It was discovered in London in the Thames River mud and has been dated back to 350 B.C. Again, um, note the La Tène influence

as there are spiral patterns on the three sections."

3 (D) The professor organizes the lecture by describing some of the Celtic Briton artifacts that have been found.

4 (D) When the professor says, "The reason has been debated endlessly," it can be inferred that there is not a definite answer to the student's question since people are still apparently debating the answer.

Dictation

1 It also <u>gives</u> us some <u>insight into</u> the higher levels of culture of the Celtic people.

2 A <u>widely accepted theory</u> is that the more loosely organized Celtic people preferred open warfare.

3 <u>Let me show you</u> a few images of swords that have been excavated in England.

iBT Practice Test

p. 154

Answers

PART 1

1 2, 4 2 (B) 3 (D) 4 (A) 5 (B)
6 (A) 7 (C) 8 (A)
9 Fact: 1, 3, 4 Not a Fact: 2 10 (B) 11 (D)
12 (D) 13 (D) 14 (B) 15 (B) 16 (C)
17 (B)

PART 2

1 (B) 2 (A) 3 (D) 4 (C) 5 (B)
6 (C) 7 (A) 8 (C) 9 (D) 10 (A)
11 (C)

PART 1

Conversation [1–5]

| Script |

Listen to part of a conversation between a student and a career center employee.

M Student: Good morning. I'm graduating this May, so I have to find a job. Is there someone here who can assist me with my résumé? I have one, but I don't think it's very, uh, professional looking.

W Career Center Employee: Well, that's what we at the career center are here for. But we aren't accepting walk-ins these days because we're so busy. You'll have to make a reservation to see one of our experts.

M: Sure. That makes sense. Is there a signup sheet or something here?

W: You can do that on our webpage. Do you know the address of the career center's webpage?

M: Um . . . No, I don't.

W: Here . . . This is a brochure with all the information you need. You can see the address clearly listed up at the top.

M: Great. Thanks a lot. Oh, uh, what's this advertisement here about a workshop?

W: The workshop will be held next Saturday. It's going to be divided into two parts, the first of which will be the process of writing a résumé. You know, uh, it will explain what should and shouldn't be included on one. The second part will be about the interview process, so you'll learn various ways to ace any interviews you have.

M: Awesome. Are there still any seats available?

W: Yes, there are about ten or so left. You can sign up for one online as well. I recommend doing it as quickly as possible though since this is annually one of our most popular events.

M: Great. Thanks again.

W: You're welcome. So . . . is there anything else you need?

M: In fact, there's one more thing I came here for.

W: Yes?

M: I'm thinking of applying for two jobs. One of them is a short-time position, but it looks kind of interesting, and the second is an internship.

W: An internship? But aren't you graduating soon? Those kinds of positions are usually reserved for sophomores or juniors.

M: It's going to be a paid internship, and the advertisement specifically mentions that this year's graduates are encouraged to apply. Apparently, if you do a good job during the six-month internship period, you stand a better-than-average chance of getting hired for a full-time position.

W: That sounds good. So, uh, what's your question about the jobs?

M: I'm a Graphics Design major, and it's necessary for me to prepare a portfolio of my work to apply for both jobs. I've got a few things to add to it, but it doesn't look very, uh, professional. Do you think I should hire someone to improve how it looks?

W: No, I don't think so.

M: Huh? Why not?

W: Anyone looking at your application won't expect a professional-looking portfolio since you're still a student. Instead, people are going to consider the work in your portfolio to see if you have the potential to be a good graphics designer in the future.

M: Ah, that makes sense.

W: But you can have someone here check out your portfolio if you like. We have a couple of individuals on staff who can give you some pointers on how to improve it.

M: All right. I guess I have to sign up for that online as well, right?

W: Actually, I'm one of those people, so if you brought your portfolio with you, I can glance at it now since it appears as though the student scheduled for this time isn't coming.

1 **Gist-Purpose Question**

② , ④ The student says, "Is there someone here who can assist me with my résumé? I have one, but I don't think it's very, uh, professional looking." Then, he adds, "In fact, there's one more thing I came here for," and he starts asking for advice about some positions that he is applying for.

2 **Detail Question**

Ⓑ The woman tells the student, "Here . . . This is a brochure with all the information you need."

3 **Understanding Organization Question**

Ⓓ The woman explains about the workshop after the student asks, "Oh, uh, what's this advertisement here about a workshop?"

4 **Making Inferences Question**

Ⓐ When the woman states, "I recommend doing it as quickly as possible though since this is annually one of our most popular events," she implies that the workshop has been held in previous years.

5 **Detail Question**

Ⓑ The woman comments, "Actually, I'm one of those people, so if you brought your portfolio with you, I can glance at it now since it appears as though the student scheduled for this time isn't coming."

Lecture #1 [6–11]

| Script |

Listen to part of a lecture in an anthropology class.

W Professor: Our profession frequently requires us to go out into the field to dig deep in the ground in search of artifacts, but, oftentimes, um, much to our chagrin, we come up with nothing. There are, however, fortunate occasions where our work is already done for us. I'm referring to instances when farmers or construction workers find artifacts in the course of doing their jobs. Among the stranger things that have been discovered in this manner are what are collectively termed the carved stone balls of Scotland. These are small, rounded stones, um, mostly between eighty and 110 millimeters in diameter, which often have protruding knobs on them. The knobs range in number from three large ones to dozens of small ones. The majority of the stone balls have elaborate etchings on them, uh, often in spiral patterns. Up here on the screen is a picture of one . . . and here's

another . . . and another. At present, more than 420 stone balls have been found. Most were unearthed in Scotland, but some were found in England.

Let's examine one in more detail . . . This is a picture of the Towie Stone. Ah, that's spelled T-O-W-I-E. It was found in 1860 near Towie in Aberdeenshire, Scotland. Interestingly enough, more than fifty carved stone balls have been found in that region. As you can see from this picture . . . and this one as well . . . the Towie Stone has four large knobs, three of which are decorated with spirals, dots, and rings. The Towie Stone is also perfectly symmetrical. Notice in this picture here . . . that the tops of its knobs are all equidistant from the center of the stone. Yes? Your hand is up?

M Student: What kinds of stones were used to make these balls?

W: A wide variety, including sandstone, greenstone, and quartzite. And for your edification, I don't think there's any particular importance to the type of stone they were made with. In all likelihood, the creators simply used whatever stones were available to them.

Ever since the first stone balls were discovered in the middle of the 1800s, there have been questions regarding their age and purpose. In case you aren't aware why we want to know this information, well, um, it's ideal to know how old the stone balls are so that we can understand more about the people who made them. And, um, just so you know, we are absolutely certain that they were carved and didn't form naturally. Unfortunately, however, these balls weren't found at well-organized dig sites. For the most part, they were found by regular people on their land, mostly by farmers who were digging in their land or planting crops. As a result, while they were considered curiosities, they didn't attract widespread attention or study for some time. That makes the job of understanding them harder since the exact places they were found are frequently unknown. We did, however, get lucky in one place. The finding of four carved stone balls at Neolithic settlements in the Orkney Islands suggests that those stones were made between 3000 and 2500 B.C., which was during the Stone Age.

Yet who made them, uh, and why, remain uncertain. ⌂11 **The history of Stone Age cultures is full of gaps despite the fact that we're slowly learning more about them. As for the carved stone balls, well, they could have been used in a variety of ways. One suggestion is that they were weights for the bottoms of fishing nets, but that sounds more like something a common stone would be used for, not something that a person spent a great deal of time carving.** Another theory is that they were used as weapons, um, perhaps in slingshots or bolas. Er . . . a bola is a long rope weighted at each end which is then spun over the wielder's head and thrown at an enemy to entangle him. A third possibility is that the carved stone balls were used as weights for measuring grain or other foodstuffs. A fourth hypothesis is that they were status symbols. They might have been symbols of authority, uh, such as a badge of office for a high-ranking member of society. It has also been suggested that the stone balls were passed from person to person in meetings, and only the person who was in possession of the ball was allowed to speak.

Interestingly, some of the people who have examined the balls have commented on their similarity to the five Platonic solids. These are five shapes named for the Greek philosopher Plato and which are said to represent the purest geometric shapes. Here they are up on the screen. Let me point them out to you . . . They are the tetrahedron . . . the hexahedron . . . the octahedron . . . the dodecahedron . . . and the icosahedron . . . If you compare these five shapes with the carved stone balls, you'll notice many similarities. This suggests that the balls may have had a mathematical purpose. Or perhaps they were carved simply to express the beauty of these pure geometric shapes and had no practical function. Ultimately, we may never know for sure, but we can still speculate about them.

Answer Explanations

6 **Understanding Organization Question**

Ⓐ While talking about the Towie Stone, the professor shows pictures to the students and then points out various aspects of the stone on the pictures.

7 **Detail Question**

Ⓒ The professor states, "For the most part, they were found by regular people on their land, mostly by farmers who were digging in their land or planting crops."

8 **Gist-Purpose Question**

Ⓐ The professor remarks, "Interestingly, some of the people who have examined the balls have commented on their similarity to the five Platonic solids. These are five shapes named for the Greek philosopher Plato and which are said to represent the purist geometric shapes. Here they are up on the screen. Let me point them out to you . . . They are the tetrahedron . . . the hexahedron . . . the octahedron . . . the dodecahedron . . . and the icosahedron . . . If you compare these five shapes with the carved stone balls, you'll notice many similarities."

9 **Detail Question**

Fact: ①, ③, ④ Not a Fact: ②

The professor says, "These are small, rounded stones, um, mostly between eight and 110 millimeters in diameter, which often have protruding knobs on them. The knobs range in number from three large ones to dozens of small ones." Then, she notes, "One suggestion is that they were weights for the bottoms of fishing nets." She also adds, "A third possibility is that the carved stone balls were used as weights for measuring grain or other foodstuffs." However, the stones have not been

found exclusively in Scotland as the professor mentions, "Most were unearthed in Scotland, but some were found in England."

10 **Making Inferences Question**

Ⓑ The professor gives several theories on the purpose of the carved stone balls, so it can be inferred that she is not sure what their purpose was.

11 **Understanding Attitude Question**

Ⓓ When the professor points out, "The history of the Stone Age cultures is full of gaps," she means that there is much that people do not know about the Stone Age today.

Lecture #2 [12–17]

| Script |

Listen to part of a lecture in an education class.

M1 Professor: Another experiment in educational reform took place at Black Mountain College from 1933 to 1957. It was located near Asheville, North Carolina, and was a liberal arts college where art was emphasized. The curriculum was loosely structured and gave a wide amount of freedom to the students, who often had a, uh, had a hand in deciding what they wanted to study and how the college was run. While this may sound a bit odd, it developed from the educational ideas of John Dewey, who was one of the great philosophers of education. He believed that education was a social and interactive process and that schools were not only places to acquire knowledge but also places to learn how to live and how to be members of a democratic society. He further stressed that students would learn more and thrive if they could be part of the process of deciding what and how they should study.

Just so you are aware, all of this was quite radical thinking for the early and mid-twentieth century, a time when education was more formalized and rigid. Back then, the teacher was in charge while students had little to no role in deciding what to study. Nevertheless, Dewey's ideas were adopted by the founders of Black Mountain College. It was established by a group of four professors who had been dismissed by a college in Florida for failing to take a pledge of loyalty to the school. Again, the notion of pledging loyalty to an educational institution may sound odd to us—I surely didn't have to do that when I took this job—but, um, such things were once common. The leader of the group, John Andrew Rice, decided that he wanted to work at a place which emphasized learning in an open and free atmosphere, which was not to be found on most of the formal and rigid college campuses of his time.

The school opened in the rural environment near Asheville in 1933. The main objective at this new college was to create an atmosphere where students could learn through a balanced combination of academic teaching, the development of artistic talent, and manual labor. This was done in an egalitarian society of democracy, so, um, everyone had a say in how things would be done. The school was unique in many ways. There were no course requirements, professors didn't hand out grades, and students didn't graduate until they themselves believed they were ready to do so. ∩17 In essence, it wasn't a place students attended for a set number of years and then received a piece of paper noting that they had done well and completed all of the necessary courses. Instead, it was a place where students could allow their minds to be set free and could be as creative as they wanted to be.

M2 Student: **It sounds to me like that was a recipe for chaos.** How did they manage to make everything work?

M1: It mostly worked thanks to the talented people whom Rice managed to attract to serve as faculty members. It also worked because of the time period when the school was founded. This was the 1930s, and many people in Europe were afraid of the rise of fascism which was happening there at the time, so large numbers of them fled to the United States. Rice managed to hire several of these people, some of whom were highly talented artists, as professors. Chief among them was Josef Albers, a German artist and educator who had worked in the German Bauhaus School. The Bauhaus School was an art school famed for bringing all art disciplines into one place where students could absorb knowledge about each of them. This, by the way, included architecture, for which that school of thought later achieved widespread fame. The Bauhaus School was eventually shut down due to pressure from the Nazis in 1933, but this happened only after its students had spread their ideas, many of which would have a great impact on modern design and architecture, far and wide.

Under Albers's hand, the Art Department quickly became the main focus of the college. Art studies combined the traditional fine arts of painting, sculpture, and drawing with crafts, theater, music, poetry, literature, and architecture. This unique environment attracted many students and other faculty members. Among them was Buckminster Fuller, who taught there in 1948 and 1949. It was while Fuller was at the college that he developed his ideas for the geodesic dome. Albert Einstein was another famed staff member at Black Mountain College. With such noted faculty and its philosophy, the school attracted many of the nation's greatest thinkers and artists.

Sadly, the experiment came to a dismal end. Albers left the school in 1949, and the remaining faculty fell into disagreement over the future of the college. Then, the school began accumulating debts, and the number of new students decreased. In 1957, the college closed down. Some say it was a failure, but I disagree as its legacy still lives on in the work of those who passed through its doors during its brief life.

12 **Gist-Content Question**

Ⓓ The lecture is mostly about the history of Black Mountain College.

13 **Understanding Function Question**

Ⓓ The professor lectures, "The curriculum was loosely structured and gave a wide amount of freedom to the students, who often had a, uh, had a hand in deciding what they wanted to study and how the college was run. While this may sound a bit odd, it developed from the educational ideas of John Dewey, who was one of the great philosophers of education. He believed that education was a social and interactive process and that schools were not only places to acquire knowledge but also places to learn how to live and how to be members of a democratic society. He further stressed that students would learn more and thrive if they could be part of the process of deciding what and how they should study."

14 **Detail Question**

Ⓑ The professor tells the class, "It was established by a group of four professors who had been dismissed by a college in Florida for failing to take a pledge of loyalty to the school. Again, the notion of pledging loyalty to an educational institution may sound odd to us—I surely didn't have to do that when I took this job—but, um, such things were once common. The leader of the group, John Andrew Rice, decided that he wanted to work at a place which emphasized learning in an open and free atmosphere, which was not to be found on most of the formal and rigid college campuses of his time."

15 **Making Inferences Question**

Ⓑ Since Josef Albers was influential at Black Mountain College and he was greatly influenced by the Bauhaus School, the professor implies that the Bauhaus School had a great effect on the college.

16 **Understanding Organization Question**

Ⓒ The professor says, "Albert Einstein was another famed staff member at Black Mountain College."

17 **Understanding Function Question**

Ⓑ When the student makes his comment, he is offering his opinion.

PART 2

Conversation [1–5]

| Script |

Listen to part of a conversation between a student and a professor.

W Student: Professor Nelson, do you have a moment, please? I have an urgent problem.

M Professor: Sure, Alice. What's going on?

W: It's the vase I'm making for my class project. I just went down to the art room where the kiln is. Apparently, my vase was removed from the kiln a couple of hours ago, but there's an enormous crack in it.

M: What happened?

W: Apparently, I shouldn't have put it in the kiln when I did since it wasn't ready for baking.

M: I see . . . You know, um, I distinctly recall telling you that the bottom of your vase was too thin and that it was going to put stress on the rest of the vase, but you apparently didn't listen to me, did you?

W: No, sir. I didn't. I wanted to finish my project early, so I put it in the kiln. You're right. I should have listened to you.

M: So . . .

W: So what?

M: So what will you do? The due date is next Friday.

W: Do I have time to make another vase?

M: Let me think . . . You'll need a couple of days to shape the pot. Then, you'll have to let the clay get completely dry.

W: Oh, no. I remember you telling us that it normally takes two weeks for clay to get bone dry. There's no way I can finish on time.

M: Yes, that's normally the case. However, the weather conditions can have a tremendous effect on how fast or slow clay dries. For instance, in humid weather, it could take clay at least two weeks to dry. But in dry conditions, uh, like those we're experiencing, clay can dry in as few as seven days.

W: Only one week? Okay, that takes me to next Wednesday. After it dries, I can put it in the kiln, right?

M: Yes. And luckily for you, we're planning to fire up the kiln next Thursday. So if your clay is totally dry, you can put your vase in the kiln on that day. But you're planning on glazing your vase, aren't you? That process takes two to three days, so I don't see how it would be possible for you to complete your vase on time. And, uh, to be frank, you can't afford to submit work late if you want to get an A. You've got either an eighty-eight or an eighty-nine right now, so you need an A on this project to improve your grade. But it's my policy to deduct twenty points for late work, so . . .

W: Yeah, I see your point. Um . . . 🎧5 I don't have to make a vase, do I?

M: Not at all. If you remember, I said you could submit any type of artwork so long as we learned how to make it in class.

W: Well, I can't make mosaics. And I'm not particularly talented at sculpting either.

M: How about making a painting with oils? We did that during the first couple of weeks of the semester. I know you made an oil painting, but I don't remember how it turned out.

W: I painted a still life of a bowl of fruit. It wasn't the best work, but I don't think I have too many options available, so I guess I'll do something similar.

M: Good luck.

Answer Explanations

1 Gist-Content Question

Ⓑ The student tells the professor, "Apparently, my vase was removed from the kiln a couple of hours ago, but there's an enormous crack in it."

2 Detail Question

Ⓐ The professor notes, "But in dry conditions, uh, like those we're experiencing, clay can dry in as few as seven days."

3 Gist-Purpose Question

Ⓓ The professor says, "And, uh, to be frank, you can't afford to submit work late if you want to get an A. You've got either an eighty-eight or an eighty-nine right now, so you need an A on this project to improve your grade. But it's my policy to deduct twenty points for late work, so . . ." So he explains his grading policy to point out that the student should not turn in her project late if she wants to get an A in his class.

4 Understanding Attitude Question

Ⓒ The professor shows that he believes the student is the cause of her problem when he remarks, "You know, um, I distinctly recall telling you that the bottom of your vase was too thin and that it was going to put stress on the rest of the vase, but you apparently didn't listen to me, did you?"

5 Understanding Function Question

Ⓑ First, the professor comments, "If you remember, I said you could submit any type of artwork so long as we learned how to make it in class." So in saying, "And I'm not particularly talented at sculpting either," the student implies that her class studied sculpting earlier in the semester.

Lecture [6–11]

| Script |

Listen to part of a lecture in a zoology class.

M Professor: One of the most common fossils that people find all around the world are trilobites. These marine animals first appeared in the oceans around 520 million years ago and died out approximately 250 million years ago. This range covers the time encompassed by the Cambrian and Permian periods in the Earth's history. Paleontologists first began examining trilobite fossils in the late 1800s. Since then, they've uncovered huge numbers of these fossils, which have provided us with a better understanding of trilobites.

First, let's examine what they look like and what they are.

As I talk, pay attention to the screen because you'll see several pictures of fossils as well as artists' renditions of what we believe trilobites actually looked like. Trilobites are a form of arthropods, which today include all insects and other species like prawns, crabs, scorpions, spiders, and mites. Trilobites evolved into a variety of species during their long period of existence. While they lived on the Earth, there were several extinction events during which large numbers of species vanished. Yet, uh, somehow, trilobites managed to survive. Not all lived, mind you, but trilobites were diverse enough that some species survived. So far, experts have classified more than twenty thousand trilobite species in the fossil record.

Despite there being large numbers of trilobites, every species shared some basic characteristics. For instance, they all had an exterior hard shell—called an exoskeleton—on their upper bodies. See it here . . . The underside was softer and lacked a hard shell. Soft body parts rarely fossilized, so most trilobite fossils show only the top side of the body. Trilobites had three body parts: a head, a thorax, and a tail. The thorax had many jointed segments, uh, as you can see in this photo . . . here . . . Trilobites also had three side-to-side sections that consisted of a central axis and two lateral lobes. Look at these . . . The term trilobite actually means "three lobes" and comes from these three side-by-side sections. Trilobites varied a great deal in size. The smallest were less than a millimeter in length while the largest . . . here's one . . . were up to sixty centimeters long. During their lives, as they grew, they would molt their exoskeletons, which fell off, broke into pieces, and descended to the ocean floor. Often, we paleontologists find pieces of shells rather than complete trilobites.

One thing you definitely should know about trilobites concerns their eyes. You can understand how diverse they were simply by knowing the following information. Some had no eyes, and it's thought that these species dwelled on the ocean floor and used other senses to move around to find food. Some paleontologists speculate that they lacked eyes because they lived in the deep ocean, where there wasn't any light to see. Nevertheless, most species had eyes. Some were small, simple eyes, and those surely stayed close to the ocean floor, where they searched for food and avoided predators. Other species had large, highly complex eyes allowing them to look in many directions. We believe those animals swam freely— perhaps close to the surface—and used their keen eyesight to search for food and to avoid danger.

Trilobites also had legs and antennae, but they were soft, so they're rarely found in fossils. On the head were a pair of long multiple-jointed antennae. Also on the head were three pairs of legs. On the body, the number of legs depended on the number of thorax segments. Each segment had a pair of legs. Most trilobites had between five and sixteen thorax segments. The legs were small and

many jointed and were likely used to crawl around the ocean floor. The antennae were probably used as sensory devices to search for food.

Now, uh, what did they eat . . . ? Well, some were hunters while others scavenged dead marine life on the ocean floor, and others consumed plankton. It's likely that the diverse types of food they ate helped trilobites survive for so long before they died out.

Well, that's a good way to introduce the topic of their extinction. The fact is, uh, we don't know exactly why they disappeared from the fossil record around 250 million years ago. One theory suggests that they had evolved too narrowly into a group of a few species that were wiped out during a single extinction event. Perhaps they had evolved only to live in shallow coastal waters. At the time they died out, sea levels fell dramatically around the world. This may have been the result of what we call the Permian Extinction Event, which happened around 252 million years ago. We don't know exactly what happened, but we do know the results. Basically, uh, ninety percent of all marine life died out, and up to seventy percent of all land animals died, too. Theories for what happened involve an asteroid impact, climate change, and increased volcanic activity. Whatever it was that happened, it likely caused the end of the trilobite.

Answer Explanations

6 Gist-Content Question

Ⓒ During the lecture, the professor mainly discusses the physical characteristics of trilobites.

7 Detail Question

Ⓐ The professor comments, "While they lived on the Earth, there were several extinction events during which large numbers of species vanished. Yet, uh, somehow, trilobites managed to survive. Not all lived, mind you, but trilobites were diverse enough that some species survived."

8 Understanding Organization Question

Ⓒ While discussing the bodies of trilobites, the professor shows slides to the students as he provides explanations.

9 Understanding Function Question

Ⓓ The professor focuses on the large amount of variety between trilobite species when he states, "One thing you definitely should know about trilobites concerns their eyes. You can understand how diverse they were simply by knowing the following information."

10 Making Inferences Question

Ⓐ In saying, "Trilobites also had legs and antennae, but they were soft, so they're rarely found in fossils," the professor implies that complete trilobite fossils containing all body parts are rare.

11 Understanding Organization Question

© The professor associates the Permian Extinction Event with the disappearance of trilobites when he lectures, "The fact is, uh, we don't know exactly why they disappeared from the fossil record around 250 million years ago. One theory suggests that they had evolved too narrowly into a group of a few species that were wiped out during a single extinction event. Perhaps they had evolved only to live in shallow coastal waters. At the time they died out, sea levels fell dramatically around the world. This may have been the result of what we call the Permian Extinction Event, which happened around 252 million years ago."

| Vocabulary Review

p. 164

Answers

A
1 beholder   2 scavenge
3 similarities   4 burst from   5 dismal

B
1 a   2 b   3 b   4 a   5 b
6 a   7 a   8 b   9 b   10 b

Practice with Short Passages

p. 168

A

Answers

1 Ⓑ

2 Visiting France: ①, ③ Staying at School: ②, ④

| Script |

Listen to part of a conversation between a student and a professor.

W Student: I appreciate your answering my question about the midterm exam, Professor Young. But before I leave, do you mind if I ask you one more question?

M Professor: Not at all, Rhonda. What is it?

W: I've been thinking about this summer and am trying to decide what to do.

M: What are your choices?

W: I could stay here at school, get a part-time job, and take a couple of summer school classes. Or, um, I could go on an archaeological dig in France.

M: The dig sounds interesting. Why don't you tell me about that?

W: Professor Hamilton in the Archaeology Department is leading it. He's going to be excavating a site in central France. He's been going there for the past, uh, three years, I think. He searches for relics from a culture that's more than 2,000 years old.

M: And how would you benefit from being one of the people helping with the dig?

W: Hmm . . . For starters, it would be a unique experience that would provide me with some hands-on training in the field of archaeology. It's also something that I'm interested in. On the other hand, it would be expensive since I wouldn't earn any money and would have to pay for everything, including my airfare there.

M: And what are the advantages of staying here for the summer term?

W: I'd get the opportunity to earn some money, which would help me during the fall semester because I wouldn't have to work so much then. And I could either take a couple of electives or focus on a core course or two during the summer session. Oh, yeah, and several of my friends will be here this summer whereas I won't know anyone on the dig in France.

M: Well, if you ask me, it seems like you already know which option has more benefits.

W: Yeah, that's true, but I badly want to go abroad. This seems like the opportunity of a lifetime, and I'd love to have the experience.

M: Since Professor Hamilton appears to go to that excavation site regularly, perhaps you could stay here this year and then go on the dig the following summer. How would you feel about doing that?

Answer Explanations

1 Ⓑ When discussing the advantages of staying at school in the summer, the student states, "I'd get the opportunity to earn some money, which would help me during the fall semester because I wouldn't have to work so much then." So if she goes to France in the summer and does not make any money, one likely outcome is that she will get a part-time job during the fall semester.

2 Visiting France: ①, ③ Staying at School: ②, ④
Regarding visiting France, the student mentions that she would be working with Professor Hamilton. She also notes, "It would be expensive since I wouldn't earn any money and would have to pay for everything, including my airfare there." As for staying at school, the student points out, "I'd get the opportunity to earn some money," and she also says, "Oh, yeah, and several of my friends will be here this summer whereas I won't know anyone on the dig in France."

B

Answers 1 Ⓐ   2 Suburbs: ① Cities: ②, ③, ④

| Script |

Listen to part of a lecture in a sociology class.

W Professor: Large numbers of people live in suburbs these days. Just so that we're clear on the definition of a suburb, it's a small town or city located near a larger urban center. Well, uh, it's not necessarily small, but it's smaller than the city it's located close to. For the next few minutes, I'd like to discuss some general differences between cities and suburbs and focus on how they affect the people residing in them. The majority of these differences can be divided into the following categories: structure, density, greenery, transportation, employment, education, crime, and pollution.

Let's examine structure first. In general, suburbs consist of residential housing, uh, typically single-family units or apartment complexes, yet there aren't many—if any—high-rise complexes. There may be office buildings, but nothing like you see downtown in major cities. Additionally, suburbs feature schools, shopping malls, parks, and other recreational facilities. In cities, skyscrapers are normal and serve as both office buildings and apartments. There may be some individual houses, but toward the centers of cities or their downtown areas, these types of homes are quite rare. Businesses and shopping areas dominate downtown areas. As for factories, they may be located in various parts of cities, but they're typically situated on the edges in designated business parks.

The population density is much higher in cities than it is in suburbs and fluctuates during the day. As workers come into the city from the suburbs, the population density increases in metropolitan areas, and it decreases when workers depart to go home. People also frequently visit cities at night for entertainment purposes, particularly to see movies, to attend theatrical presentations, and to go to sporting events. On the other hand, city dwellers tend to visit the suburbs or countryside on weekends to get fresh air and to enjoy greener environs. Suburbs, of course, almost always have more green spaces than cities. Parks, uh, and even tracts of forests, can be found in suburbs whereas they're mostly absent in cities.

M Student: But some urban centers, um, such as New York City, are becoming greener these days.

W: Yes, it's true that there's a current trend toward making rooftops in cities green, and more trees are being planted alongside streets. But the bottom line is that suburbs are still much, much greener than cities are.

Obviously, there's lots of movement back and forth between cities and suburbs. All of this movement is aided by dense transportation networks both within them and connecting them. Most cities have bus systems while many have subways or similar forms of transportation, and large metropolises usually have enormous fleets of taxis ready to take people anywhere. There are commuter trains that bring people to these cities from the suburbs as well. Within suburbs, however, transportation systems are much less complex. There is rarely a subway system, there are limited bus routes that make occasional stops, and there are much fewer taxis. Therefore, the primary mode of transportation in suburbs is the automobile. Interestingly, in big cities, there are large numbers of people in their forties and fifties who not only don't own cars but also lack driver's licenses and might not even know how to drive. That simply isn't the case in suburbs.

We still have a few more topics to go, but I think it's time that we stop and take a break. Let's take ten minutes off, and when we start up again, we'll begin by discussing the differences in employment between the two.

Answer Explanations

1 (A) The professor comments, "Within suburbs, however, transportation systems are much less complex. There is rarely a subway system, there are limited bus routes that make occasional stops, and there are much fewer taxis. Therefore, the primary mode of transportation in suburbs is the automobile." Therefore, it can be inferred that more

people drive personal vehicles than take the bus.

2 Suburbs: ☐ Cities: ☐, ☐, ☐
About the suburbs, the professor states, "Suburbs, of course, almost always have more green spaces than cities. Parks, uh, and even tracts of forests, can be found in suburbs whereas they're mostly absent in cities." Regarding cities, the professor notes, "Most cities have bus systems while many have subways or similar forms of transportation, and large metropolises usually have enormous fleets of taxis ready to take people anywhere. There are commuter trains that bring people to these cities from the suburbs as well." She also remarks, "There may be some individual houses, but toward the centers of cities or their downtown areas, these types of homes are quite rare." And she points out, "The population density is much higher in cities than it is in suburbs and fluctuates during the day. As workers come into the city from the suburbs, the population density increases in metropolitan areas, and it decreases when workers depart to go home."

C

Answers

1 ⓒ
2 Mutualism: ☐ Commensalism: ☐, ☐ Parasitism: ☐

| Script |

Listen to part of a lecture in a biology class.

M Professor: Another common type of relationship in the natural world is symbiosis. In this type of relationship, two organisms interact with each other, and there are benefits either to both or only one of them. There are three basic types of symbiotic interactions: mutualism, commensalism, and parasitism. Mutualism occurs when one organism helps another and, in return, receives benefits of its own. Basically, uh, it's nature's way of saying you scratch my back, and I'll scratch yours. In commensalism, one organism benefits while the second does not, yet the second one isn't harmed in any manner. As for parasitism, one organism receives an advantage while harming the other organism. Let me give you some specific examples to more clearly illustrate what I'm referring to.

First up is mutualism . . . The acacia tree is commonly found in the tropics. Most species of acacia trees have alkaloids in their leaves, so that helps them avoid having their leaves eaten. Why . . . ? Well, the alkaloids leave a bitter taste in insects and other animals that consume their leaves. However, one species, the bullhorn acacia of Central America, lacks this defensive system. Instead, it relies upon a symbiotic relationship with ants. The ants live in hollows in the tree's thorns and consume the sweet nectar it produces. Those are the benefits the ants receive. These ants, by the way, are of the stinging variety and can cause painful wounds to animals and other insects. Whenever animals start eating the leaves, the ants attack them and therefore protect the tree. So the tree provides shelter and food while the ants provide protection.

How about an example of commensalism . . . ? Ah, here's one . . . This involves a bird called the cattle egret and cows as well as other large herbivores. The cattle egret is a large bird found in subtropical and tropical regions. Its main food source is insects. The cattle egret has developed a way easily to capture insects. Insects often hide in vegetation, which makes it hard for animals to find them. But when cattle and other large herds of herbivores move through an area, they disturb the vegetation and thereby cause the insects to leave their hiding spots. The cattle egret follows herd animals and consumes the insects they expose. The herds don't reap any benefits, so this is clearly an example of commensalism.

All right, um, on to parasitism . . . Common parasites are bacteria in our bodies, viruses, and many small insects, such as fleas and mosquitoes. Parasites may harm their hosts so much that they cause illness or even death, but, of course, not all parasites do that. Some merely harm the host yet don't cause enough damage to kill it since they need the host to survive. Many viruses are like that. Basically, they survive in a host until they can be passed on to another one. In some cases, the harm, such as a flea or mosquito bite that draws blood but doesn't otherwise cause injury, may be mild. But if that creature is a vector insect and thus one that spreads diseases like malaria, then great harm, including death, can be caused to the host.

W Student: I thought some parasites are beneficial, not harmful, and can provide mutual benefits.

M: Well, it's true that some creatures we generally regard as being parasites can provide benefits, but, uh, according to the definitions I just gave you, they aren't engaging in parasitism, are they? Instead, they're engaging in either mutualism or commensalism. Still, um, that's a good point you brought up, Clarice, so let me give you a couple of examples. Let's talk about *E. coli* bacteria . . .

Answer Explanations

1 Ⓒ The professor discusses how both the bullhorn acacia and the cattle egret benefit from the symbiotic relationships that they are in.

2 Mutualism: ④ Commensalism: ②, ③ Parasitism: ①
About mutualism, the professor states that the bullhorn acacia and ants have that type of relationship. Regarding commensalism, the professor points out that the cattle egret and cow have that kind of relationship. He also says, "In commensalism, one organism benefits while the second does not, yet the second one isn't harmed in any manner." As for parasitism, he notes, "As for parasitism, one organism receives an advantage while harming the other organism."

D

| Script |

Listen to part of a lecture in a physiology class.

W Professor: Everybody sleeps, yet, uh, surprisingly, most of us aren't aware of exactly how we sleep. We know we sleep and dream, but that's it, uh, for the most part. Well, I'm going to explain the process of sleep to you. There are several phases, and scientists have a pretty decent understanding of each one nowadays. We mostly study sleep in order better to understand it and to assist people having trouble sleeping. Let's see what we've learned about sleep . . .

There are five widely recognized phases of sleep. The first four are stages one to four while the fifth is called REM sleep. That, by the way, stands for rapid eye movement, and it happens to be the stage during which people dream. But I don't want to get ahead of myself, so let me cover each stage for you.

Stage one happens when you're drifting off to sleep. It's a light sleep, uh, sort of like a twilight area between being asleep and being awake, and you can easily wake up from it. However, your body reacts slowly during this stage, and you may have muscle contractions and experience a sensation like you're falling. Stage two refers to the onset of deeper sleep. You become more relaxed, and your breathing and heart rate become more regular. Your body, uh, body temperature drops a bit, and you're disconnected from the real world and your surroundings. Eye movement stops, and your brainwave activity slows a great amount.

Stage three and stage four are the deepest part of sleep and can be recognized on brain scans by the presence of delta waves, so we sometimes call this delta sleep. Look at the pictures of the brain scan on page 104 of your books . . . The top picture shows normal brain activity, which features bursts of rapid jumps at high frequencies. The bottom picture, on the other hand, depicts a brain scan of a person sleeping deeply. Notice the delta waves, uh, the long, shallow brainwaves. In stage three, the delta waves are combined with some sharp bursts of brain activity, but, by stage four, there are only delta waves. During stage four, the body is in such a deep sleep that it's incredibly hard to wake someone up. Your breathing slows down, your blood pressure gets lower, your muscles relax, and you get a lot of restorative rest, which, um, which recharges the body.

The fifth stage is REM sleep, which, as I already noted, is when you dream. This stage is characterized by the eyes moving rapidly yet not opening. All this movement takes place under the eyelids. During REM sleep, your body becomes totally rigid with all the muscles tense. We aren't positive, but we believe the reason this happens is so that you don't react during a dream by lashing out, kicking, falling out of bed, or doing some other potentially harmful activity. Basically, it's nature's way of keeping you from hurting yourself while dreaming. And here's something else of importance: Dreaming isn't just something that entertains, uh, or frightens, I guess, you at night. Instead, dreaming helps you get a full rest and recharged batteries. Just so you know, the average person spends about twenty-five percent of his sleeping time in REM sleep.

M Student: How long does each stage last?

W: It depends on the person, so the exact time varies. But a person progresses through all five stages every ninety to 110 minutes, so in the course of eight hours, a person might go through the cycle five times.

Answer Explanations

1 ⓑ About stage 4 sleep, the professor mentions, "Your breathing slows down, your blood pressure gets lower, your muscles relax, and you get a lot of restorative rest, which, um, which recharges the body." So it is likely that a person who gets a lot of it will wake up well rested.

2 ⓓ About stage 2 sleep, the professor points out, "Eye movement stops." As for REM sleep, the professor comments, "This stage is characterized by the eyes moving rapidly yet not opening." So she compares how much the eyes move in each stage.

Practice with Long Passages   p. 172

A

| Answers | 1 Ⓐ | 2 Ⓓ | 3 Ⓒ | 4 Ⓐ |

| Script |

Listen to part of a conversation between a student and a student activities office employee.

M1 Student: Hi there. Is this where I'm supposed to go to sign up for some extracurricular activities?

M2 Student Activities Office Employee: Actually, you were supposed to do that a couple of days ago. We had a special event at the campus center where virtually every club and sports league on campus was present to try to attract new members. Didn't you hear about it?

M1: 🎧4 Uh, yeah, I think I remember reading something about it in the school newspaper, but I was sort of busy on that day, so I wasn't able to get to the campus center then. So, um . . . is it possible for me to sign up for any clubs here?

M2: **I'm afraid not.**

M1: Oh, that's too bad.

M2: However, um, I can give you some information about them, including when they're going to have their first meeting. Most clubs are still actively seeking members, so they almost never turn down anyone who wants to join.

M1: That makes sense. I mean, uh, for what possible reason could a club reject a student who wants to belong to it?

M2: I can think of a couple. For instance, if you don't have your own camera, you're probably not going to be welcome at any photography club meetings.

M1: Yeah, that's a good one.

M2: Anyway, um, how about telling me which activities you're interested in doing? Then, I can provide you with some information about the clubs that would be appropriate for you.

M1: All right. Is there a cycling club here? I used to go cycling every day back home, and I have my mountain bike at my apartment, but I don't get a chance to ride it very often nowadays. I'd love to do some cycling with other students.

M2: Unfortunately, there isn't a cycling club. There was one here maybe, uh . . . I guess it was around two or three years ago. But there weren't enough people interested in it, so it sort of just faded away and disappeared after a while.

M1: That's terrible. Do you think I could start up a cycling club this semester?

M2: No, you can't because applications for new clubs had to be submitted by last week. You could always put an ad in the school paper requesting that like-minded people meet you to go riding though.

M1: That's a cool idea. If enough people are interested, we could try to start the club up again next spring.

M2: That would probably be effective.

M1: So, uh, is there a basketball or soccer intramural league here? I'd like to do something active that would help me stay in shape, and either of those would be fine.

M2: The basketball intramural league doesn't start until October, but the soccer league is still accepting new players. Do you want some more information about it?

M1: Yeah, that would be awesome.

Answer Explanations

1 Ⓐ When the student enters the office, he asks, "Is this where I'm supposed to go to sign up for some extracurricular activities?"

2 Ⓓ When talking about putting an ad in the paper, the student remarks, "If enough people are interested, we could try to start the club up again next spring." The employee agrees, so a likely outcome would be that the cycling club will be restarted during a later semester.

3 Ⓒ The student requests that the employee tell him more about the soccer league, so he is interested in learning more about it.

4 Ⓐ When the employee says, "I'm afraid not," in response to the student's inquiry, "Is it possible for me to sign up for any clubs here?" he means that the student cannot register for any clubs.

Dictation

1 Is this where I'm <u>supposed</u> to go to <u>sign up for</u> some extracurricular activities?

2 <u>How about telling me</u> which activities you're interested in doing?

3 <u>Do you think</u> I could start up a cycling club this semester?

B

Answers

1 Ⓐ   **2** Ⓑ–Ⓓ–Ⓐ–Ⓒ   **3** Ⓑ   **4** Ⓓ

| Script |

Listen to part of a lecture in a biology class.

M Professor: Bacteria are all around us and live in every kind of environment on the Earth. To survive, they have adapted some rather unique ways of living. 🎧4 One such way is to form a colony of bacteria that is much stronger and more resistant than individual cells are. This colony is called a biofilm. And, uh, no, it's not a documentary about a famous person. **Biofilm is bacteria, and it's all around us in a plethora of forms.** Some are harmless while some can be quite deadly.

Biofilm can attach itself to nearly any kind of surface, including living creatures and inanimate objects. So long as it has moisture and nutrients to support the bacteria in the biofilm, just about anything can support it. For instance, that gunk you feel on your teeth in the morning prior to brushing them is a type of biofilm. You may be surprised to hear that there are 500 species of bacteria found in typical dental plaque. I imagine that makes a few of you want to spend a bit more time brushing your teeth each day, doesn't it . . . ? Anyway, uh, back to the topic at hand . . . In nature, one type of biofilm is the slime that appears on rocks in rivers. Now that I think of it, slime is a pretty good way to describe biofilm since it tends to be, well, slimy in appearance. Oh, uh, I should mention one thing . . . Biofilm doesn't just contain bacteria. In nature, all kinds of things can join bacteria in creating biofilm. What things . . . ? Well, there can be fungi, algae, yeast, protozoa, and debris such as plant matter and soil in biofilm.

W Student: Professor Harper, how do bacteria join and then stick together once they've formed biofilm?

M: That's a good question as the process is rather interesting.

Permit me to explain . . . The bacteria produce sugary molecular strands that essentially glue them all together. These sugary strands are called extracellular polymeric substances, or EPS, for short. When bacteria form these EPS strands and then come together, they can create biofilm which may eventually grow to be many centimeters thick and may have a complex three-dimensional structure that provides both strength and protection. Here's what happens . . . First, a few bacteria form on a surface, and they become connected thanks to the EPS strands. The biofilm extracts water from moisture and absorbs nutrients in various ways so that it can be sustained. Gradually, more and more bacteria—as well as other substances—join the biofilm and make it increase in size. Interestingly, this can happen in only a few hours. Now, uh, once a biofilm colony is growing and secure, it sends off small packets of bacteria to nearby areas to form new biofilm. Basically, it sends out other bacteria to colonize new places.

W: Are all biofilm harmful?

M: No, all of them aren't, but many are, and these can cause both illnesses and damage. For that reason, scientists have been studying biofilm for years to learn how to destroy it. It's a rather difficult task though. The primary issue concerns how we first began studying bacteria decades ago. Back then, scientists looked at individual bacteria cells and devised ways to kill them. From their research, they developed numerous antibacterial drugs that can be utilized to combat infections. But what these scientists didn't understand was the nature of biofilms, some of which are found in the human body. So while the medicines they created are effective at killing small amounts of bacteria that are by themselves, they are generally ineffective against biofilm colonies, which are able to resist them.

But the news isn't all bad since biofilm can also be beneficial. Right now, some researchers, including myself, are studying ways to use non-harmful biofilm to protect water and soil resources from harmful bacteria. We can also use biofilm to destroy hazardous waste that resists other means of destruction. Let me show you a short video of the work my team is doing. I think you'll find it interesting.

Answer Explanations

1 Ⓐ The professor states, "These sugary strands are called extracellular polymeric substances, or EPS, for short. When bacteria form these EPS strands and then come together, they can create biofilm which may eventually grow to be many centimeters thick and may have a complex three-dimensional structure that provides both strength and protection. Here's what happens." So he talks about them to explain the process that allows bacteria to create biofilm.

2 Ⓑ–Ⓓ–Ⓐ–Ⓒ The professor tells the class, "When

bacteria form these EPS strands and then come together, they can create biofilm which may eventually grow to be many centimeters thick and may have a complex three-dimensional structure that provides both strength and protection. Here's what happens. . . First, a few bacteria form on a surface, and they become connected thanks to the EPS strands. The biofilm extracts water from moisture and absorbs nutrients in various ways so that it can be sustained. Gradually, more and more bacteria—as well as other substances—join the biofilm and make it increase in size."

3 Ⓑ The professor lectures, "From their research, they developed numerous antibacterial drugs that can be utilized to combat infections. But what these scientists didn't understand was the nature of biofilms, some of which are found in the human body. So while the medicines they created are effective at killing small amounts of bacteria that are by themselves, they are generally ineffective against biofilm colonies, which are able to resist them."

4 Ⓓ The professor means that there are lots of different types of biofilm that can live in various places.

Dictation

1 Biofilm is bacteria, and it's all around us in a plethora of forms.

2 These sugary strands are called extracellular polymeric substances, or EPS, for short.

3 But the news isn't all bad since biofilm can also be beneficial.

iBT Practice Test   p. 176

Answers

PART 1

1 Ⓓ   2 Ⓒ   3 Ⓐ

4 Fact: [1] Not a Fact: [2], [3], [4]   5 Ⓑ

6 Ⓓ   7 Ⓑ   8 Ⓓ   9 Ⓑ

10 House of York: [2], [3] House of Lancaster: [1], [4]

11 Ⓓ   12 Ⓒ   13 Ⓑ

14 First Law of Motion: [2] Second Law of Motion: [1], [4]

Third Law of Motion: [3]   15 Ⓐ   16 Ⓑ

17 Ⓓ

PART 2

1 Ⓑ   2 Ⓓ   3 Ⓐ   4 [1], [2]   5 Ⓑ

6 Ⓒ   7 Ⓑ   8 Ⓓ

9 Rational Consumer: [2], [4] Irrational Consumer: [1], [3]

10 Ⓑ   11 Ⓒ

PART 1

Conversation [1–5]

| Script |

Listen to part of a conversation between a student and a professor.

W1 Professor: Lisa, you said you wanted to meet me to speak about something of importance. What's going on?

W2 Student: It's about the midterm exam, Professor Sigmund.

W1: Wasn't I clear about what information will be on the test and what types of questions will be asked?

W2: You were crystal clear regarding them. But my problem is that I can't take the test at the scheduled time.

W1: Why won't you be able to do that? The test is going to be during our regular class time, so I'm not sure what could possibly interfere with your making it to the exam.

W2: 🎧5 Um, I'm a member of the school's volleyball team, and we've got a big tournament which is being held next Wednesday, Thursday, and Friday.

W1: In the middle of the week? What kind of person would schedule a tournament then? **That sort of event should be held on the weekend to avoid interfering with so many student-athletes' classes.**

W2: I totally agree with you, ma'am, but, uh, I didn't have anything to do with the schedule. The tournament is taking place in Akron, which is five hours away from here, so we're departing on Tuesday afternoon and won't return to campus until Sunday. I've already talked to Professor Dawson in the English Department, and he's letting me take my exam early.

W1: When?

W2: I'll be taking it in his office next Tuesday afternoon. The test is scheduled for next Friday, but he's allowing me to take it a few days early.

W1: What about your other professors?

W2: I've spoken with Professor Allston in the Chemistry Department. In fact, I visited her office a few minutes ago. She's having me take the exam this Friday. That's a bit earlier than I had wanted since it only gives me two days to prepare for it, but I'm just pleased she's permitting me to take the test early. And those are the only professors I have to speak with.

W1: You're only taking three classes this semester?

W2: Oh, no, ma'am. I'm enrolled in five classes, but only three have exams. As for my other two classes, I have to turn in papers by the end of next week, and I can submit them by email once I finish them.

W1: Ah, okay. That makes sense.

W2: So . . . Would it be all right to take the exam at an alternative time?

W1: Well, it would be unkind of me not to extend you that

courtesy since your other professors are doing that. When would you prefer to take the exam?

W2: How does next Monday around, um . . . eleven or so sound? I've got free time from eleven to one then.

W1: Sorry, but I've got a class starting at eleven. What's your schedule like on Tuesday?

W2: I've got classes all morning, and then I'm taking my English exam at one thirty. Oh, and the bus leaves at four.

W1: Your English exam will take an hour, right?

W2: That's correct.

W1: In that case, what about coming here after it ends? You ought to arrive here a bit after two thirty, and then you can take my exam, which should only require forty-five minutes or so. That will give you enough time to finish and to get to wherever the bus is leaving from.

W2: It's a bit tight, but I think I can make it.

Answer Explanations

1 Gist-Content Question

ⒹThe student and professor are mostly talking about the need for the student to take her test at an alternative time.

2 Connecting Content Question

ⒸThe student tells the professor when she is going to take the exams for those two professors, so that is the comparison she makes.

3 Making Inferences Question

ⒶWhen talking about her papers, the student says, "As for my other two classes, I have to turn in papers by the end of next week, and I can submit them by email once I finish them." Since she will be at the tournament next week, she implies that she will work on her papers while she is there.

4 Detail Question

Fact: ① Not a Fact: ②, ③, ④

It is a fact that the students are supposed to take the professor's test during the regular class time. But it is not a fact that the students can choose between writing a paper or taking a test. They must take a test. Nor is it a fact that the test will cover two weeks' worth of material or that it will take two hours to complete.

5 Understanding Function Question

ⒷThe professor makes the statement to show that she is displeased about when the tournament is scheduled. She doesn't want it to interfere with the students' class schedules.

| Script |

Listen to part of a lecture in a history class.

W Professor: The death of England's King Henry V in 1422 set off a chain of events that eventually led to the Wars of the Roses. The main protagonists in the wars were two noble houses, the House of Lancaster and the House of York, which were branches of the royal House of Plantagenet. The wars lasted from 1455 to 1485, but don't be mistaken in believing that there were thirty years of continuous warfare as there were extensive lulls in the fighting at times. The conflict ended when a member of the House of Lancaster, Henry Tudor, emerged victorious at the last battle at Bosworth Field and was crowned King Henry VII. But, um, I'm getting a bit ahead of myself. For the next few minutes, I'd like to examine the root causes of the wars and then cover some of the more dramatic events and battles that happened during them. Your hand is up. Yes?

M Student: Why are they called the Wars of the Roses?

W: It has to do with the heraldic symbols of the two houses. The House of York was represented by a white rose whereas one of the symbols of the House of Lancaster was a red rose. All right, as I said a moment ago, Henry V died in 1422 and left behind an infant son, who was crowned King Henry VI. Without the strong, guiding hand of his father, Henry VI grew up to become a weak-willed man who also had a touch of mental illness. And, um, just so you know, Henry VI represented the Lancaster side of the family in the forthcoming dispute.

🎧11 Henry's reign as king was challenged by Richard, Duke of York, who's more commonly referred to as Richard of York. **Richard's claim to the throne was based on family ties going back to King Edward III, whom we studied in the previous class.** Richard was quite a unique individual. Unlike the king, he was a strong man, um, a man of action, and he had played a prominent role in the Hundred Years' War with France that was being fought while Henry was still a growing child. Richard was also one of the wealthiest men in England and spent a great deal of his own money supporting the English army that was fighting in France.

After assuming the throne, Henry VI failed to produce a male heir for many years, and it was long assumed that Richard of York, who was a decade older than the king, would be his successor. Henry's rule was further weakened by the troublesome people who surrounded him at court. Bear in mind that he became king when he was only nine months old, so, uh, for most of his life, he had people around him who wielded power as regents. And, unfortunately, for the most part, they improperly used that power to better themselves rather than the realm. Henry also married a strong-willed woman, Margaret of Anjou, who was a niece of the French king,

Charles VII. The marriage took place in 1445 and was in part an attempt to bring about peace between England and France. Yet that gambit failed, the fight renewed, and through bad management and a series of military reversals, the English lost virtually all of their possessions in France when the war came to its conclusion.

Back in England, Richard of York led a faction that desired to renew the war against France, but he was opposed by those surrounding the king. Then, in 1453, Henry and Margaret finally produced a male heir, who was named Edward. Henry, however, soon suffered a mental breakdown, and those around him took advantage of his weakness. Something else you should know is that at that time, there were a large number of noble families that had disputes with one another, and many of them started clashing. Since most nobles had their own private armies, that led to growing unrest throughout the land. There was also a great deal of unhappiness regarding the king, his wife, and their advisors. Richard of York was the focal point of the sentiment against the king and those at court, but Margaret managed to force Richard out of court life and started plotting for ways to reduce his power.

That was too much for Richard, who had sacrificed a great amount of his wealth in the unsuccessful wars in France. He was no longer the heir to the throne, and he was suddenly being challenged by the king's wife, who happened to be French. Richard gathered a force of men and marched on London as he was determined to remove those around Henry who were advising him. On May 22, 1455, the two sides met at the First Battle of St. Albans, which took place north of London and was the first physical encounter of the Wars of the Roses. Richard's forces won the battle, and Richard took over the affairs at court. He pushed Margaret aside and was named Protector of the Realm, um, so he pretty much became the main advisor to the king. However, with Henry still suffering from mental lapses, Richard was, for all intents and purposes, the ruler of England. This was just the beginning of war though. The fighting renewed in 1459. Let me tell you what happened during that year.

Answer Explanations

6 Gist-Content Question

(D) The professor focuses on the major events that happened prior to the Wars of the Roses breaking out.

7 Making Inferences Question

(B) About Richard of York, the professor says, "Henry's reign as king was challenged by Richard, Duke of York, who's more commonly referred to as Richard of York. Richard's claim to the throne was based on family ties going back to King Edward III, whom we studied in the previous class. Richard was quite a unique individual. Unlike the king, he was a strong man, um, a man of action, and he had played a prominent role in the Hundred Years' War with France that was being fought

while Henry was still a growing child." She therefore implies that Richard was more of a warrior than Henry VI was.

8 Understanding Attitude Question

(D) The professor comments, "Bear in mind that he became king when he was only nine months old, so, uh, for most of his life, he had people around him who wielded power as regents. And, unfortunately, for the most part, they improperly used that power to better themselves rather than the realm."

9 Detail Question

(B) The professor tells the students, "On May 22, 1455, the two sides met at the First Battle of St. Albans, which took place north of London and was the first physical encounter of the Wars of the Roses. Richard's forces won the battle, and Richard took over the affairs at court."

10 Connecting Content Question

House of York: ②, ③ House of Lancaster: ①, ④
About the House of York, the professor notes, "Back in England, Richard of York led a faction that desired to renew the war against France." She also states, "That was too much for Richard, who had sacrificed a great amount of his wealth in the unsuccessful wars in France. He was no longer the heir to the throne, and he was suddenly being challenged by the king's wife, who happened to be French. Richard gathered a force of men and marched on London as he was determined to remove those around Henry who were advising him." Regarding the House of Lancaster, the professor proclaims, "Henry VI represented the Lancaster side of the family in the forthcoming dispute." She adds, "Henry, however, soon suffered a mental breakdown, and those around him took advantage of his weakness."

11 Understanding Function Question

(D) After mentioning King Edward III, the professor notes, "Whom we studied in the previous class," so she is implying that the students should know who he was.

Lecture #2 [12–17]

| Script |

Listen to part of a lecture in a physics class.

M Professor: 🎧17 Sir Isaac Newton's three laws of motion are some of the mainstays of our understanding of the physical universe. I'm sure that you all studied them in high school, so most of what I say will, uh, hopefully, be a refresher for you. Nevertheless, this is important, so I need to tell you both about Newton himself and then explain all three of the laws. **If you don't mind, hold your questions until I'm done, please.**

First, a bit about Newton . . . He was an English mathematician who was born in 1642 and died in 1726. He's well known for his work in optics and for discovering the principles of calculus, which was accomplished pretty much simultaneously by a German named Gottfried Leibniz. Newton's most famous work, which we're discussing today, covered both gravity and the laws of motion. I'm talking, of course, about his work published in 1687 and entitled *Mathematical Principles of Natural Philosophy*.

In the work, Newton described the three laws of motion. Let me tell you about them. Newton's first law of motion states that an object at rest remains at rest or an object in motion stays in motion at the same speed and direction unless it is acted upon by an outside force. A simpler way of saying that is that all objects keep doing whatever they are doing unless some kind of external force affects them. A key point we need to take note of here is exactly what kind of outside force acts on the object. There are two types of forces about which you need to be aware: balanced forces and unbalanced forces. A balanced force is one where there's a state of equilibrium. As an example, um, aha . . . Look at my desk. Notice how the textbook is just sitting there. The force of gravity is holding it down while another force, often called the normal force, is pushing up on the book from the table. These two forces . . . gravity and the normal force . . . are of equal magnitude and pushing in opposite directions, which is why the book remains at rest.

But what happens if I push the book . . . ? Watch . . . Notice how it slides across the desk. The reason is that I placed an unbalanced force on it. Eventually, it stops moving because another unbalanced force—friction from the desk—stops it. So the energy from my push is unbalanced because nothing initially counters it. And the friction is unbalanced because I stopped pushing. So these unbalanced forces started the movement of the book and then stopped it. That's how Newton's first law works. Outside forces that are balanced leave an object at rest, and outside forces that are unbalanced cause an object to move, stop, or change directions.

Newton's second law of motion is a bit more complex. It states that the acceleration of an object depends upon the net forces acting on it as well as its mass. As the force acting on the object increases, its acceleration increases. But if the mass of the object increases, then its acceleration decreases, and more net force is needed to increase its acceleration. To understand this law, first, um, you need to realize that there's an unbalanced force accelerating the object. It's also crucial to remember that when we talk about the net force, we're referring to all of the forces that are acting on the object. This net force is expressed by the formula F = MA, in which F stands for the net force, M is the mass of the object, and A is the acceleration of the object. We can also use numerical values to reach what's called a standard metric unit of force, which is, uh, unsurprisingly, called a Newton. One Newton is the force required to move a one-kilogram

mass one meter per second squared. As an example of this law, think about how a small iron ball and a large iron ball would move if you push them. It will obviously take more net force to move the large ball as far as you move the small ball because of its greater mass.

And last is the third law of motion, which states that for every action, there is an equal and opposite reaction. In other words, actions come in pairs. Here's an example of what this law means . . . Think about a rocket that's blasting off to go into space. The rocket burns fuel, so hot exhaust gas is pushed out of its rear. As a reaction, a force called thrust is produced, and it pushes the rocket up into the air, thereby allowing it to get into space. Another example is a moving car . . . As a car moves, its tires spin, grip the road, and move forward, right . . . ? Well, not exactly. In reality, the spinning tires are pushing the road backward while the road is pushing the tires forward. Both the tires and the road are pushing with equal force in opposite directions. All right, um, I think that's enough, so do you have any questions for me regarding this matter, or should I move on . . . ? Yes, something on your mind . . . ?

Answer Explanations

12 Understanding Function Question

ⓒ The professor tells the students to look at his desk and then conducts a minor experiment on it.

13 Detail Question

ⓑ The professor remarks, "Eventually, it stops moving because another unbalanced force—friction from the desk—stops it."

14 Connecting Content Question

First Law of Motion: ② Second Law of Motion: ①, ④
Third Law of Motion: ③
About the first law of motion, the professor tells the students why the book on his desk does not move. Regarding the second law of motion, he says, "This net force is expressed by the formula F = MA, in which F stands for the net force, M is the mass of the object, and A is the acceleration of the object." He also comments, "It will obviously take more net force to move the large ball as far as you move the small ball because of its greater mass." As for the third law of motion, he states, "And last is the third law of motion, which states that for every action, there is an equal and opposite reaction."

15 Understanding Organization Question

ⓐ The professor gives examples of each of the laws of motion as he describes them one by one.

16 Making Inferences Question

ⓑ At the end of the lecture, the professor indicates that he will answer a question by a student when he states, "All right, um, I think that's enough, so do you have any questions for me regarding this matter, or should I move on . . . ? Yes, something on your mind . . . ?"

17 Understanding Attitude Question

Ⓓ When the professor requests that the students "hold your questions until I'm done," it can be inferred that he does not like to be interrupted by students when he is lecturing.

PART 2

Conversation [1–5]

| Script |

Listen to part of a conversation between a student and a professor.

M Student: Thank you for clearing up my confusion regarding the ancient dig site in Ethiopia, Professor Starling. Your explanation answered all of my questions.

W Professor: I'm glad to have been of assistance, Matthew.

M: I know you're busy, but I have one more thing I'd like to discuss with you at this moment. Is that all right?

W: I've got plenty of time, Matthew. My classes and office hours are both finished for the day, and I don't have any other appointments either.

M: Wonderful. So, uh, as you know, I'm going to be a senior next year, and I'd love to do a senior project in Anthropology. I wonder if you would agree to be my advisor for the project.

W: That sounds fine to . . . Wait a minute.

M: Yes?

W: I thought your major is Business Administration. Did you change majors or declare a double major recently?

M: No, ma'am. I'm still majoring in Business Administration. It's just that I've taken a few classes in Anthropology, so I'm interested in doing a senior project on it. I even have the topic I'd like to research all picked out.

W: Um, I hate to be the one to break the news to you, Matthew, but students are only permitted to do senior projects in fields they're majoring in. Unless you declare a second major, you won't be allowed to do a senior project in Anthropology. How many classes have you taken in this department?

M: Yours is the fourth. And I plan to take one each semester during my senior year.

W: Hmm . . . You know, you only need to take six classes to get a minor in Anthropology. Of course, a couple of classes are required to qualify for a minor. Have you taken Anthropology 11 and 17?

M: Oh, yeah. Professor Porter is such an entertaining lecturer.

W: Good. Those are the two only required classes to get a minor. So, um, since you're planning to take two more classes next year, why don't you declare a minor in Anthropology?

M: Sure. And then I can do a senior project, right?

W: No.

M: No? Then why do you want me to declare a minor?

W: Two reasons. First, if you are taking that many classes in one department, you should get acknowledged for it. A minor will look good on your résumé after you graduate and start applying for jobs. It will tell potential employers that you didn't merely focus on your major.

M: Okay. What's the other reason?

W: You'll be able to take an independent study course in Anthropology. It's not as prestigious as doing a senior project would be, but if you're genuinely interested in the topic, you'll be able to research it during the course of the semester and then write a long research paper on your findings. I would definitely agree to do that with you if you wanted.

M: That sounds really interesting. Thank you for the information. But let me think about it since it appears that I'm going to need to do a senior project in Business Administration. I should talk to my advisor and see if he thinks I'll be able to handle doing two research projects at the same time.

W: That's a prudent decision. Come back here once he lets you know the answer to your question.

Answer Explanations

1 Gist-Content Question

Ⓑ During the conversation, the speakers mostly talk about the student's desire to do a senior project.

2 Connecting Content Question

Ⓓ The student states, "And I plan to take one each semester during my senior year," so it can be inferred that he will take two Anthropology classes during his senior year.

3 Making Inferences Question

Ⓐ The professor asks the student if he has taken a couple of Anthropology classes. The student responds by saying, "Oh, yeah. Professor Porter is such an entertaining lecturer." The student therefore implies that Professor Porter is in the Anthropology Department.

4 Detail Question

1, 2 The professor remarks, "First, if you are taking that many classes in one department, you should get acknowledged for it. A minor will look good on your résumé after you graduate and start applying for jobs. It will tell potential employers that you didn't merely focus on your major."

5 Understanding Function Question

Ⓑ The student comments, "But let me think about it since it appears that I'm going to need to do a senior project in Business Administration. I should talk to my advisor and see if he thinks I'll be able to handle doing two research projects at the same time."

| Script |

Listen to part of a lecture in an economics class.

W Professor: Classical economic theory was established on the notion that consumers are rational. By that, I mean that consumers make choices based upon what gives them the greatest benefit from a product. This benefit may constitute satisfaction from making a good choice, it may come from a monetary benefit, or it may come from the usefulness of the product purchased. This rational behavior was considered a strong base upon which to build an economic theory. Of course, we now know that this isn't true because consumers are not always rational.

As far back as 1759, Adam Smith, the father of modern economics, discussed the idea of the perfectly rational consumer in his book *The Theory of Moral Sentiments*. Smith believed that consumers could see the rational way to make proper choices just like a well-educated economist could do. Smith argued that there were three basic principles of rational consumers. First, rational consumers had to have clearly defined preferences over a period of time. Second, Smith said rational consumers had to have keen analytical skills to make rational choices. Third, Smith stated that rational consumers had to attempt to get the greatest possible benefit from their choices.

To visualize the choices of rational consumers, economists created the indifference curve. You can find a picture of it in your textbooks on page 117 . . . Please turn there now . . . The indifference curve is the curved line drawn on the graph. Imagine that a consumer has a choice between apples and oranges. On a graph, the vertical line represents apples, and the horizontal line represents oranges. Let's say that a consumer likes both and gets satisfaction from both. However, the level of satisfaction becomes less if the consumer eats more apples than oranges or, uh, vice versa. The indifference curve line plots this changing amount of satisfaction. For example, our consumer has three apples and three oranges. If she eats three oranges and one apple, her satisfaction for oranges is less because they are too familiar to her. Likewise, if she eats more apples than oranges, she'll be less satisfied with apples. So a balance between apples and oranges, such as by eating two of each, would result in the ultimate point of satisfaction on the indifference curve.

However, economists added another line, uh, the budget line. It's the straight line on the graph. The budget line determines how many apples and oranges can be bought based upon how much money a consumer has. So where the ultimate satisfaction point is located for a rational consumer is where the indifference curve line and the budget line intersect on the graph. Economists used this to understand the buying habits of consumers for a long time. Today, we know that they didn't get it quite right.

This brings us to the habits of irrational consumers. Irrational consumers are driven by their emotions rather than by logic. Consumers sometimes buy goods because of how those purchases make them feel. For example, you may want coffee beans. There are numerous inexpensive brands that produce delicious coffee. But you acquire a more expensive brand since that company treats coffee bean growers well or talks about protecting the environment. Rational consumers would buy the most coffee beans for the best price, but irrational consumers abandon logic and buy the more expensive brand due to how it makes them feel. In essence, these consumers let their emotions determine which brands they buy.

Another aspect of the habits of irrational consumers is context. By this, I mean the situation that consumers are in, their past choices, and the variety of options available. For example, maybe a consumer has to buy a birthday present at the last moment. In this context, he's more likely to decide quickly and without much thought because there's no time to make a thoughtful, logical choice. Consumers are also influenced by their past choices. Perhaps a consumer insists on buying the same brand of cellphone when he upgrades even though there are other cheaper brands available. In his mind, if the brand was good enough in the past, it's good enough now. And let's also consider that there are sometimes too many options to choose from. Consumers are frequently overwhelmed by the variety of choices available, so they may pick something at random just to get the decision-making process over. It may not be the best choice, but they're more interested in choosing something and moving on with their lives.

Finally, let's not forget about advertising. Since the 1950s, advertising companies have used psychology to influence how people make purchases. Many ads play on people's emotions and stress how their lives would be better by making certain purchases . . . Okay, this is a topic I intend to continue discussing, but we don't have time now. We need to start our class presentations. Larry Carter, I believe you're scheduled to go first.

Answer Explanations

6 **Understanding Organization Question**

ⓒ In discussing Adam Smith, the professor focuses on describing his thoughts on rational consumers.

7 **Understanding Function Question**

ⓑ The professor tells the students, "To visualize the choices of rational consumers, economists created the indifference curve. You can find a picture of it in your textbooks on page 117 . . . Please turn there now . . . The indifference curve is the curved line drawn on the graph."

8 **Detail Question**

ⓓ The professor comments, "However, economists

added another line, uh, the budget line. It's the straight line on the graph. The budget line determines how many apples and oranges can be bought based upon how much money a consumer has."

9 Connecting Content Question

Rational Consumer: ②, ④ Irrational Consumer: ①, ③
About rational consumers, the professor notes, "This rational behavior was considered a strong base upon which to build an economic theory," and, "Rational consumers would buy the most coffee beans for the best price." As for irrational consumers, the professor points out, "Consumers are also influenced by their past choices. Perhaps a consumer insists on buying the same brand of cellphone when he upgrades even though there are other cheaper brands available. In his mind, if the brand was good enough in the past, it's good enough now."

10 Connecting Content Question

Ⓑ First, the professor states, "Irrational consumers are driven by their emotions rather than by logic." Then, she says, "Since the 1950s, advertising companies have used psychology to influence how people make purchases. Many ads play on people's emotions and stress how their lives would be better by making certain purchases." It can therefore be inferred that psychology in advertisements is effective at getting irrational consumers to make purchases.

11 Making Inferences Question

Ⓒ At the end of the lecture, the professor states, "We need to start our class presentations. Larry Carter, I believe you're scheduled to go first."

| Vocabulary Review

p. 186

Answers

A
1 surroundings   2 sentiment
3 metropolis   4 simultaneously   5 devise

B
1 b   2 b   3 b   4 a   5 b
6 a   7 a   8 b   9 b   10 a

Actual Test

Answers

PART 1 Conversation   p. 189

| Script |

Listen to part of a conversation between a student and a professor.

W Professor: Thanks for dropping by my office on time for our meeting, Brad. So, um, it's time to make your progress report on your term paper. How has the work on it been going since you spoke with me, uh, what was it . . . two weeks ago?

M Student: Yes, ma'am, that's correct. We had a meeting on October 28 to discuss everything I had done until then.

W: All right. Then tell me . . . What have you accomplished during that time?

M: Um . . . I completely changed my topic.

W: Whatever did you do that for, Brad?

M: Er . . . I had two reasons for doing so. First of all, I had a lot of trouble finding information on the topic I had initially chosen. And second, well, to be honest, I wasn't, um, particularly interested in the topic anyway, so I thought I should find something that I wanted to write about.

W: Hmm . . . Those both make sense, but you realize that you're running out of time, don't you? Your paper's due in two and a half weeks. Are you going to be able to complete it by the due date?

M: I think so. I've done quite a bit of work on it.

W: Tell me about it then.

M: I decided to write about the bald eagle population in this area. Apparently, the number of breeding pairs here has been increasing in the past five or so years. I thought I could study that and try to figure out what might account for the sudden increase in the bald eagle population.

W: That . . . is actually a very interesting topic, Brad.

M: Thank you.

W: What has your research indicated so far?

M: Well, um, it appears to be a combination of better weather, which has enabled the birds to breed more successfully recently, and conservation laws that are protecting the birds.

W: Okay. Now, remember that you're supposed to conduct a video interview with a noted authority as a part of your project. Have you done the interview yet?

M: No, not yet.

W: Do you have one scheduled then?

M: Yes, I do. I'm going to be interviewing Dr. Austin Fletcher at Central University. I contacted him last week, and he agreed to meet with me. Are you familiar with Dr. Fletcher and his work?

W: Very much so. We were classmates in our PhD program about twenty years ago, and we collaborate on projects every once in a while. He's a brilliant man, so I'd say you made a good choice, Brad.

M: I'm glad you feel that way.

W: Okay, one last question . . . How is the progress on your paper going?

M: Hmm . . . I've only written about five pages thus far, so I've still got around twenty more to go. 🎧5 But I'm waiting until after I meet Dr. Fletcher to write the bulk of my paper because I've got a long list of questions to ask him.

W: **All right, Brad, I was pessimistic when you first started, but I'm feeling more optimistic about your work after considering what you have told me.** Keep working on your project and contact me if you run into any problems. Oh, um, by the way, I'll give Austin a call in a few minutes and put in a good word for you. That might help you out a bit.

M: Thanks, Professor Jackson. I truly appreciate your doing that for me.

Answer Explanations

1 Gist-Purpose Question

Ⓑ The student and professor talk about an assignment the student is working on, so that is the reason he visits her office.

2 Detail Question

[2], [3] The student comments, "I had two reasons for doing so. First of all, I had a lot of trouble finding information on the topic I had initially chosen. And second, well, to be honest, I wasn't, um, particularly interested in the topic anyway, so I thought I should find something that I wanted to write about."

3 Understanding Function Question

Ⓐ About Dr. Fletcher, the professor remarks, "Very much so. We were classmates in our PhD program about twenty years ago, and we collaborate on projects every once in a while." So she is making the student aware that she knows both him and his work.

4 Making Inferences Question

Ⓒ The professor states, "Oh, um, by the way, I'll give Austin a call in a few minutes and put in a good word for you."

5 Understanding Attitude Question

Ⓓ The professor's statement indicates that she had felt negatively about the student's assignment at first. However, after speaking with him, she feels much better.

PART 1 Lecture #1   p. 192

| Script |

Listen to part of a lecture in an English literature class.

W Professor: There are two major controversies surrounding the works of William Shakespeare. The first, which we discussed in, um, last Thursday's class, concerns whether or not he wrote the works himself or if some—or all, I suppose—of the works attributed to him were penned by another individual. The second controversy concerns fake plays. By that, I'm referring to plays written by other individuals who then claimed they had discovered lost works authored by Shakespeare. Many false attempts took place centuries ago, so few details of them have survived until today. However, we have extensive knowledge of two such forgeries. Both were initially dismissed as fakes, but, as you'll find out momentarily, one of them might not be a fake at all.

The first story takes us back to the year 1796. A play entitled *Vortigern and Rowena* was staged in London in April. It was an historical play based on mythical events said to have taken place in fifth-century Britain. The names of the two characters in the title were legendary figures from that time. It was claimed that this was a lost play written by Shakespeare, but it was, in actuality, a hoax. The originator of this fraud was William Henry Ireland, whose father Samuel was a publisher of travel books and also happened to be quite knowledgeable about Shakespeare and his works.

Now, uh, to set the stage, so to speak, you need to

understand that we have very few examples of William Shakespeare's own writing. 🎧11 For instance, there aren't any plays of his written in his own hand that have survived to the present time.

M Student: What examples of his handwriting do we have? Letters? Poems?

W: His signature.

M: **Really? That's all we have?**

W: Sadly, that's it. There are a mere six signatures that are verified as having been made by Shakespeare. While there may be other examples of writing that he made, there's nothing else experts agree on.

So, uh, all of his handwritten plays have been lost, and that has provided plenty of opportunities for forgers to create documents and to declare they were penned by Shakespeare. As for William Henry Ireland, he claimed to have been provided the play in addition to documents supporting its authenticity by someone who wished to remain anonymous. He showed the play and papers to his father, who seemed to believe they were authentic. Thus a theater group was hired, and preparations for the play to be staged for the first time in decades—or perhaps a couple of centuries—were made . . . Or so some thought.

Controversy surrounded the play before its opening night though. Numerous critics denounced it as fake with only a few claiming it was the real thing. Finally, the play was staged—for one night and one performance only—and the consensus was that, while rather good, the play simply could not have been written by Shakespeare because it lacked his flair and plotting while the characters had no depth. William Henry Ireland later confessed to having made up the entire thing. He subsequently wrote a book about how he did it and published the play as an original work of his own. However, his reputation was shattered, and he died in poverty.

Now, uh, here's another example from earlier in the eighteenth century . . . In 1727, playwright Lewis Theobald presented a play entitled *Double Falsehood*. He claimed it was a reimagining of Shakespeare's lost play *The History of Cardenio*, which was based on a minor section of Cervantes's masterpiece *Don Quixote*. Shakespearian experts believe *The History of Cardenio*, which is usually simply called *Cardenio*, was performed in 1613 and was written by Shakespeare and John Fletcher, a playwright known to have collaborated with Shakespeare on some plays. However, the manuscript was lost and never published like most of Shakespeare's plays were. Theobald claimed to have found a copy of the manuscript and used it as the basis for *Double Falsehood*. While the play is similar to the story in *Don Quixote*, Theobald changed the characters' names and parts of the plot.

Controversy dogged Theobald like it would later affect Ireland since Theobald never proved he had the original manuscript . . . or at least he never showed it to anyone who could verify its authenticity. So was it a fake or not? Until modern times, most people believed it was an attempt at duplicity. But many experts have, well, they've changed their minds in recent years. They believe the wording and plotting are so similar to Shakespeare and Fletcher's other collaborations that the hands of both Fletcher and Shakespeare must be in there somewhere, and I agree with them.

M: Isn't that way of analyzing writing rather subjective?

W: To some extent, yes, it is. There's a lot of room for error when comparing writing styles in various works. That's particularly true for Shakespeare since many experts love his work so much. The thought of finding a lost play of his would create a great amount of excitement and surely bias Shakespearean scholars in their analyses. In fact, skeptics who doubt Theobald's claim bring this up as a major point against them. But let me show you a few passages from *Double Falsehood* that may convince you that Theobald really did have a copy of *Cardenio*.

Answer Explanations

6 Gist-Content Question

Ⓐ The lecture is mostly about two plays that people claimed had been originally written by Shakespeare.

7 Detail Question

Ⓒ The professor says that after the play was staged, "William Henry Ireland later confessed to having made up the entire thing. He subsequently wrote a book about how he did it and published the play as an original work of his own."

8 Connecting Content Question

Vortigern and Rowena: ②, ④ *Double Falsehood*: ①, ③ About *Vortigern and Rowena*, the professor notes, "William Henry Ireland later confessed to having made up the entire thing. He subsequently wrote a book about how he did it and published the play as an original work of his own." She also says, "Finally, the play was staged— for one night and one performance only." Regarding *Double Falsehood*, the professor remarks, "In 1727, playwright Lewis Theobald presented a play entitled *Double Falsehood*. He claimed it was a reimagining of Shakespeare's lost play *The History of Cardenio*, which was based on a minor section of Cervantes's masterpiece *Don Quixote*." She further adds, "But many experts have, well, they've changed their minds in recent years. They believe the wording and plotting are so similar to Shakespeare and Fletcher's other collaborations that the hands of both Fletcher and Shakespeare must be in there somewhere, and I agree with them."

9 Understanding Organization Question

Ⓐ In her lecture, the professor separately talks about two plays that were written during the eighteenth century.

10 Understanding Attitude Question

Ⓑ The professor proclaims, "They believe the wording and plotting are so similar to Shakespeare and Fletcher's other collaborations that the hands of both Fletcher and Shakespeare must be in there somewhere, and I agree with them."

11 Understanding Function Question

Ⓒ When the student responds to the professor's comment by asking, "Really? That's all we have?" he is expressing his surprise. In this case, it is important to listen to his tone of voice to hear how surprised he is.

PART 1 Lecture #2 p. 195

| Script |

Listen to part of a lecture in a zoology class.

M Professor: Another way animals move is by gliding. And by gliding, I don't mean that they fly in the air, glide for a bit, and then fly again. Instead, I'm talking about animals that cannot fly but are capable of leaping into the air and using their bodies to glide long distances. Examples of gliding animals are some species of fish, lemurs, snakes, lizards, geckos, frogs, possums, and squirrels. Many times, these animals have the moniker "flying" attached to the name of their species, but don't be mistaken: This doesn't mean that they're true fliers. A true flying species is one that can take off, maintain sustained flight over a long distance, and land again in a controlled fashion. These animals typically have wings and, uh, strong shoulder muscles capable of flapping their wings at great speeds to maintain both thrust and lift. Gliding animals, in contrast, lack wings like birds and insects have, and most of them can't take off from the ground. They need to leap from high places, um, such as trees, to be able to glide. One exception is the flying fish, which leaps from the water. Ah, and gliding animals cannot glide long distances since gravity fairly quickly pulls them back to the ground or water.

W Student: Professor Nelson, if they don't have wings, then how exactly are they capable of gliding in the air?

M: Well, Jenny, they can glide due to the shapes of their bodies. You see, uh, most gliding animals have membranes that they can extend from their bodies to make them more aerodynamic. Look up here at the screen. Here are a flying lemur . . . a possum . . . and a squirrel. Did you notice that all of them have membranes between their front and rear legs on both sides of their bodies . . . ? When the animals extend those membranes and glide from tree to tree, their bodies assume a square shape. Here's a short video . . . See how the squirrel leaps . . . and extends its body so that it's shaped like a square . . . and that's it. It simply glided from one tree to another. Now, uh, flying lizards, like this one here . . . have membranes, but their membranes are more wing shaped with rounded tips, and they don't extend the full length of their bodies between the front and rear legs. See that . . . ?

Other gliding animals have different body structures. Flying frogs, like this one . . . have webbed feet that permit them to glide short distances. They can use their large, webbed feet to make small changes in their gliding paths to maneuver to where they want to go. Flying snakes have no special membranes but can flatten their bodies to give them greater aerodynamic shapes before they leap from trees. While the flying fish has appendages that resemble wings . . . they're more like pectoral fins than wings. Flying fish use great speed to propel themselves from the water and to glide short distances before landing back in the water and leaping again. Their fins flap like wings, but they don't provide lift for sustained flight like birds as they serve only to provide aerodynamic surfaces to allow gliding. In addition, flying fish often use their tailfins to strike the water, which pushes them higher in the air and gives them some thrust so that they can stay in the air for relatively long distances.

You may be wondering why these animals glide . . . For the most part, they do it either to find food or to avoid becoming food. For tree-dwelling animals, gliding from tree to tree helps them avoid predators and enables them to move to other trees to find food without having to descend to the ground and climb up another tree. Doing that wastes energy and may expose them to predators on the ground. As for flying fish, they usually leap from the water when predators are nearby. On the other hand, flying snakes tend to be predators, so gliding from tree to tree allows them to catch prey unaware.

As a general rule, gliding animals reside in tropical regions where dense forests give them plenty of high places to leap from. One exception is the flying squirrel, which resides in the temperate regions of North America and Europe. Now, uh . . . yes, Jenny? Another question?

W: Yes, please. I'm curious . . . Did gliding animals start evolving to become fliers but have their evolution, uh, arrested at some point?

M: That's a complex question, but I can safely say that, for the most part, the answer is no. Gliding animals never developed the basic body structures that would indicate they were meant to become fliers. The most obvious thing is their lack of wings or even the beginnings of wings. Other than the flying fish, gliding animals have nothing like wings, which all flying creatures use to achieve flight. There is, however, the bat. Some zoologists believe it was once a gliding animal but then evolved to become a flying animal later. You know what? This is an interesting topic, so let's talk about the bat's evolution for a moment.

12 Gist-Content Question

Ⓒ The lecture is mostly about the way that some gliding animals are capable of moving through the air.

13 Connecting Content Question

Ⓐ The professor remarks, "Flying frogs, like this one . . . have webbed feet that permit them to glide short distances. They can use their large, webbed feet to make small changes in their gliding paths to maneuver to where they want to go. Flying snakes have no special membranes but can flatten their bodies to give them greater aerodynamic shapes before they leap from trees." So he compares the form of the body part that enables each animal to glide.

14 Detail Question

Ⓓ The professor comments, "In addition, flying fish often use their tailfins to strike the water, which pushes them higher in the air and gives them some thrust so that they can stay in the air for relatively long distances."

15 Understanding Organization Question

Ⓐ The professor focuses on the fact that the flying squirrel does not live in the tropics in stating, "As a general rule, gliding animals reside in tropical regions where dense forests give them plenty of high places to leap from. One exception is the flying squirrel, which resides in the temperate regions of North America and Europe."

16 Understanding Function Question

Ⓑ The student asks a question about the evolution of gliding animals, so the professor talks about it to respond to her inquiry.

17 Detail Question

Fact: ①, ② Not a Fact: ③, ④
The professor notes, "Many times, these animals have the moniker 'flying' attached to the name of their species, but don't be mistaken: This doesn't mean that they're true fliers." He also says, "Well, Jenny, they can glide due to the shapes of their bodies." It is not true, however, that there are more gliding animals that are predators than prey animals, nor is it true that many gliding animals evolved like the bat did.

PART 2 Conversation

p. 198

| Script |

Listen to part of a conversation between a student and a Registrar's office employee.

W Registrar's Office Employee: Hello. I believe you're next in line. What can I do for you today?

M Student: Hello. I'm here for a couple of things. First of all, I need to get a copy of my transcript since I'm applying for jobs at several different companies.

W: Sure, we can do that. But, um, did you just say that you want a single copy of your transcript?

M: Yes, that's right.

W: I'm sorry, but you are planning to apply to more than one company, aren't you? I'm pretty sure you said that.

M: Er . . . Yes, that's what I'm doing. Why do you ask?

W: 🎧5 If you intend to submit applications to several companies, don't you need more than one copy of your transcript so that you can send one to each of them?

M: Oh, I'm just going to copy the transcript and send that instead.

W: **I'd highly advise that you not do that.**

M: Yeah? Why not?

W: First of all, sending a photocopy of your transcript isn't very professional and is likely to result in your application being discarded. Second of all, the people at virtually every company you're going to apply to expect to get a sealed copy of your transcript sent directly from this office.

M: Oh . . . I was unaware of that.

W: Shall I assume you don't have the addresses of the companies with you?

M: Uh, yeah. Right. Okay, I've never done this before, so would you mind explaining to me what the process is?

W: It's no problem at all. What you need to do is fill out, um, this form here . . . Take a look at the form . . . Notice that you need to write the name of the company or the person you're sending your transcript to, the address it should be sent to, and how many copies should go to each individual or company.

M: That's convenient. Um . . . who pays for the postage?

W: That's included in the price of your transcript. By the way, it costs $5 for each transcript. Why don't you take a couple of these forms with you, fill them out at your home, and then come back here later when you know exactly where each transcript should go?

M: Okay. Thanks.

W: My pleasure.

M: Oh, uh, I have to get one more thing, please. I also need a copy of my diploma.

W: You are going to be graduating this spring, right?

M: Yes, that's correct.

W: In that case, you can't get a copy of your diploma until July. One will be sent to you a week after graduation, but we don't print duplicate copies until one month after the ceremony is held. So, uh, unfortunately, you're going to have to wait until then to receive another copy. You can, however, fill out an online form and submit it to the office. We'll process your request, but we won't send you anything until we're allowed to. Just so you know, it costs

$200 to get a second copy of your diploma.

M: Wow, that's kind of steep. You know, um, I didn't know any of what you just told me. Thanks so much for taking the time to explain the situation to me. Not everyone would do that. I appreciate it.

W: Thanks for the compliment. It's always a pleasure to help students out.

Answer Explanations

1 Gist-Purpose Question

Ⓒ The student goes to the Registrar's office to get copies of his transcript and his diploma, both of which are official documents.

2 Detail Question

Ⓒ The woman gives the student a form to fill out and says, "What you need to do is fill out, um, this form here."

3 Making Inferences Question

Ⓐ The woman tells the student, "Why don't you take a couple of these forms with you, fill them out at your home, and then come back here later when you know exactly where each transcript should go?" The student agrees, so it can be inferred that he will go back to the Registrar's office another time.

4 Understanding Attitude Question

Ⓓ At the end of the conversation, the student says, "You know, um, I didn't know any of what you just told me. Thanks so much for taking the time to explain the situation to me. Not everyone would do that. I appreciate it." So he is pleased with how she has helped him.

5 Understanding Function Question

Ⓑ When the woman advises the student not to do what he just said he intends to do, she is implying that the student needs to come up with another idea.

PART 2 Lecture   p. 201

| Script |

Listen to part of a lecture in a physics class.

M Professor: If you've ever been seriously ill or injured in an accident, you probably had a scanning procedure done to determine the illness or the extent of your injuries. Nowadays, the most common types are the CAT scan and the MRI scan. These acronyms stand for computerized axial tomography for the CAT scan and magnetic resonance imaging for the MRI scan. Both have been used for decades and require large machines that scan the body and then employ computers to interpret the data they collect. There's also a relatively new offshoot of the MRI machine that's called the fMRI. It stands for functional magnetic resonance imaging. And please note that the acronym fMRI uses a lower-case f while the other letters are capitalized. For the next few moments, I'd like to discuss how MRI and fMRI technologies are both similar and different.

The primary way they're the same concerns what they do. They both enable doctors to look deep inside the body to find out what's happening. Without these tools, doctors would most likely have to open up their patients' bodies to find out what's going on inside them. In addition, each of them utilizes expensive machines and computers to do the work. And, um . . . well, that's just about it for the similarities.

As for the differences . . . To begin with, MRI technology is older, having been developed in the 1970s, and it essentially gave birth to fMRI technology, which didn't appear until the early 1990s. Another key difference concerns which body parts they're used on. MRI scans can be performed on virtually any part of the body whereas fMRI scans are used exclusively on the brain. 🎧11 Would anyone like to guess why?

W Student: I think I know the answer, Professor Freeman.

M: **Well, don't keep us in suspense then, Wendy.**

W: Uh, right. Sorry, sir. I believe the reason they're used on different body parts concerns the way the two scans function.

M: Well done. Would you happen to know how each of them functions?

W: No, sir, I don't. I just remember reading somewhere that it's one of the differences between the two machines.

M: Okay, class, since Wendy isn't sure, let me tell you. And this is important because the way each machine functions is integral to understanding how they're different. Firstly, MRI technology is based on studying the anatomical structure of the body. So it provides doctors with a scan of the body part's structure and nothing else. It accomplishes this by using large magnets to align the nuclei of the water molecules in your body. From these aligned water molecules, the MRI scanner's computers can form images of the interior of the body. Basically, uh, it highlights the differences in space between various parts of the body, such as bones, muscles, and organs. From these images, a doctor can determine if a patient has a problem such as a disease or injury. MRI technology is frequently used to detect tumors, such as cancer, and to look for injuries in the bones and tissue following accidents.

fMRI technology, on the other hand, has another function and operates differently. Its main purpose is to examine the metabolic functions of body parts, so fMRI technology isn't used to look for tumors or injuries. Instead, doctors employ it to determine how a body part is working. Thus far, the technology has only been used on the brain. As for how it works, well, fMRI technology, like the MRI, uses magnetic power to align the water molecules in the brain, but the fMRI machine also calculates the level of oxygen in the blood going to the brain in real time. When brain activity increases, more red blood cells flow there, and the brain's blood vessels widen. This is something an fMRI machine is capable of picking up on. In essence, the machine can determine which parts of the brain are active in real time. As the machine scans the brain, the doctor may have the patient perform certain tasks or may ask the patient questions. When the patient responds, the machine records the level of oxygen flowing to certain parts of the brain.

So . . . what's the purpose of fMRI technology? First, the brain remains something of a mystery to us. In the last two decades, we've taken great steps forward thanks to the use of fMRI technology though. We can map the brain and understand which parts of it control specific parts of the body. And we can do that without having to open up a patient's skull and endangering that individual's life through surgery. Second, fMRI technology is useful in the field of mental health as doctors employ it to examine patients with cognitive disabilities. By taking scans of these patients, they try to determine why their brains are unable to function as nondisabled people's brains do.

W: Is fMRI technology as common as MRI technology?

M: No, it's not, um, for two main reasons. First, fMRI machines are much more expensive to manufacture. Second, the technology is used in a highly specialized area of medical research and patient care whereas MRI scans are much more regularly done on patients.

Answer Explanations

6 Gist-Content Question

Ⓒ The professor spends most of the lecture explaining the way that two types of scanning technology, the MRI and the fMRI, work.

7 Making Inferences Question

Ⓐ The professor says, "They both enable doctors to look deep inside the body to find out what's happening. Without these tools, doctors would most likely have to open up their patients' bodies to find out what's going on inside them." In stating that, he implies that doctors can avoid doing surgery on some patients thanks to those technologies.

8 Connecting Content Question

Ⓓ The professor remarks, "This is something an fMRI machine is capable of picking up on. In essence, the machine can determine which parts of the brain are active in real time. As the machine scans the brain, the doctor may have the patient perform certain tasks or may ask the patient questions. When the patient responds, the machine records the level of oxygen flowing to certain parts of the brain." It is therefore likely that a person doing an activity while having an fMRI scan done will enable the doctor to learn which part of the patient's brain is being used.

9 Connecting Content Question

MRI: ②, ③ fMRI: ①, ④

Regarding the MRI, the professor notes, "Firstly, MRI technology is based on studying the anatomical structure of the body," and further states, "MRI technology is frequently used to detect tumors, such as cancer." As for the fMRI, the professor comments, "Second, fMRI technology is useful in the field of mental health as doctors employ it to examine patients with cognitive disabilities." He also remarks, "No, it's not, um, for two main reasons," when a student asks if fMRI technology is as common as MRI technology.

10 Understanding Organization Question

Ⓓ The professor talks about each type of technology independent of the other in his lecture.

11 Understanding Function Question

Ⓐ When the professor tells the student, "Well, don't keep us in suspense then, Wendy," he is encouraging her to answer his question. He says this in response to the student stating, "I think I know the answer."

PART 3 Conversation   p. 204

| Script |

Listen to part of a conversation between a student and a professor.

W1 Student: Professor Landers, I'm here for our two o'clock appointment.

W2 Professor: Good afternoon, Emily. Please come in and take a seat.

W1: Thank you very much, ma'am.

W2: So . . . you requested this meeting. How about going ahead and telling me what's on your mind?

W1: Sure. Basically, I'm thinking of taking on a second major, and I'd like to have your opinion of that.

W2: Which major are you considering adding? Knowing that will enable me to determine whether it's a good idea or not.

W1: Ah, right. Well, I've been thinking . . . Since the world is becoming more and more interconnected these days, it's probably not smart for me only to major in Economics. I mean, uh, what happens in other countries affects us here, so I think I should be aware of what's going on in places around the world.

W2: So you're contemplating majoring in History then?

W1: I gave that some thought, but many of the requirements for a History major are for ancient and medieval history, which I'm not particularly interested in. 🎧4 Instead, I believe I'd like to get a second major in International Relations. By doing that, I could see the connections between countries much better, and I'm positive that

would help me as a budding economist.

W2: **You may be on to something there, Emily.**

W1: So you like my proposal?

W2: That's affirmative. I've had quite a few students do the same two majors in my one and a half decades here at this school, and not one of them has ever expressed any regret for that decision.

W1: Wow, that sounds great.

W2: However . . .

W1: Yes?

W2: You're currently in the fall semester of your sophomore year, so, uh, starting next semester, you're really going to have to focus on taking the right classes. The International Relations major here requires students to take an abnormally large number of classes, so you're going to be busy for the remainder of your time at school. By that, I mean that you should expect to take a full load of classes each semester. You'll need to attend summer school as well.

W1: Yes, ma'am. I researched that and figured out that I'm probably going to have to take at least three summer school classes over the next two years in order to graduate on time.

W2: You don't mind doing that?

W1: 🎧5 Not at all. I stayed here this past summer and worked on campus. It was a good experience, so I'll probably try to get another summer job. It won't be a problem for me to take classes as well.

W2: **Okay, it looks like you've got that covered.** Have you selected an advisor in the International Relations Department yet?

W1: I have yet to do that because I've only taken one course in that department. I don't have to declare a second major until the fall semester in my junior year, so I don't think it's necessary for me to rush. I'll take two classes in that department next year and one or two summer school classes, so I'd prefer to meet some of the other professors there before I make a decision.

W2: Good thinking. You wouldn't want to make a hasty choice.

W1: I agree.

W2: Well, it looks like you're going to have little free time from now on. I wish you the best of luck, Emily.

W1: Thanks for saying that.

Answer Explanations

1 Gist-Content Question

Ⓐ The student and professor mostly talk about the student's decision to double-major while at school.

2 Detail Question

②, ④ The professor tells the student, "The International

Relations major here requires students to take an abnormally large number of classes, so you're going to be busy for the remainder of your time at school. By that, I mean that you should expect to take a full load of classes each semester. You'll need to attend summer school as well."

3 Making Inferences Question

B When talking about deciding on an advisor in her new major, the student states, "I have yet to do that because I've only taken one course in that department. I don't have to declare a second major until the fall semester in my junior year, so I don't think it's necessary for me to rush. I'll take two classes in that department next year and one or two summer school classes, so I'd prefer to meet some of the other professors there before I make a decision." So it can be inferred that she will find a new advisor during her junior year.

4 Understanding Function Question

A When the professor says, "You may be on to something there, Emily," she is expressing her support for the student's decision.

5 Understanding Attitude Question

C When the professor mentions, "Okay, it looks like you've got that covered," she is implying that she is satisfied with what the student just told her.

PART 3 Lecture   p. 207

| Script |

Listen to part of a lecture in a history class.

M Professor: All right, let's get started . . . We're going to begin today's lecture by talking about a significant event in English history which took place in 1381. I'm referring, of course, to the Peasants' Revolt. It started in the regions of Essex and Kent in southeast England and later spread to the northern and western parts of the country. Many government officials were killed during it, and, um, for a time, London itself was occupied by rebels. For the most part, the revolt involved mobs of peasants led by clergymen and artisans. It began in late May of 1381 and wasn't completely put down until November. Estimates of the number of dead vary, but it's certain that several thousand people died during this period of turmoil.

So . . . what caused it? Well, a variety of things did. The primary cause was the lingering effects of the Black Death, the epidemic that swept through England in the late 1340s and killed more than a third of the entire population. As a result of the Black Death, the country experienced both social and economic upheaval. Suddenly, peasant labor was in great demand since such a large number of people had died, so, for once, the peasants had an advantage over the nobles and therefore began making demands for

better working conditions. Among these demands were, um, were higher wages and the right to move to new locations in search of better work, something they weren't allowed to do under feudalism. Soon, English lords and landowners were clashing over access to the reduced pool of labor. In 1351, the government passed a law called the Statute of Laborers. It stated that peasants couldn't be paid more than what they had earned in 1346, which was prior to the onset of the Black Death. It additionally banned lords and landowners from offering higher wages. A third clause stated that no peasants could move off the land they lived on to seek work elsewhere. In essence, the law solidified the country's feudal traditions.

Naturally, the peasants were upset by the law, which instilled in them a fatalistic view that their lives would never improve no matter what happened. After all, um, they were tied to the land, their wages were frozen, and they had to continue providing free labor for their lords and the Church as often as two days a week. On top of all that, inflation started in the following decades. Well, wages increased slightly, um, but not enough to keep up with rising prices. As you can see, they had difficult lives, so it's no wonder that they eventually rebelled due to the harshness they endured. For the peasants, the proverbial straw that broke the camel's back came because of England's long war with France, which was later termed the Hundred Years' War. To pay for the war, the government increased taxes. In 1377, a poll tax on every adult in the kingdom was imposed. It was supposed to be a one-time affair, but the need for money to finance the war was so great that it was levied twice more. When the poll tax was levied for the third time in 1380, the revolt began soon afterward.

It started in Essex, where many peasants had outright refused to pay the 1380 poll tax or went into hiding to avoid the tax collectors. In spring of 1381, the government sent more tax collectors out. On May 30, one collector assembled the people of three villages in Essex and instructed them that they not only had to pay the tax but that they also had to pay for the people who didn't show up. The peasants naturally became irate, so a riot began, during which the tax collector was beaten and some of the men accompanying him were killed. The rioting spread, and before long, much of the countryside was in revolt with people attacking landowners, burning manor houses, and causing general mayhem.

W Student: Where was the army? Why didn't they put down the revolt?

M: Most of the army was in France fighting the war, so, um, initially, there were few armed men to stop the revolt. As a result, the unrest spread to Kent, and a few leaders emerged. They included a clergyman named John Ball and a peasant named Wat Tyler. The peasants marched on London, where the mobs looted the Tower of London, killed some high officials, and destroyed tax records.

King Richard II, who was but fourteen years of age and extremely inexperienced, met the peasants on June 14 and acceded to all their demands. At another meeting the next day, the king's men feared Wat Tyler was going to attack Richard, so they killed Tyler, which took some of the steam out of the rebels. Then, the government raised a 4,000-man force in and around London, and the bloodshed really began. John Ball and several other leaders were captured and executed. Throughout the long summer and into the fall, the rebels were attacked and dispersed. Ultimately, Richard didn't give into their demands except to end the poll tax. He claimed his promises had been made under duress, so he therefore didn't have to fulfill them.

Answer Explanations

6 Gist-Purpose Question

Ⓐ Before talking about the Black Death, the professor states about the Peasants' Revolt, "So . . . what caused it? Well, a variety of things did. The primary cause was the lingering effects of the Black Death, the epidemic that swept through England in the late 1340s and killed more than a third of the entire population."

7 Detail Question

②, ④ About the Statute of Laborers, the professor remarks, "In 1351, the government passed a law called the Statute of Laborers. It stated that peasants couldn't be paid more than what they had earned in 1346, which was prior to the onset of the Black Death. It additionally banned lords and landowners from offering higher wages. A third clause stated that no peasants could move off the land they lived on to seek work elsewhere."

8 Understanding Attitude Question

Ⓐ The professor notes that he understands why the peasants revolted in commenting, "Naturally, the peasants were upset by the law, which instilled in them a fatalistic view that their lives would never improve no matter what happened. After all, um, they were tied to the land, their wages were frozen, and they had to continue providing free labor for their lords and the Church as often as two days a week. On top of all that, inflation started in the following decades. Well, wages increased slightly, um, but not enough to keep up with rising prices. As you can see, they had difficult lives, so it's no wonder that they eventually rebelled due to the harshness they endured."

9 Detail Question

Ⓑ The professor says, "For the peasants, the proverbial straw that broke the camel's back came because of England's long war with France, which was later termed the Hundred Years' War. To pay for the war, the government increased taxes. In 1377, a poll tax on every adult in the kingdom was imposed."

10 Making Inferences Question

Ⓓ The professor remarks, "At another meeting the next day, the king's men feared Wat Tyler was going to attack Richard, so they killed Tyler, which took some of the steam out of the rebels." In stating that the death of Wat Tyler "took some of the steam out of the rebels," the professor implies that Tyler was influential amongst the peasants.

11 Understanding Organization Question

Ⓑ The professor talks about the events in the Peasants' Revolt in the order that they happen, so he uses chronological order to describe them.